MORGAN FOUR
OWNERS WORKSHOP MANUAL

By R. Clarke

Morgan Four-Four, Series 1 to 5 1936-68
Morgan Four-Four 1600 1968-81
Morgan Plus-Four 1950-69
Morgan Plus-Four-Plus 1963-66

Distributed by
Brooklands Book Distribution Ltd.
'Holmerise', Seven Hills Road,
Cobham, Surrey, England
Printed in Hong Kong

BROOKLANDS BOOKS

The following Autobook Workshop Manuals are currently available from Brooklands Book Distribution

Alfa Romeo Alfasud 1972-1983 OWM 864
Alfa Romeo Alfasud 1973-1979 OWM 959
Alfa Romeo Giulia-Spider 1962-1978 OWM 724*
BMW 1800 1964-1971 OWM 813
BMW 2000, 2002 1966-1976 OWM 601
BMW 2500, 2800, 3.0 3.3, Bavaria 1968-1977 OWM 906
BMW 518, 520, 1973-1981 OWM 911*
Datsun 260Z 1974-1978 OWM 852
Datsun 280Z 1975-1978 OWM 936
Fiat X/19 1974-1982 OWM 928
Jaguar 'E' Type 1961-1972 OWM 758
Land Rover Mk2, 2A, 3 1959-1983 OWM 895*
Mazda 1000, 1200, 1300 1969-1978 OWM 708
Morgan Four 1963-1981 OWM 796*
Peugeot 204 1965-1976 OWM 841
Peugeot 304 1970-1980 OWM 716
Peugeot 504 1968-1982 OWM 783
Porsche 356 1957-1965 OWM 827*
Reliant Scimitar 1968-1979 OWM 896*
Rover 2000, 2200 1963-1967 OWM 890
Rover 3500, SE, V8S, Vanden Plas, Vitesse 1976-1984 OWM 921

*New enlarged Brooklands edition

ISBN 1 870642 635

First Edition 1968
Second Edition, fully revised 1970
Third Edition, fully revised 1973
Fourth Edition, fully revised 1977
Fifth Edition, fully revised 1979
Reprinted 1982
Reprinted 1984
Reprinted 1985
Enlarged Edition 1989

© Brooklands Books 1989   Printed in Hong Kong

OWM 796

BROOKLANDS
BOOKS

CONTENTS

BROOKLANDS BOOKS SERIES

AC Ace & Aceca 1953-1983
AC Cobra 1962-1969
Alfa Romeo Alfasud 1972-1984
Alfa Romeo Alfetta Coupes GT.GTV.GTV6 1974-1987
Alfa Romeo Giulia Berlinas 1962-1976
Alfa Romeo Giulia Coupés 1963-1976
Alfa Romeo Spider 1966-1987
Allard Gold Portfolio 1937-1958
Alvis Gold Portfolio 1919-1967
Aston Martin Gold Portfolio 1972-1985
Austin Seven 1922-1982
Austin A30 & A35 1951-1962
Austin Healey 3000 1959-1967
Austin Healey 100 & 3000 Collection No. 1
Austin Healey 'Frogeye' Sprite Collection No. 1
Austin Healey Sprite 1958-1971
Avanti 1962-1983
BMW Six Cylinder Coupés 1969-1975
BMW 1600 Collection No. 1
BMW 2002 1968-1976
Bristol Cars Gold Portfolio 1946-1985
Buick Automobiles 1947-1960
Buick Riviera 1963-1978
Cadillac Automobiles 1949-1959
Cadillac Automobiles 1960-1969
Cadillac Eldorado 1967-1978
Camaro 1966-1970
Chevrolet Camaro & Z-28 1973-1981
High Performance Camaros 1982-1988
Chevrolet Camaro Collection No. 1
Chevrolet 1955-1957
Chevrolet Impala & SS 1958-1971
Chevelle & SS 1964-1972
Chevy II Nova & SS 1962-1973
High Performance Corvettes 1983-1989
Chrysler 300 1955-1970
Citroen Traction Avant 1934-1957
Citroen DS & ID 1955-1975
Citroen 2CV 1948-1988
Cobras & Replicas 1962-1983
Cortina 1600E & GT 1967-1970
Corvair 1959-1968
Daimler Dart & V-8 250 1959-1969
Datsun 240Z 1970-1973
Datsun 280Z & ZX 1975-1983
De Tomaso Collection No. 1
Dodge Charger 1966-1974
Excalibur Collection No. 1
Ferrari Cars 1946-1956
Ferrari Dino 1965-1974
Ferrari Dino 308 1974-1979
Ferrari 308 & Mondial 1980-1984
Ferrari Collection No. 1
Fiat-Bertone X1/9 1973-1988
Fiat Pininfarina 124+2000 Spider 1968-1985
Ford Automobiles 1949-1959
Ford Fairlane 1955-1970
Ford Falcon 1960-1970
Ford RS Escort 1968-1980
High Performance Escorts MkI 1968-1974
High Performance Escorts MkII 1975-1980
High Performance Mustangs 1982-1988
Honda CRX 1983-1987
Hudson & Railton Cars 1936-1940
Jaguar Cars 1957-1961
Jaguar Cars 1961-1964
Jaguar XK120 XK140 XK150 Gold Portfolio 1948-1960
Jaguar E-Type Gold Portfolio 1961-1971
Jaguar E-Type 1966-1971
Jaguar E-Type V12 1971-1975
Jaguar XJ6 1968-1972
Jaguar XJ6 Series II 1973-1979
Jaguar XJ6 & XJ12 Series III 1979-1985
Jaguar XJ12 1972-1980
Jaguar XJS Gold Portfolio 1975-1988
Jensen Cars 1946-1967
Jensen Cars 1967-1979
Jensen Interceptor Gold Portfolio 1966-1986
Jensen Healey 1972-1976
Lamborghini Cars 1964-1970
Lamborghini Cars 1970-1975
Lamborghini Countach Collection No. 1
Lamborghini Countach & Urraco 1974-1980
Lamborghini Countach & Jalpa 1980-1985
Lancia Stratos 1972-1985
Land Rover 1948-1973
Land Rover Series II & IIa 1958-1971
Land Rover Series III 1971-1985
Land Rover 90 & 110 1983-1989
Lotus Cortina 1963-1970
Lotur Elan Gold Portfolio 1962-1974
Lotus Elan Collection No. 2
Lotus Elite 1957-1964
Lotus Elite & Eclat 1974-1981
Lotus Turbo Esprit 1980-1986
Lotus Europa 1966-1975
Lotus Europa Collection No. 1
Lotus Seven 1957-1980
Lotus Seven Collection No. 1
Marcos Cars 1960-1988
Maserati 1965-1970
Maserati 1970-1975
Mazda RX-7 Collection No. 1
Mercedes 190 & 300SL 1954-1963
Mercedes 230/250/280SL 1963-1971
Mercedes 350/450SL & SLC 1971-1980
Mercedes Benz Cars 1949-1954
Mercedes Benz Cars 1954-1957
Mercedes Benz Cars 1957-1961
Mercedes Benz Competition Cars 1950-1957
Metropolitan 1954-1962

MG TC 1945-1949
MG TD 1949-1953
MG TF 1953-1955
MG Cars 1957-1959
MG Cars 1959-1962
MG Midget 1961-1980
MGA Collection No. 1
MGA Roadsters 1955-1962
MGB Roadsters 1962-1980
MGB GT 1965-1980
Mini Cooper 1961-1971
Morgan Cars 1960-1970
The Morgan 3-Wheeler Gold Portfolio 1910-1952
Morgan Cars Gold Portfolio 1968-1989
Morris Minor Collection No. 1
Oldsmobile Automobiles 1955-1963
Old's Cutlass & 4-4-2 1964-1972
Oldsmobile Toronado 1966-1978
Opel GT 1968-1973
Packard Gold Portfolio 1946-1958
Pantera 1970-1973
Pantera & Mangusta 1969-1974
Plymouth Barracuda 1964-1974
Pontiac Fiero 1984-1988
Pontiac GTO 1964-1970
Pontiac Firebird 1967-1973
Pontiac Firebird and Trans-Am 1973-1981
High Performance Firebirds 1982-1988
Pontiac Tempest & GTO 1961-1965
Porsche Cars 1960-1964
Porsche Cars 1964-1968
Porsche Cars 1968-1972
Porsche Cars in the Sixties
Porsche Cars 1972-1975
Porsche 356 1952-1965
Porsche 911 1965-1969
Porsche 911 1970-1972
Porsche 911 1973-1977
Porsche 911 Carrera 1973-1977
Porsche 911 SC 1978-1983
Porsche 911 Turbo 1975-1984
Porsche 914 Gold Portfolio 1969-1976
Porsche 914 Collection No. 1
Porsche 924 Gold Portfolio 1975-1988
Porsche 928 1977-1984
Porsche 944 1981-1985
Reliant Scimitar 1964-1986
Riley 1½ & 2½ Litre Gold Portfolio 1945-1955
Rolls Royce Silver Cloud 1955-1965
Rolls Royce Silver Shadow 1965-1980
Range Rover Gold Portfolio 1970-1988
Rover 3 & 3.5 Litre 1958-1973
Rover P4 1949-1959
Rover P4 1955-1964
Rover 2000 + 2200 1963-1977
Rover 3500 1968-1977
Rover 3500 & Vitesse 1976-1986
Saab Sonett Collection No. 1
Saab Turbo 1976-1983
Studebaker Hawks & Larks 1956-1963
Sunbeam Tiger and Alpine Gold Portfolio 1959-1967
Thunderbird 1955-1957
Thunderbird 1958-1963
Thunderbird 1964-1976
Toyota MR2 1984-1988
Triumph 2000-2.5-2500 1963-1977
Triumph Spitfire 1962-1980
Triumph Spitfire Collection No. 1
Triumph Stag 1970-1980
Triumph Stag Collection No. 1
Triumph TR2 & TR3 1952-1960
Triumph TR4.TR5.TR250 1961-1968
Triumph TR6 1969-1976
Triumph TR6 Collection No. 1
Triumph TR7 & TR8 1975-1982
Triumph GT6 1966-1974
Triumph Vitesse & Herald 1959-1971
TVR Gold Portfolio 1959-1988
Volkswagen Cars 1936-1956
VW Beetle 1956-1977
VW Beetle Collection No. 1
VW Golf GTi 1976-1986
VW Karmann Ghia 1955-1982
VW Scirocco 1974-1981
VW Bus-Camper-Van 1954-1967
VW Bus-Camper-Van 1968-1979
VW Bus-Camper-Van 1979-1989
Volvo 1800 1960-1973
Volvo 120 Series 1956-1970

BROOKLANDS MUSCLE CARS SERIES

American Motors Muscle Cars 1966-1970
Buick Muscle Cars 1965-1970
Camaro Muscle Cars 1966-1972
Capri Muscle Cars 1969-1983
Chevrolet Muscle Cars 1966-1972
Dodge Muscle Cars 1967-1970
Mercury Muscle Cars 1966-1971
Mini Muscle Cars 1961-1979
Mopar Muscle Cars 1964-1967
Mopar Muscle Cars 1968-1971
Mustang Muscle Cars 1967-1971
Shelby Mustang Muscle Cars 1965-1970
Oldsmobile Muscle Cars 1964-1970
Plymouth Muscle Cars 1966-1971
Pontiac Muscle Cars 1966-1972

BROOKLANDS ROAD & TRACK SERIES

Road & Track on Alfa Romeo 1949-1963
Road & Track on Alfa Romeo 1964-1970
Road & Track on Alfa Romeo 1971-1976
Road & Track on Alfa Romeo 1977-1989
Road & Track on Aston Martin 1962-1984
Road & Track on Auburn Cord & Duesenberg 1952-1984

Road & Track on Audi 1952-1980
Road & Track on Audi 1980-1986
Road & Track on Austin Healey 1953-1970
Road & Track on BMW Cars 1966-1974
Road & Track on BMW Cars 1975-1978
Road & Track on BMW Cars 1979-1983
Road & Track on Cobra, Shelby & Ford GT40 1962-1983
Road & Track on Corvette 1953-1967
Road & Track on Corvette 1968-1982
Road & Track on Corvette 1982-1986
Road & Track on Datsun Z 1970-1983
Road & Track on Ferrari 1950-1968
Road & Track on Ferrari 1968-1974
Road & Track on Ferrari 1975-1981
Road & Track on Ferrari 1981-1984
Road's Track on Fiat Sports Cars 1968-1987
Road & Track on Jaguar 1950-1960
Road & Track on Jaguar 1961-1968
Road & Track on Jaguar 1968-1974
Road & Track on Jaguar 1974-1982
Road & Track on Jaguar 1983-1989
Road & Track on Lamborghini 1964-1985
Road & Track on Lotus 1972-1981
Road & Track on Maserati 1952-1974
Road & Track on Maserati 1975-1983
Road & Track on Mazda RX7 1978-1986
Road & Track on Mercedes 1952-1962
Road & Track on Mercedes 1963-1970
Road & Track on Mercedes 1971-1979
Road & Track on Mercedes 1980-1987
Road & Track on MG Sports Cars 1949-1961
Road & Track on MG Sports Cars 1962-1980
Road & Track on Mustang 1964-1977
Road & Track on Peugeot 1955-1986
Road & Track on Pontiac 1960-1983
Road & Track on Porsche 1951-1967
Road & Track on Porsche 1968-1971
Road & Track on Porsche 1972-1975
Road & Track on Porsche 1975-1978
Road & Track on Porsche 1979-1982
Road & Track on Porsche 1982-1985
Road & Track on Porsche 1985-1988
Road & Track on Rolls Royce & Bentley 1950-1965
Road & Track on Rolls Royce & Bentley 1966-1984
Road & Track on Saab 1955-1985
Road & Track on Toyota Sports & G T Cars 1966-1986
Road & Track on Triumph Sports Cars 1953-1967
Road & Track on Triumph Sports Cars 1967-1974
Road & Track on Triumph Sports Cars 1974-1982
Road & Track on Volkswagen 1951-1968
Road & Track on Volkswagen 1968-1978
Road & Track on Volkswagen 1978-1985
Road & Track on Volvo 1957-1974
Road & Track on Volvo 1975-1985
Road & Track Henry Manney at Large & Abroad

BROOKLANDS CAR AND DRIVER SERIES

Car and Driver on BMW 1955-1977
Car and Driver on BMW 1977-1985
Car and Driver on Cobra, Shelby & Ford GT40 1963-1984
Car and Driver on Datsun Z 1600 & 2000 1966-1984
Car and Driver on Corvette 1956-1967
Car and Driver on Corvette 1968-1977
Car and Driver on Corvette 1978-1982
Car and Driver on Corvette 1983-1988
Car and Driver on Ferrari 1955-1962
Car and Driver on Ferrari 1963-1975
Car and Driver on Ferrari 1976-1983
Car and Driver on Mopar 1956-1967
Car and Driver on Mopar 1968-1975
Car and Driver on Mustang 1964-1972
Car and Driver on Pontiac 1961-1975
Car and Driver on Porsche 1955-1962
Car and Driver on Porsche 1963-1970
Car and Driver on Porsche 1970-1976
Car and Driver on Porsche 1977-1981
Car and Driver on Porsche 1982-1986
Car and Driver on Saab 1956-1985
Car and Driver on Volvo 1955-1986

BROOKLANDS MOTOR & THOROUGHBRED & CLASSIC CAR SERIES

Motor & T & CC on Ferrari 1966-1976
Motor & T & CC on Ferrari 1976-1984
Motor & T & CC on Lotus 1979-1983

BROOKLANDS PRACTICAL CLASSICS SERIES

Practical Classics on Austin A 40 Restoration
Practical Classics on Land Rover Restoration
Practical Classics on Metalworking in Restoration
Practical Classics on Midget/Sprite Restoration
Practical Classics on Mini Cooper Restoration
Practical Classics on MGB Restoration
Practical Classics on Morris Minor Restoration
Practical Classics on Triumph Herald/Vitesse
Practical Classics on Triumph Spitfire Restoration
Practical Classics on VW Beetle Restoration
Practical Classics on 1930S Car Restoration

BROOKLANDS MILITARY VEHICLES SERIES

Allied Military Vehicles Collection No. 1
Allied Military Vehicles Collection No. 2
Dodge Military Vehicles Collection No. 1
Military Jeeps 1941-1945
Off Road Jeeps 1944-1971
V W Kubelwagen 1940-1975

INTRODUCTION

This do-it-yourself Workshop Manual has been specially written for the owner who wishes to maintain his vehicle in first class condition and to carry out the bulk of his own servicing and repairs. Considerable savings on garage charges can be made, and one can drive in safety and confidence knowing the work has been done properly.

Comprehensive step-by-step instructions and illustrations are given on most dismantling, overhauling and assembling operations. Certain assemblies require the use of expensive special tools, the purchase of which would be unjustified. In these cases information is included but the reader is recommended to hand the unit to the agent for attention.

Throughout the Manual hints and tips are included which will be found invaluable, and there is an easy to follow fault diagnosis at the end of each chapter.

Whilst every care has been taken to ensure correctness of information it is obviously not possible to guarantee complete freedom from errors or omissions or to accept liability arising from such errors or omissions.

Instructions may refer to the righthand or lefthand sides of the vehicle or the components. These are the same as the righthand or lefthand of an observer standing behind the vehicle and looking forward.

The Morgan Four/4 was introduced in 1936 and derived its name from having four wheels and four cylinders. The construction of the Four/4 followed closely the design of the Morgan three-wheeler, which had been made at Malvern for over twenty-five years.

The four-seater was introduced in 1937, followed the next year by the coupé version. These three body styles have always been available and were added to in 1963 with the Plus/4/Plus, a hard top two-seater with a fibre-glass body, which has now been discontinued; about 60 were produced.

The engines fitted to Morgans have always been supplied by well-known manufacturers. The original Four/4 was Coventry Climax powered, and this continued up to 1939 when the Standard Special unit was first offered as an option and soon afterwards became the regular equipment. This engine was the Standard 10 engine of the period with pushrod overhead valves replacing the normal side valve head. In 1950 the Standard Vanguard engine was fitted and because of the dramatic increase in performance, was called the Plus/4. This engine with all its TR variations is still being used. In the mid-fifties Triumph engines were in short supply and so Morgans, to keep production at about nine cars a week, started to fit Ford 100E units, and so was born the Four/4 Series II. Since that time a Ford engined model has always been in the range but with growing performance more in keeping with Morgans sports car image.

Morgans

IN 1975 the Morgan Motor Company are a remarkable survival, on the surface at any rate. They were founded by the present managing director's father before the First World War, making their name with those famous three-wheelers which unlike all modern tricycle cars had the engine in the right place, between the two front wheels, so that the centre of gravity was more favourably placed (though you could still turn one over).

They continued, after the last war, with a four-wheeled, classic style of sports-car, mostly two-seater, which up to the end of the 1950s at least was more or less in the style of the times, although it was beginning to look old-fashioned compared even with the offerings of such a conservative firm as MG. The remarkable thing is that the Morgan has stayed basically the same through the 1960s and as far as we've got into the 1970s. It 'shows no sign of changing.

And why should the Morgan change? The one time they did essay a modern, all-enveloping bodywork, it was not well received. One theory to explain that is the likelihood that whilst one might accept a very hard ride and a twisting chassis in a traditional sports car, such defects were not so charming or in place in a vehicle which at any rate looked as if it wanted to be compared with modern contemporaries.

Those of us on *Autocar's* staff who are Morgan lovers admit with great readiness that, without wishing to seem presumptuous, we are sure that the car could easily be improved with a better chassis, and proper, modern all-independent suspension and steering — without altering the car's bodywork nota-bly. Because that body, with its cutaway doors, raked slab back, exposed spare wheel, sweeping wings and louvred, centre-hinged bonnet is certainly a main reason for the Morgan's continued success, both here and abroad. We like it that way, and so obviously do a lot of other people.

What is it like to drive a Morgan? It is a sad fact that only one present member of *Autocar's* staff has driven a Ford-engined 4/4 1600 in anger, as it were, on Road Test; the last time we had one in current form it was not run-in, and was with us for photographic purposes

Tyre wear can be high if one yields too often to the temptations of V8 power
The joy of motoring, albeit on a closed airfield track and with a Plus 8 to play with (inset)

This article first appeared in Autocar 20 December 1975 and has been reprinted with their permission. All prices refered to are those applicable in 1975.

only. Our experience is based almost wholly therefore on the marvellous Plus 8 — marvellous, with reservations. It might not help anyone who, like most of us, might only afford the smaller Morgan, to say that one opinion shared by all of us is that the Plus 8 is made by its superb, light-alloy 3½-litre V8 Rover engine. To be fair, that engine's most pleasing qualities would be made insignificant if the car weighed much more than it does. But since it scales only 17.7 cwt against an MGB V8's 21½ cwt, the Plus 8's performance is sheer delight, not only in standing start acceleration but, thanks to its smoothness and spread of power, in top gear urge. If one feels lazy, the gearbox on a Plus 8 becomes virtually a range selector; during the Road Test, with the aid of only a little clutch-slipping, (up to just below 300 rpm, 6 mph), we recorded a quite respectable 22.9sec for the standing quarter-mile in top gear all the way.

To climb in and sit behind the steering wheel is to return to at least 25 years ago. The wheel is close, by the standards of today, making what seems at first a

Left: Family four-seater under its home hills, the Malverns

Below left: Four-seater 4 /4, an attempt to keep the family man happily Morgan's a little longer

slightly cramped cockpit if you are at all large. As you adapt, the feeling of confinement disappears. Drivers with small feet find the pedals a bit high, though partly thanks to the traditional Morgan roller throttle pedal, heel and toe changes are simplicity. Throttle control is smooth, or should be.

The ride is almost incredible if you are used to nearly any other 1970s car. Every bump is felt, more or less, and on an uneven corner the car will skitter outwards a little if upset. Its roadholding nevertheless is quite good, though not exceptional. Behaviour is better than you might expect, remembering the ride. It is above all fun, which is the principle purpose of a sports car, which any Morgan most undoubtedly is.

The best feature of the Plus 8 is the engine, if not its accessibility

Traditional dashboard on the Plus 8: only up-to-date features are the rocker switches

Morgan retain ash framing for the body and door frames

Cast alloy wheels are a recognition feature of the Morgan Plus 8; the extra 2in. of wheelbase is not so obvious

Hood-up vision is restricted; no Morgan should be driven in this condition

What to look for

For the information in this section, we are indebted to Peter May, sales manager of Mike Duncan Ltd., who are Morgan dealers for the Midlands, based at Windmill Hill, Colley Gate, Halesowen.

On the older cars, especially the TR-engined ones, it does not surprise us to learn that you should check for cracked chassis, notably close by the engine mounts. Morgan's ever-faithful and to many eyes dubious looking Z-section frame members cannot be expected to resist the fatigue effects of a lifetime of flexing for ever. This defect is less likely to be found at present in later models.

The car uses a traditional light wood frame for its scanty bodywork. Naturally enough then, again on the notably older models, there is a chance of wet rot, most commonly found in the door pillars.

The car has always used one of the earliest forms of independent front suspension, which has the virtues of potentially very low unsprung weight, strength and simplicity, and the vices of making no compensation for body roll as a wishbone arrangement can be made to, plus almost certainly marked wear. (Lancia used the same sliding pillar set-up for years too, though not lately.) The Morgan ifs does have a definitely limited wear life — about 20,000 miles we gather — after which the sliding axle and bronze bushes must be renewed. It is obviously simple to check this; start by trying to shake a front wheel sideways, making sure how much of any movement at the rim is due to wheel bearing slop by repeating the procedure with a friend applying the brakes hard.

Steering is by worm and nut, and whilst not as absolutely precise as a good rack and pinion, should not betray excessive slop. If it does, check how much of this is due to suspension play, since it does not wear badly.

The usual inspection for corrosion is needed of course, though thanks partly to its construction, the Morgan is not rust-prone; if there are damaged panels, replacement is said to be easy. Steel body panels are standard, but at various times some panels such as the rear and the bonnet ones have been optionally made in light alloy.

Inspect the gearbox thoroughly, particularly if the car you are thinking of uses the Moss box, for which spares are now very difficult. It is a very robust unit strong enough to cope comfortably with the power and torque of earlier Plus 8s; but, with abuse, first gear gets bashed and suffers accordingly. The Rover box used on later Plus 8s has a very good record of reliability in this application.

On the engine side, the first signs of crankshaft bothers on TR versions is a leak from the back main bearing; as a rough check, make

Morgan enthusiasm seen at a rally; the aerodynamic car was not a success

sure that when warm the oil pressure is at least 50 psi. Piston trouble is the most usual with the generally reliable Ford units, revealing itself once the engine is warm with what Mr May delightfully calls "heavy breathing" — blow by forced oil vapour from the rocker cover. The Rover engine not surprisingly has an excellently unclouded reputation on the whole, except for a batch around 1971-72 which suffered from noisy cam followers. Head gaskets have been troublesome in some instances. Don't be alarmed by apparently low oil pressure on Plus 8s; 30 psi is quite acceptable. □

Performance data

Road Test in *Autocar* of

Morgan Plus 8

12 September 1968

Mean maximum speed (mph)	124
Acceleration (sec)	
0-30 mph	2.3
0-40	3.5
0-50	5.2
0-60	6.7
0-70	8.6
0-80	11.8
0-90	14.5
0-100	18.4
0-110	25.7
0-120	42.9
Standing ¼-mile (sec)	15.1
Top gear (sec)	
10-30 mph	5.8
20-40	5.0
30-50	4.8
40-60	4.6
50-70	4.5
60-80	5.2
70-90	6.0
80-100	7.4
90-110	10.9
100-120	13.8
Overall fuel consumption (mpg)	18.3
Typical fuel consumption (mpg)	21
Dimensions	
Length	12ft 8in
Width	4ft 9in
Height	4ft 2in
Weight	17.7cwt

Approximate selling prices

Price range	4/4 1600	Plus 8
£700-£850	1968	—
£850-£1,050	1969	—
£1,050-£1,250	1970	1969
£1,250-£1,350	1971	—
£1,350-£1,550	1972	1970
£1,550-£1,750	1973	1971
£1,750-£2,100	1973	1972
£2,100-£2,400	1974	1973
£2,400-£2,900	—	1974

Spare prices

Component or sub-assembly	4/4 1600 (Ford)	Plus 8 (Rover V8) Moss box	Plus 8 (Rover V8) Rover box
Engine (short)	£111.50		
Gearbox assy.	£80.61	£189.00ex.	£191.00
Clutch assy.	£17.28	£21.66	£28.34
Rear axle less hubs, brakes	£113.40ex.		£189.00
Brake pads	£5.15		£8.05
Brake shoes	£5.68		£5.68
Radiator assy.	£42.20		£86.83
Alternator	£22.86ex.		£26.86ex.
Starter motor	£10.32ex.		£31.74ex.
Bumper (front & rear)	£19.44		£19.44
Windscreen, laminated	£43.20		£43.20
Exhaust system, complete	£49.00	£46.63	£50.61

Milestones and Chassis identification

		Series	Chassis No.
January 1968: 4/4 1600 introduced, with 1,599 c.c. 81x77.7mm Ford cross-flow engine fitted in place of Series IV (1,340 c.c., 1961-1965) and Series V (1,498 c.c., 1965-1967)	(Tourer) (Competition)	1600B 1600GT	1600 1605
October 1968: Plus 8 starts, with 2in. longer wheelbase to fit Rover 3,528 c.c. 88.9x71.12mm V8 engine, bucket seats, cast light alloy wheels	R		7001
November 1968: Competition 4-seater starts		1600B	1740
January 1969: Plus 4 Triumph-engined 2,138 c.c. models dropped (produced first in 1962) — last chassis no.	—		6853
October 1969: 4/4 1600 given dash similar to Plus 8, rev counter to right of steering wheel, other instruments and new rocker switches in oval panel mid-dash	(Tourer) (comp. 2-str.) (comp. 4-str.)	1600B 1600GT 1600B	2014 2017 2031
November 1970: 4/4 1600 fitted with collapsible steering column, standard engine and Competition designation dropped	(2-str.) (4-str.)	1600GT 1600B	2276 2281
December 1970: 4/4 1600 Tourer model dropped — last chassis no.		1600B	2321
February 1971: 4/4 1600 fitted with Ford 2265E with prefix A: mechanically worked clutch		1600GT	2381
October 1971: All models given dual line brakes, more dash padding, protruding instead of flush back lamps	(4/4 2-str.) (4/4 4-str.) (Plus 8)	B B R	2559 2565 7426
May 1972: Plus 8 fitted with Rover 3500S gearbox in place of now defunct Moss one	R		7482
May 1973: Improved fresh-air heater fitted all models	(4/4)	B	3060
October 1973: Plus 8 gearing raised, track widened	(Plus 8)	R R	7602 7660

CHAPTER 1

THE ENGINE

PART A   THE COVENTRY CLIMAX ENGINE

1A : 1   Engine type

The Coventry Climax engine was a popular power unit in 1936 when the Morgan 4/4 made its debut, and was to be found in the Triumph Gloria, the Crossley and many other makes. The unit fitted to the Morgan had a cubic capacity of 1,122 cc and developed 34 bhp at 4,500 rpm. (RAC rating 9.8 hp).

The exhaust valves are arranged at the side of the cylinders and the inlet valves are overhead and are operated by pushrods and rockers.

Late in 1936 the arrangement of the cup and ball joint was inverted so that the cup was at the top of the pushrod, where it will retain lubricant, and the ball is attached to the rocker. At the same time a number of other changes were made including the method of adjusting the tappets, and the connection from the bottom of the radiator was moved and enlarged. Moving with the times an air cooled dynamo was fitted and was driven by belt instead of by chain. The ignition distributor which was previously combined with the dynamo was redesigned to be driven independently by skew gears, and the engine mountings were changed to utilize rubber instead of being bolted rigidly to the chassis.

The engine is well lubricated. The course of the oil from the sump is as follows:

Upon being drawn up the suction pipe, the mouth of which is situated about $\frac{1}{4}$ inch from the bottom of the sump, oil passes through a gravity operated ball valve to a gear type pump. From here it is fed under pressure to a gallery case in the cylinder block and in turn by branch ducts to the main bearings of the crankshaft, which, being drilled, permits oil to be conducted to the connecting rod big-ends. An overhead rocker feed pipe also takes its supply from the gallery above-mentioned. Here oil is led through drilled bosses in the cylinder head to the base of the rocker bracket; this in turn is drilled both down the pedestal and through the rocker pivot arms. Lastly the rocker itself is drilled to allow oil to get to the pad in contact with the inlet valve and also the pushrod cup-end. Flow of oil is restricted to these latter parts by the insertion of wick in the oil holes in the rocker. Should this wick become unserviceable it can be replaced successfully by string. Provision for the removal of surplus oil is made by channels cast in the cylinder head, these channels leading to holes in the head of the cylinder block, through which the pushrods operate. Flowing down these, the oil finds its way back through the crankcase to the sump, lubricating the tappets at the same time. To enable the timing chain to be lubricated, surplus oil from the oil release has been arranged to play upon the chain and chain wheels direct. Cylinder bores are lubricated by crankcase oil vapour flung from the big-ends.

The oil pressure under normal conditions of running, with engine hot, should be about 40 lb/sq in. This pressure is higher when the engine is cold and the viscosity of the oil greater. If difficulty is experienced in maintaining oil pressure it is possible that foreign matter has lodged under the ball valve of the oil release. This is located at the front of the engine, on the near side, and after removing the aluminium cover the ball and spring should be examined and if the ball is pitted or ridged it should be renewed. Main bearing wear will also cause falling off in pressure.

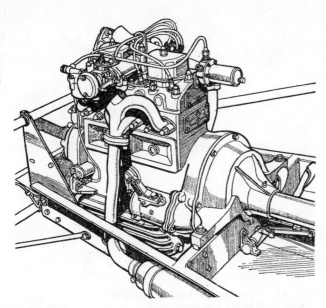

FIG 1A : 1   Coventry Climax Engine in situ (Four/4 1936)

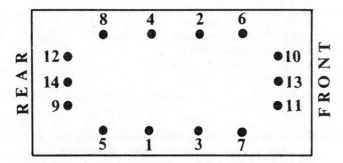

FIG 1A : 2   Cylinder head nut tightening sequence

1A : 2   To remove cylinder head

Drain off water from radiator; take off dynamo belt and disconnect top water pipe; remove ignition wires from sparking plugs, carefully noting the position of each plug cable. Remove the two overhead inlet valve rocker covers and disconnect the brass unions which convey the oil pressure feed via copper pipes to the overhead valve rocker oil system. Disconnect the pipes from carburetter and induction pipe and after releasing the ball joint and 'Rich Mixture' wire on the carburetter levers, detach carburetter and induction pipe (in one unit) from cylinder head and exhaust manifold. Following this, unscrew the large hexagon nuts which hold down the overhead rocker mountings, then the rocker mountings, each with its pair of rockers may be lifted. Withdraw the pushrods upwards and remove the cylinder head holding down nuts. The cylinder head may now be lifted from the cylinder block, care, of course, being taken of the combustion chamber gasket, although it is generally advisable to use a new gasket. If the head should be tight it will assist in freeing it if it is tapped under the lugs which will be found at the side.

1A : 3   Valve grinding

The valve springs should be pressed to enable the cotters to be removed and the valves ground in with a very fine emery powder moistened with oil. It will be found convenient when grinding in valves, to place a light spring under the valve head to lift the valve off its seat; it is necessary that the valve should be turned round from time to time during the grinding process to avoid the formation of ridges on the seating. When this operation is completed, the valves, ports and combustion head should be freed from all traces of carbon and emery powder, the valves and springs replaced and the tappet clearance adjusted and checked in accordance with the details that follow.

When replacing the cylinder head, it is advisable to see that the gasket is perfectly flat and in good condition and to apply a small quantity of good quality jointing compound to each side of the gasket before replacing. It is important that the cylinder head nuts should be tightened evenly to avoid excessive pressure in one spot.

They should be tightened down as per diagram **(FIG 1A : 2)**. It is essential to go over the nuts again with a spanner after the engine has been warmed up. *Note:* The inlet valve tappet clearance cannot be checked until the pushrods, rockers and rocker mountings have been replaced. Also the head holding down nuts should be finally tightened when the rocker mountings and induction pipe have been bolted home. Do not replace rocker covers until the engine has been run for at least ten minutes and the holding down nuts retightened and tappets finally adjusted.

The firing order of the engine is 1, 3, 4, 2.

1A : 4   Decarbonizing gasket set

Cylinder head gasket
Inlet rocker cover washers (2)
Exhaust tappet washer
Exhaust manifold washers (3)
Induction Bracket Washer
Exhaust pipe washer
Water—outlet manifold washers (4)
Rocker—bracket base washers (2)

1A : 5   Induction pipe

There is a correct way to tighten the induction pipe which must be followed. Do not tighten down on to the exhaust manifold, but first tighten down the three nuts on the cylinder head. Then ascertain if the washer between the pipe and the exhaust manifold is of requisite thickness before finally tightening. Pack, if necessary, to prevent strain being imposed.

1A : 6   Rocker and exhaust tappet covers

Carelessness in fitting the above parts can result in the leakage of oil, which in addition to increasing consumption, smothers the engine and keeps it in a continual state of untidiness. All these covers have cork joint washers. It is essential that the holes in the rocker covers register with the dowel in the cylinder head, and also that the holes in the joint washers fit over the dowels. No amount of tightening will prevent loss of oil if these precautions are not observed.

The long joint washer on the exhaust valve cover has a tendency to sag in the middle when the cover is being replaced **(FIG 1A : 3)**. Smearing a little grease round the edge of the cover will avoid this.

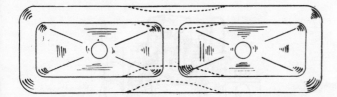

FIG 1A : 3 Exhaust valve cover, showing joint washers tendency to sag

1A : 7   Tappets

Tappets should be adjusted to the following clearances when the engine is cold. **(FIG 1A : 4 and 1A : 5)**.

Inlet—.006 inch.
Exhaust—.008 inch.

The tappets should be set when the piston in the corresponding cylinder is at the top of the compression stroke.

1A : 8   Valve timing

If the valve timing is disturbed it should be reset as follows. It is best to set from the inlet closing point and check the exhaust opening, as the other points are very close to the dead centre, making accurate measurement difficult. The timing is given in relation to degrees of crankpin movement and also in relation to piston movement.

The inlet valve commences to open when the crankpin is 10 deg. before t d c, the piston being within $\frac{3}{64}$ inch of the top of its stroke, and closes when the crankpin is 50 deg. past b d c, the piston being $3\frac{1}{32}$ inch from the top of its stroke.

The exhaust valve commences to open when the crankpin is 50 deg. before b d c, the piston being $3\frac{1}{32}$ inch from the top of its stroke, and closes when the crankpin is 10 deg. past t d c, the piston being $\frac{3}{64}$ inch from the top of its stroke.

N.B: It is important to see that tappet clearances are correct when applying the above.

1A : 9   Ignition timing

The distributor has a centrifugal advance and vernier timing adjustment located on the drive housing by a clamp plate. This should be set to the midway position. A two bolt cap at the bottom of the drive housing retains the skew gear, the contact breaker points should be set to open at the t d c and the gap adjusted to .012—.015 inch.

1A : 10   Timing chain

To check tension of the chain remove the plug from the timing cover and a finger can then feel the slackness which should be approx. $\frac{1}{4}$ inch. To adjust the timing chain when necessary, the three bolts holding the distributor drive housing should be slackened off a little, then the aluminium flange, together with the drive housing, can be pivoted about the bottom securing bolt, thus by swinging the assembly outwards the chain is automatically tightened. The chain, however, must not be run dead tight. When correct adjustment has been obtained the housing securing bolts should be re-tightened, care being taken not to alter the adjustment while so doing.

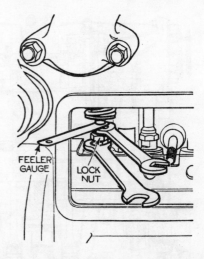

FIG 1A : 4   Adjusting exhaust valve clearance

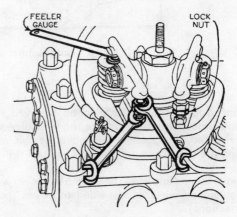

FIG 1A : 5   Adjusting inlet valve clearance

1A : 11   To remove the timing chain

1 Remove radiator, etc.
2 Remove dynamo belt and pulley, etc.
3 Remove dynamo
4 Remove timing chain cover
5 Remove 3 bolts out of distributor drive housing. Tip same and remove chain.

Replace in the reverse order, remembering to line up the marks on the sprockets.

1A : 12   To adjust dynamo belt

Slack off the securing bolts and swing dynamo outwards and upwards (this movement being governed by the pivoting bosses on the water outlet pipe and the adjustment link plate). When correct belt tension has been obtained ($\frac{1}{2}$ inch play), retighten securing bolts. Length of dynamo belt 3 feet $5\frac{5}{8}$ inches.

1A : 13   Removing the engine and gearbox

Except for major overhauls and attention to the clutch it should seldom be necessary to remove the engine from the chassis.

The most straight forward way is to remove engine, clutch housing and gearbox as one unit. It will follow that, in order to allow the gearbox to clear as the unit is raised and at the same time 'tilted', certain portions of

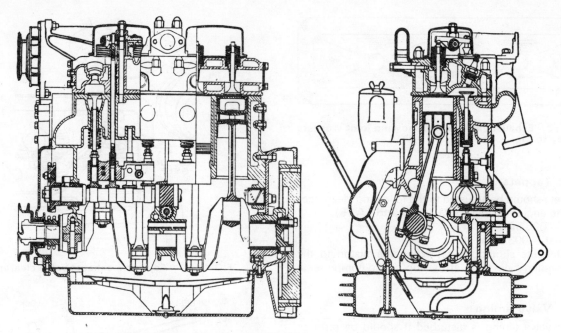

FIG 1A : 6   Longitudinal and Cross Section of Coventry Climax Engine

the front woodwork will have to be removed. If the following procedure is carried out, no difficulty should be experienced. It is possible to remove the unit without removing the radiator, but it is much easier if it is taken away.

1 Remove bonnet and swing headlamp bar down without disconnecting wires, except side lamp wires (pull out connections).
2 Remove radiator (two bolts at bottom of side pieces and tie-rod).
3 Disconnect all pipes, wires and controls from engine, the exhaust pipe can be swung out of the way without removing from silencer.
4 Remove pedal board and take out screws holding board which carries coil and cut out, enabling it to lift to allow gearbox to clear.
5 Take off battery (4 seater only).
6 Remove mounting bolts and lift engine preferably with a loop attached to the near side front and off side rear cylinder head bolts, tilting it to clear front upper tube.

Replace engine in reverse order to the above noting if the mounting bolts drop in easily as this is a good guide to chassis alignment.

1A : 14 Stripping the bottom of the engine (with engine removed)

1 Remove sump.
2 Remove spark plugs.
3 Remove caps off big-ends, and remove con-rods together with pistons through the bottom of the engine (will not go through bores).
4 Remove clutch and flywheel.
5 Remove timing chest cover and take off sprocket, together with timing chain.
6 Remove the 3 main bearing caps.
   The crankshaft should now drop away.
   Re-assemble in the reverse order.

ENGINE OVERHAUL

1A : 15 The crankshaft

The crankshaft runs in three bronze-backed white metal-lined shells dowelled in housings. The running clearance being .0015–.002 inch. End float is controlled by the front main bearing which has a thrust washer behind the timing gear, .003–.007 inch.

The bearings may be scraped to fit and caps may be filed to take up slight wear.

Crankshaft data

	Mains			Crankpins
	No. 1	No. 2	No. 3	
Dia.	$1\frac{3}{4}$ inch	2 inch	$1\frac{3}{4}$ inch	$1\frac{1}{2}$ inch
Length	$1\frac{5}{16}$ inch	$1\frac{5}{8}$ inch	$2\frac{5}{16}$ inch	$1\frac{3}{4}$ inch

The flywheel with integral starter gear (88/10 teeth) is bolted to the crankshaft flange and locked by tab washers. Always use new tab washers when re-assembling.

Round felt oil seals are fitted in grooves in the sides of the rear bearing cap, check and replace if necessary. The sump flange fits round the bottom of the timing cover at the front, and the oil thrower disc inside the timing cover.

1A : 16 Connecting rods and pistons

The big-ends are direct white metal in the con-rods. The running clearances are .0015–.002 inch with side clearance of .002–.0055 inch. The small ends are bronzed bushed, and the gudgeon pins should be a thumb push fit when cold. Aerolite pistons are fitted with a clearance at the bottom of the skirt on the thrust side of .0000–.0005 inch, clearance at top of skirt on same side .002–.003 inch.

Two compression rings and one scraper ring are fitted and should be gapped in the bores to read .015 inch. There should be a free fit without play in the grooves.

The gudgeon pin should be a thumb push fit in the piston when piston is warm.

1A:17 Camshaft drive

The camshaft on the nearside is driven by a duplex roller endless chain which then drives the distributor high up on the off side through skew gears. The distributor drive housing is slotted for chain adjustment, and the tension can be felt through the plug in the timing cover. The camshaft chain wheel is hub keyed on to the end of the shaft, and the chain wheel is bolted against the hub flange by bolts with chamfered heads. End float is controlled by front bush bolted to crankcase. Of the three camshaft bearings the front and rear are bushed whilst the centre one runs direct in the crankcase. (The engine must be removed for alteration to the timing gear on the camshaft). No timing marks are provided and therefore wheels should be marked before dismantling. Inlet opens and exhaust closes at same angle either side of t d c.

1A:18 Valves and tappets

The inlet and exhaust valves are not interchangeable. The inlet valves have a stem dia. of .311 inch, a head dia. of 1.433 inch and a face angle of 45 deg., and are located by split cone cotters. The exhaust valves have a stem dia. .309 inch, a head dia. 1.224 inch and a face angle of 45 deg., and are located by flat cotters in slots in stems. Double valve springs to inlet valve and single to exhaust. The inlet valve guides are shouldered whilst the exhaust are without, press in with chamfer inwards, leaving $\frac{9}{16}$ inch projecting downwards into valve chest.

Mushroom tappets are employed in two detachable blocks of four, dowelled and bolted to the crankcase. The exhaust tappets situated at the outer ends of each block have screw and locknut adjustment. Inlet tappets are recessed for pushrods and have a different diameter.

A detachable bracket carries each pair of inlet rockers on head at an angle. The rockers are located by circlips on early models and later by nuts.

1A:19 Fault diagnosis (see Section 1E:20).

PART B THE SPECIAL STANDARD TEN O H V ENGINE

1B:1 Engine type

Just before the war, the Morgan Co. offered as an alternative to the Coventry Climax engine, a specially built Standard engine. This unit has a bore of 63.5 mm and stroke of 100 mm. It has a compression ratio of 6.8 to 1 and gives 38.8 bhp at 4,500 rpm.

The overhead valves are vertical and in line but are offset from the centre of the cylinder. In plan the combustion chamber is more or less oval and its length is greater than the cylinder diameter but its width is considerably less.

The valves are all overhead and the inlet valves are larger than the exhaust. The 14 mm sparking plugs have $\frac{3}{4}$ inch reach, and the connecting rods are steel stampings. The pistons are light alloy Aerolites with split skirts. Single springs are used on the valves and there is a return spring at the foot of each pushrod. The overhead rockers are simple forgings and adjustment of valve clearance is by ball-ended setscrew in the rocker, the ball fitting into the cupped top of the pushrod. At the bottom these rods are themselves rounded to fit into the cupped tops of the tappets.

The cam is so designed that the clearance is gradually taken up before the valve starts to open so that quiet operation is obtained.

A feature of the lubrication system is that oil is fed along the overhead rocker shaft to each rocker bearing and through it to passages drilled at each end of every rocker; this therefore means that a supply of oil is always in the clearance between the rocker and valve stem as well as in the cupped top end of the pushrod. This has a distinct cushioning effect and cuts out any form of metallic hammering. The lubrication for the rest of the engine is of a normal nature. Oil is fed to the three main bearings and through passages drilled in the counter-balanced crankshaft to the big-end bearings. The crankshaft has suitable oil return worms embodied at the front and rear which prevents oil leaking along the shaft. The cylinder bores and the small end bearings receive their lubricant by splash, the top of each connecting rod being cupped and drilled. Then, forced feed lubrication is provided by a gear pump submerged in the cast aluminium oil sump and driven from a vertical shaft by a skew gear on the centre of the camshaft. The pump has a gauze covered floating intake submerged just below the oil level, so as to avoid picking up sludge. The camshaft that drives the pump continues upwards and drives the distributor head.

Thermosyphon cooling is adopted and this is supplemented by a two-bladed fan—the capacity of the system being 16 pints.

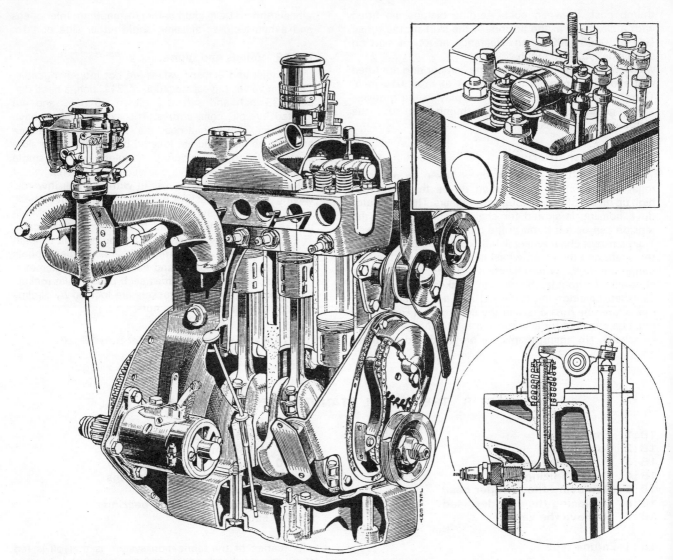

FIG 1B:1 Sectional view of Standard special engine (1939), showing manifold and Solex carburetter. Top inset shows overhead rockers and pushrods. Bottom inset shows combustion chamber and position of valve

The engine mounting is slightly changed from its predecessor. Diagonally placed rubber pads arranged partly in compression and partly in shear support the front end of the engine in brackets carried by the frame side members. In the region of the flywheel housing a transverse bracket with a Silentbloc bushing at each end provides a support, whilst a further pair of rubber blocks support the gearbox, the latter being joined to the engine by a large diameter tube containing the clutch shaft.

1B:2 Lubrication

The level on the dipstick should read between the high and low mark. Oil should be changed every 2,500 miles and sump removed from car and flushed out every 10,000 miles. Care should be taken not to remove the oil gauze which surrounds the pump as the set screws also hold the pump cover in place. The by-pass oil filter should be washed out in petrol every 2,500 miles and should be replaced every 10,000 miles.

1B:3 Fitting new oil filter element

1 Disconnect inlet and outlet pipes, loosen mounting straps and remove filter.
2 Blow through inlet and outlet pipes (after removing from engine) and check for cleanliness, also take a look at the calibrated orifice in the inlet union for the same reason.
3 Transfer all fittings from old to new filter and install same, check for damage and tighten the unions.
4 Run engine and check for leaks then tighten again. The oil pressure gauge should read 40/60 lb/sq in. under normal running conditions (slightly higher when cold).

1B:4 Decarbonizing

Pinking of the engine when being driven hard is the usual indication of whether the engine is in need of decarbonization or not. This state usually occurs after 10,000 to 15,000 miles of normal running.

1B : 5 Removing the cylinder head

1 Drain cooling system, remembering to keep coolant if antifreeze is used.
2 Disconnect radiator hose.
3 Remove rocker cover and undo the two nuts at the base of the distributor tower, and remove distributor and coil together, complete with plug leads. Do not slacken the clamp bolt on the distributor body as this would upset the timing.
4 Remove petrol pipe and control connections to the carburetter.
5 Uncouple the exhaust pipe and remove manifold nuts, take off inlet and exhaust manifolds.
6 Remove water outlet pipe from top of cylinder head.
7 Undo nuts at top of towers and remove rockers complete with shaft and towers.
8 The oil pipe from the oil gallery to the head, which is the feed to the rockers should now be undone, together with the bolt which is screwed into the head to assist the fixing of the dynamo.
9 Remove cylinder head nuts, remembering to slacken them off first commencing from the centre and working outwards diagonally. This is to prevent distortion of the head.

The cylinder head should now be free. If any difficulty is experienced in removing the head, turn the engine over by hand so that the compression will break the seal. Do **not** try to lever it off with a screwdriver.

1B : 6 Replacing the cylinder head

The order for replacing the components is the reverse of the previous section, a few points however may be helpful.
1 Use new gasket and jointing washers if possible.
2 Smear gasket with a little grease or household soap, this is to help with the next removal and prevent sticking.
3 Tighten cylinder head nuts a little at a time, working from the centre outwards to the front and rear crossing diagonally.
4 Check clearances (see Technical Data section) of valves.
5 If a new cylinder head gasket has been fitted run the engine for a short time and then retighten—repeat this operation again after about 100 miles again checking the valve clearance.
Note: When the cylinder head is removed, the distributor vertical driving shaft may have lifted out of engagement with the oil pump at the bottom end. Before attempting to replace the distributor check to see that the lower end of the shaft engages with the pump by pressing on to the top end whilst the engine is turned over by hand. To engage the distributor spindle with the top half of the driving shaft remove the distributor cover and turn the spindle until it is felt to engage. As there is only one position where this can happen the timing will not have been disturbed. Use no force when refitting the vertical bracket and distributor, when the shafts are correctly engaged the bracket will touch the cylinder head flange and the nuts can then be safely tightened.

1B : 7 Remove the valves

1 Remove cylinder head as previously described.

2 Fabricate a small block of wood which is slightly smaller but a little thicker than the combustion chamber and place it on the workbench.
3 Place cylinder head on top of block so that it rests on the valve head which is to be removed—depress the valve springs and remove the split collets. The valve will now be free and can be removed—repeat process with all eight valves.
4 The valves and cylinder head on this engine are appropriately numbered but a previous owner may not have been able to get a correctly numbered valve when replacing at some earlier time—a good way of keeping the valves in the correct order is to take an old shoe box and turn it upside down, punch eight holes in it and mark them and then place each valve as it is removed into the appropriate hole.

1B : 8 Replacing the valves and checking the clearances

Replacing the valves is a straightforward procedure, but care is necessary to make sure that the right valve is placed in the correct valve guide. With the rocker cover removed the valves can be checked. Turn the engine over with the starting handle half a revolution beyond the point where the valve to be adjusted has fully closed. The gap should be .022 inch for inlet and exhaust when cold. To adjust the gap slacken off the locknut on the rocker and adjust the ball pin until the gauge is a close sliding fit between the valve stem and rocker.

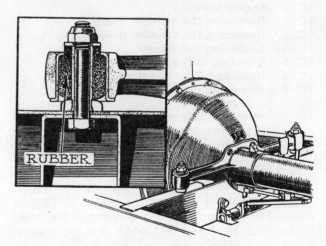

FIG 1B : 2 Front engine mounting

1B : 9 Valve timing

It is important that if any part affecting the valve timing is removed to take note of the markings on the chainwheel teeth. If these are indistinct make marks of your own before removing the chain. Should this have been neglected it will be necessary to retime as follows:
Inlet   opens 10 deg. before t d c.
Inlet   closes 50 deg. after b d c.
Exhaust opens 50 deg. before b d c.
Exhaust closes 10 deg. after t d c.

1B : 10 Replacing the timing chain

1 Remove headlamps and radiator.

2 Remove fan pulley, etc.
3 Remove timing cover.
4 Knock back lock washers on timing wheel bolts and then remove sprocket and chain, etc.

To check chain hold back tensioner and feel for a $\frac{1}{4}$ inch movement, if excessive fit new chain.

Reverse the order for re-assembling remembering to check for the marks on the chain wheels.

1B : 11 Replacing big-end bearings

It is possible to replace the big-end bearings without removing the engine or conrods, but should the crankshaft need grinding the engine must be removed. To renew the big-end bearings only drain and remove the sump, this exposes the big-end caps which can then be removed and the bearing shells can be pushed out. Slip in the new shells and replace the caps, doing the nuts up tight. If the pistons need to be removed they can be drawn through the bottom of the block.

1B : 12 Engine removal

1 Drain radiator, etc.
2 Disconnect all controls and pipes to carburetter and fuel pump and leads to distributor, etc.
3 Disconnect exhaust system.
4 Remove radiator and headlamps, etc.

5 Remove pedal board and disconnect clutch operating lever.
6 Disconnect gearbox and remove.
7 Undo front engine mountings and clutch housing mountings.

The engine should now be free and can be removed.

1B : 13 Renewing the main bearings

1 Remove engine as previously described.
2 Remove timing chest cover and withdraw sprockets with timing chain.
3 Remove front and rear engine bearer plates.
4 Remove clutch and flywheel, etc.
5 Remove big-end caps.
6 With the removal of the main bearing caps the crankshaft will be found to be free.

Reassemble in the reverse order to dismantling remembering to replace the bearing caps from whence they came—they are all numbered which will be of some assistance. Care should be taken in refitting the timing chain sprockets so as not to disturb the valve timing.

Note: This engine is an overhead valve version of the Standard Ten engine of the same period.

1B : 14 Fault diagnosis (see Section 1E : 20).

PART C THE FORD 100E ENGINE

1C : 1 Engine type

The Morgan 4/4 Series II introduced in 1955 is powered by the Ford 100E engine, which is also fitted in the 1953–59 Prefect and Anglia and the Popular introduced in 1959.

This unit, together with the clutch and gearbox is 'as fitted' to the above cars with the exception of a modified gear lever.

One of the advantages of this engine fitted to the Morgan (over the Prefect, etc.) is that the sump can be removed whilst the engine is *in situ* and therefore operations like renewing the big-ends, etc. do not call for the removal of the engine.

The 1172 cc side valve engine has inlet valves with larger heads than the exhaust valves, to allow improved engine breathing, and all valves have adjustable tappets and split taper cotter retainers. Solid valve guides are fitted direct into the cylinder block. Autothermic type pistons are used, having the piston pin holes offset $\frac{1}{16}$ inch towards the thrust side of the engine.

1C : 2 Removing the cylinder head

1 Drain cooling system.
2 Disconnect the choke wire at the carburetter and the throttle control at the throttle lever.
3 Disconnect the HT leads at the sparking plugs and the coil HT and LT leads at the distributor.
4 Note the position of the index scale in relation to the cylinder head and remove the screw which holds the distributor index scale to the cylinder head, and lift out distributor.
5 Detach top hose.
6 Remove dipstick and engine breather cap.
7 Unscrew cylinder head bolts and the sparking plugs.
8 Remove cylinder head, tapping gently on one side if necessary.

1C : 3 Replacing the cylinder head

1 Clean up head and block faces.
2 Smear high melting point grease on both sides of the gasket—the word ENFO should be uppermost on the gasket.

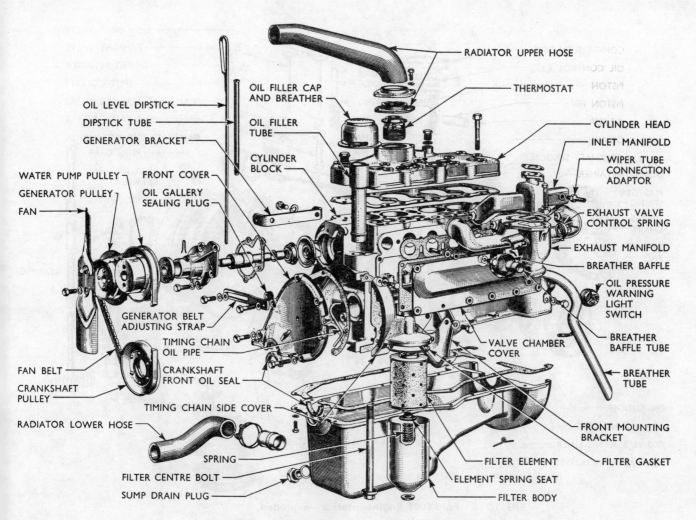

FIG 1C : 1   Ford 100E Engine exterior—exploded

Labels (from the figure):

RADIATOR UPPER HOSE
THERMOSTAT
CYLINDER HEAD
INLET MANIFOLD
WIPER TUBE CONNECTION ADAPTOR
EXHAUST VALVE CONTROL SPRING
EXHAUST MANIFOLD
BREATHER BAFFLE
OIL PRESSURE WARNING LIGHT SWITCH
BREATHER BAFFLE TUBE
BREATHER TUBE
FRONT MOUNTING BRACKET
FILTER GASKET
FILTER ELEMENT
ELEMENT SPRING SEAT
FILTER BODY
VALVE CHAMBER COVER

OIL FILLER CAP AND BREATHER
OIL LEVEL DIPSTICK
DIPSTICK TUBE
OIL FILLER TUBE
GENERATOR BRACKET
CYLINDER BLOCK
WATER PUMP PULLEY
GENERATOR PULLEY
FRONT COVER
OIL GALLERY SEALING PLUG
FAN
GENERATOR BELT ADJUSTING STRAP
TIMING CHAIN OIL PIPE
CRANKSHAFT FRONT OIL SEAL
FAN BELT
CRANKSHAFT PULLEY
TIMING CHAIN SIDE COVER
RADIATOR LOWER HOSE
SPRING
FILTER CENTRE BOLT
SUMP DRAIN PLUG

3 Replace cylinder head—tighten a little at a time in the order given in **FIG 1C : 3**.
4 Replace all items detached for removal—See Chapter 3 for 'Ignition Timing'.
5 After running the engine for a short while retighten head bolts again.

1C : 4 Removing the valves

1 Remove cylinder head as described.
2 Disconnect the exhaust pipe from the manifold.
3 Disconnect petrol pipe at carburetter.
4 Undo 4 bolts that secure inlet and exhaust manifolds. and remove same, together with carburetter, etc.
5 Remove fuel pump and gasket (2 bolts).
6 Unscrew the bolts holding the valve chamber cover to the cylinder block and the sump screw which holds the ventilation tube bracket.
7 Disconnect the oil pressure pipe and detach the cover, ventilation tube and cover gasket. The valve mechanism will now be exposed.
8 Block the two holes which connect with the crankcase.
9 Compress springs with compressor tool and remove split taper cotters—remove compressor tool and draw valve through top of guide and then spring and seats can be eased off guide, care being taken to keep

valves in the correct order and the springs, cotters and spring seats with the correct valve.

1C : 5 Grinding-in the valves

This is quite a standard operation and the only equipment necessary is a rubber suction cup valve tool (**FIG 1C : 4**). Before grinding in the valve check that it is in its lowest position. After the grinding operation clean all valves and valve seats thoroughly.

1C : 6 Re-assembling the valves

1 Check for wear between the valve and guides and replace if excessive.
2 Fit the valves lubricating each beforehand.
3 Place a valve spring and spring seat over each valve stem and compress them with a compressor.
4 Insert valve cotters.
5 Adjust the valve clearances. The valve clearance is set by turning the adjuster which screws into the tappet. As the adjusters are self-locking, no separate locknuts are necessary.
6 Make sure that the valve to be adjusted is fully closed and hold the tappet with spanner. With a second spanner turn the adjuster until a clearance of .0115 to .0135 inch is established between the adjuster and the valve foot.

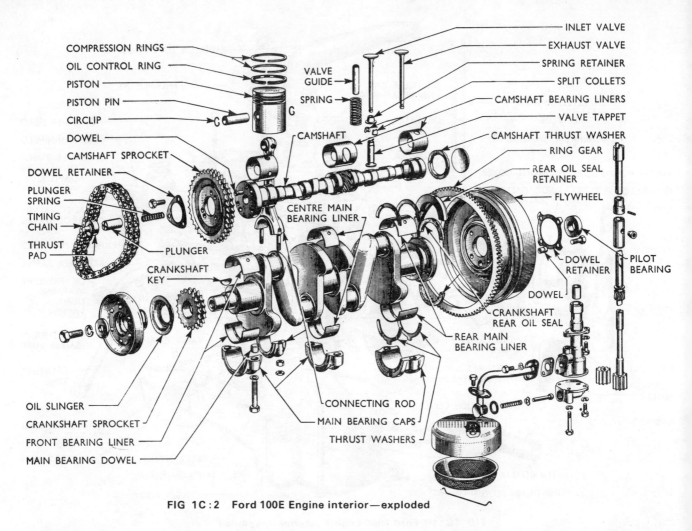

FIG 1C:2   Ford 100E Engine interior—exploded

Labels in figure:

COMPRESSION RINGS
OIL CONTROL RING
PISTON
PISTON PIN
CIRCLIP
DOWEL
CAMSHAFT SPROCKET
DOWEL RETAINER
PLUNGER SPRING
TIMING CHAIN
THRUST PAD
PLUNGER
CRANKSHAFT KEY
OIL SLINGER
CRANKSHAFT SPROCKET
FRONT BEARING LINER
MAIN BEARING DOWEL

VALVE GUIDE
SPRING
CAMSHAFT
CENTRE MAIN BEARING LINER
CONNECTING ROD
MAIN BEARING CAPS
THRUST WASHERS
REAR MAIN BEARING LINER

INLET VALVE
EXHAUST VALVE
SPRING RETAINER
SPLIT COLLETS
CAMSHAFT BEARING LINERS
VALVE TAPPET
CAMSHAFT THRUST WASHER
RING GEAR
REAR OIL SEAL RETAINER
FLYWHEEL
DOWEL RETAINER
PILOT BEARING
DOWEL
CRANKSHAFT REAR OIL SEAL

7 Refit the valve chamber cover tightening the bolts as in **FIG 1C:5.**

8 Replace all remaining components in the reverse order to dismantling.

1C:7 Removing connecting rods and pistons, etc.

1 Remove cylinder head as described.

2 Remove sump.

3 Ensure that the connecting rod and cap are suitably marked to ensure correct reassembly.

4 Turn crankshaft until piston is in lowest position and undo lock and main nuts on the big-end cap and remove the cap. The piston and conrod can now be removed through the top of the block.

5 After removing the piston and conrod refit the big-end cap, ensuring that the marks on the rod and cap are together.

6 To separate piston from rod remove circlips, warm piston in boiling water and push out gudgeon pin.
Note: It is important that all parts from one assembly are kept together and not mixed.

1C:8 Reassembling connecting rods and pistons, etc.

1 When reassembling the conrod to the piston locate the small end between gudgeon pin bosses so that when the assembly is held with the piston upwards, the arrow on the piston crown points away from you and the stamped numbers on the big-end are to the left.

2 Warm piston and refit gudgeon pin, this is locked in position with a circlip at each end.

3 Replace conrod assemblies in bore using a piston ring squeezer to prevent damaging the rings.

FIG 1C:3   Cylinder head tightening sequence

4 After inserting each piston, with the arrow to the front, and assembling the conrods to the crankpins, refit the big-end nuts and tighten to 20 to 25 lb ft. Then fit and tighten the lock nuts to 2½ to 3 lb ft.

5 Replace sump, head, etc.

1C:9 Cylinder front cover, sprockets and timing chain

1 Drain radiator and remove same, etc.

2 Remove crankshaft pulley and eight screws securing the cylinder front cover to the block (two of these screws pass up through the sump flange).

3 To remove the camshaft sprocket, extract the thrust plunger and spring from the centre of the sprocket and bend back the locking tabs. Unscrew the three bolts and detach the sprocket.

4 To remove the timing chain or crankshaft it will be necessary to first remove the sump. When replacing the sprockets, ensure that timing marks on both sprockets are lined up as in **FIG 1C:12** and that the dowels on the camshaft flange engage in the holes in the sprocket.

1C:10 Engine lubrication system

A submerged gear type pump delivers oil under pressure to the main oil gallery. A pressure relief valve is built into the pump cover to relieve the pump of heavy loads when starting in very cold weather.

The oil pump filter screen cover, **(FIG 1C:6)** situated in the bottom of the sump is connected to the pump by a short pipe.

Drilled passages from the main oil gallery at the base of the valve chamber cover feed the camshaft and crankshaft

FIG 1C:4 Hand grinding a valve

main bearings. A pipe from the front camshaft bearing feeds a controlled flow of oil to the timing chain.

The connecting rod big end bearings are lubricated through passages in the crankshaft from the main bearing journals. The connecting rod small ends are splash lubricated.

A bypass type oil filter is located beneath the lefthand side of the cylinder front cover and is fed from the camshaft front bearing. The cleaned oil from the filter is returned to the sump.

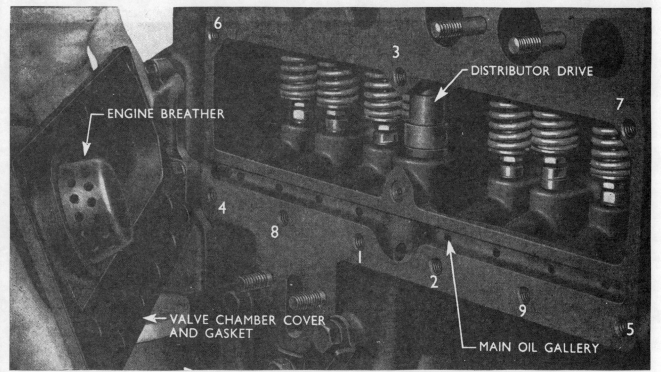

FIG 1C:5 Valve chamber cover bolt tightening sequence

FIG 1C:6 Oil pump in situ

1C:11 The oil pump

The oil pump filter screen may be removed after detaching the wire clip from the screen cover (**FIG 1C:7**). (The sump having been removed beforehand).

The oil relief valve is incorporated in the pump cover and is located beneath the large hexagon headed plug at the front of the pump.

The pump may be removed after unscrewing the two bolts securing it to the crankcase flange.

The oil pump gears may be extracted after the pump cover has been detached.

When reassembling the pump, ensure that the gaskets at either end of the pump to filter screen cover pipe are in good condition and are not allowing an air leak.

When replacing the pump cover, fit the cover with the relief valve plug towards the screen cover pipe flange on the body and ensure that the machined face of the pump is perfectly flat and is not scored.

1C:12 Engine removal

1 Remove bonnet and disconnect the rod from scuttle to radiator.
2 Drain radiator and remove water hoses, etc.
3 Disconnect all pipes and controls, to carburetter and fuel pump, etc. including oil pipe.
4 Disconnect starter and dynamo leads and all ignition leads.
5 Undo the bolts around clutch housing and release engine mounting bolts.
6 Check for any other connections which might restrict removal.

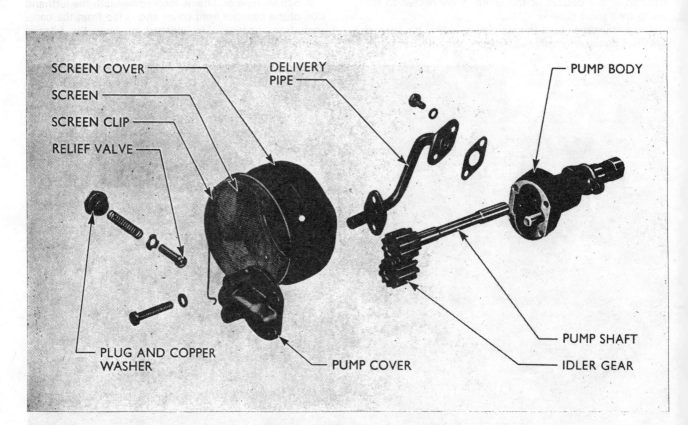

SCREEN COVER

SCREEN

SCREEN CLIP

RELIEF VALVE

DELIVERY PIPE

PUMP BODY

PLUG AND COPPER WASHER

PUMP COVER

PUMP SHAFT

IDLER GEAR

FIG 1C:7 Oil pump exploded

The engine can now be taken out, but as the radiator is still in position a slight twist and lift at the front will be necessary. (Replace in reverse order).

Note: The engine must be split at clutch to take gearbox out.

1C:13 Dismantling the engine

If possible try to mount the engine on a stand or bench which makes it accessible from all sides—this will greatly facilitate stripping.

1 Remove generator and mounting bracket.
2 Remove starter motor which is mounted on to the flywheel housing by 2 bolts.
3 Take out dipstick and unscrew the dipstick tube from the crankcase flange.
4 Remove the engine mounting brackets and near side support insulator.
   Note: It is necessary to remove the above items if you are fortunate enough to have the 'universal engine stand'.
5 Detach the top and bottom radiator hoses. When the top hose is removed the thermostat will be revealed, and this then can be lifted out.
6 Remove the clutch assembly, using a clutch compression tool. Engage the tool under the edge of the pressure plate and operate the cam lever. This will compress the openings and permit the six securing bolts to be unscrewed evenly and the clutch assembly removed.
7 Remove the fuel pump. This is located on the cylinder block and secured by two nuts on studs.
8 Remove the oil pressure warning light switch which is situated at the rear end of the valve chamber cover and is screwed into place.
9 By removing the bolt at the base of the oil filter, the oil filter body can be drawn away. Care should be taken not to tilt this as it can contain up to 1 pint of oil. For details of dismantling filter see 'oil filter' section.
10 Remove the oil filter and cap, this is a press fit in the cylinder block.
11 Remove the sparking plugs and eye-bolt if used.
12 Remove the cylinder head and gasket remembering to unscrew the nuts on the head a little at a time in the reverse order (FIG 1C:3).
13 Remove the fan and fan pulley which are secured to the water pump flange by two bolts and spring washers, and detach the fan belt.
14 Remove the crankshaft pulley. First unscrew the pulley bolt and then pull off the pulley.
15 Remove the nine bolts and spring washers which hold on the valve chamber cover and remove same. It will also be necessary to unscrew the bolt holding the lower end of the engine ventilation pipe to the crankcase flange.
16 Drain sump.
17 Turn engine over on bench, care being taken to ensure that the cylinder block surface is not scratched.
   Note: When the engine is inverted the distributor drive coupling shaft will drop out of its location in the block.
18 Remove the sump which is now secured by only 13 bolts, one of the bolts having been removed when the engine ventilation pipe was detached.

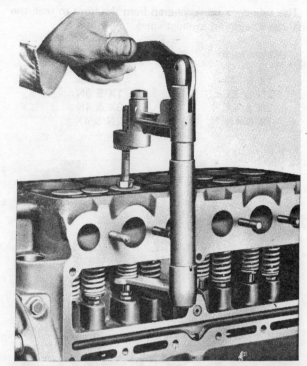

FIG 1C:8 Removing a valve with a valve-spring compressor

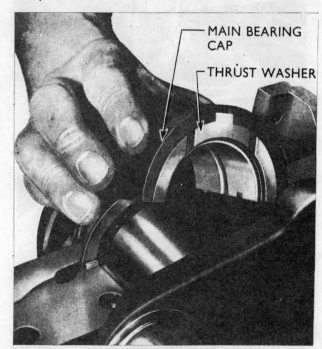

FIG 1C:9 Fitting crankshaft lower thrust washer

19 To remove the valve assemblies turn the engine over so that the valve heads are uppermost, and rotate the camshaft by means of the flywheel so that each valve in turn is fully closed before the spring is compressed. The following table will give a good guide to whether the push rod is being lifted or not.

   Key—N = Inlet valve
      X = Exhaust valve

The cylinders are numbered from the front to rear, the first valve being an exhaust valve.

Valves open	Valves to be removed or ground in
1X & 3N	1N & 2X
1N & 2X	1X & 3N
2N & 4X	3X & 4N
3X & 4N	2N & 4X

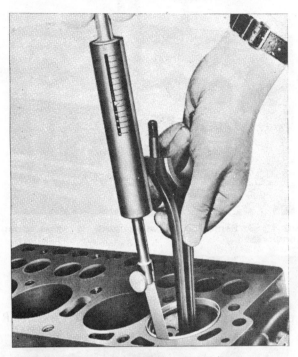

FIG 1C:10 Checking piston fit using a pull scale

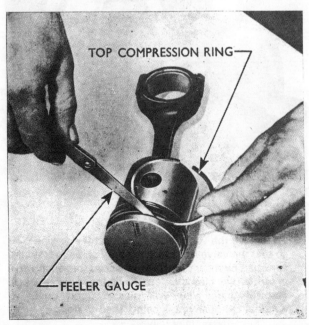

TOP COMPRESSION RING

FEELER GAUGE

FIG 1C:11 Checking the ring gap in groove

Revolve the flywheel until the exhaust valve of No. 1 cylinder and the inlet valve of No. 3 cylinder are in a position of maximum lift, then remove No. 1 cylinder inlet valve and No. 2 cylinder exhaust valve. Again revolve the flywheel until the next two valves in the 'valves open' column are fully raised and remove the corresponding valves in the opposite columns. Continue process until all valves are removed. There is a special Ford valve spring compressor (FIG 1C:8) (Tool A/CEY–6513) and this operates as follows:

Select valve and engage the lever arm of the valve spring compressor under the valve spring seat and tighten down the adjuster bolt until it rests on the head of the valve. Move the cam handle down to compress the spring and carefully remove the two split taper cotters from the stem of the valve. Remove tool, valve spring seat and valve and proceed to next valve.

20 Remove the valve guides.

21 Remove the cylinder front cover which is attached to the front of the cylinder block by six bolts and spring washers. The two bolts which pass up through the sump flange will have already been removed. Detach the spring and plunger, which are located in the front end of the camshaft; the plunger bears against a thrust pad on the front cover, thus controlling camshaft end float.
Note: The six front cover bolts are 3 lengths. The two shortest are fitted in the top and bottom lefthand holes. The longest bolt fits the bottom lefthand hole. The three medium length bolts fit in the remaining holes.

22 To remove cylinder side cover unscrew the three bolts holding same.

23 Detach the oil slinger from the front end of the crankshaft.

24 To remove the camshaft sprocket and timing chain, sever the locking wire and unscrew the 3 bolts. Detach the locking plate and remove the sprocket from the camshaft when the timing chain can be taken from the two sprockets.

25 Remove the crankshaft sprocket.
Note: The sprocket on the crankshaft is located by a key and keyway at the end of the shaft and the inside bore of the sprocket.

26 Remove the distributor drive gear and sleeve. This is retained in place by a small dowel which can be extracted by screwing a suitable bolt into the centre hole to pull it out of the cylinder block. The gear and sleeve can then be lifted out of engagement with the camshaft gear.

27 Withdraw the camshaft, first turning the engine over to allow the camshaft to clear the tappet feet.

28 The tappets may now be lifted out from their locations in the block.

29 Remove oil pump as a complete assembly (filter screen and cover) by unscrewing the two bolts securing the pump to the crankcase flange.

30 Remove the piston and connecting rod assemblies. Revolve crankshaft until the piston is at the bottom of its stroke and unscrew main and locknuts of each connecting rod stud. Carefully withdraw the cap, making a note that both the rod and cap are numbered

on the camshaft side of the engine. Check that the numbers correspond on the rod and cap. The piston can now be pushed up the bore and removed.

31 Remove the piston from the connecting rod assembly.

(a) Remove the circlips at each end of the gudgeon pin.

(b) Immerse the piston in boiling water for a few minutes, sufficient to expand the piston.

(c) Whilst still hot, gently push out the gudgeon pin; to avoid damage the piston should be supported during this operation.

32 Remove the flywheel. Bend back the locking tabs of the four bolts and unscrew same. Rotate the crankshaft until the locating dowel is uppermost, when the flywheel may be detached from the flange; a little persuasion with a hide mallet may be necessary.

The starter ring gear is shrunk on the flywheel and may be removed if necessary by cutting between two teeth with a hacksaw and splitting the gear with a chisel.

Examine the flywheel pilot bearing and replace if worn or scored.

33 Remove the main bearing caps. Each one of these is held by two bolts and spring washers and has separate steel backed white metal liners. Remove the bolts and lift off the bearing caps, together with the half liners. End float on the crankshaft is controlled by divided type washers each side of the rear main bearing.

Note: The washers in the cap have locating tabs which fit in slots in the cap to keep them stationary.

34 Remove the crankshaft by holding it firmly and raising it squarely out of the cylinder block, being careful not to damage the bearings or thrust washers.

35 Extract the upper halves of the liners from their block locations, the liners are located in the block by means of small tongues.

Note 1: It is possible to remove the liners with the crankshaft *in situ,* if one has the special tool.

Note 2: Early engines were fitted with liners containing two oil feed holes. These have now been replaced by liners containing only one hole, but double the size (.31 inch dia.).

The liners are completely inter-changeable, pair for pair.

36 Remove the upper crankshaft rear oil seal which lies behind the rear main bearing in a semi-circular retainer in the block. In the same way the lower halves of the front and rear oil seals may be removed from the annular grooves in the sump.

37 The timing chain oil pipe can be removed from the block by taking out the screw and clip. (The other end is located in a passage at the front camshaft bearing).

38 Remove the camshaft bearing liners if necessary. Before removing the bushes the blanking plug behind the rear camshaft bearing must be removed. Remove the fuel pump retaining studs if necessary.

1C : 14 Modification on the oil pump

Incorporated in the oil pump is an 'O' ring rubber seal which reduces the possibility of air leaks between the delivery pipe and pump body. The inlet hole in the pump body is counter-bored to accommodate this rubber ring, which replaces the gasket fitted on earlier engines. So when fitting a new pipe to an old pump, it may be necessary to open out the oil feed hole in the pump body, to accept the later pipe which projects approx. $\frac{3}{16}$ inch beyond the flange.

1C : 15 The oil filter

To dismantle.

1 Remove the filter element.

2 File away the raised stake marks on the bolt which secures the relief valve and spring in the filter body, then the bolt may be withdrawn and the valve and spring removed.

To re-assemble.

1 Use a new rubber gasket on centre bolt and replace.

2 Fit spring and relief valve over the centre bolt and pass the bolt with the raised side of the valve towards the open end of the filter body.

3 Restake the bolt with a chisel to retain the valve and spring in position.

4 Fit a new filter over the bolt in such a way that the end face of the filter having a raised boss faces the open end of the body, i.e. faces upwards when the filter is located on the engine.

1C : 16 Re-assembling the engine

Before re-assembling the engine make sure that the cylinder block and all its components parts are clean and that all the oil ways are clear. All wearing parts should be checked, and new parts fitted where necessary. It would be wise to replace all gaskets, oil seals and locking plates, and it should be remembered that the new crankshaft oil seals should be soaked in clean engine oil for at least 3 hours before they are fitted.

Lubricate all bearings and moving parts with clean engine oil before assembly.

1 When replacing the camshaft bearing liners make sure that the oil holes in the liners are correctly aligned with the corresponding holes in the block. When fitting a new blanking plug behind the rear camshaft bearing, it is wise to coat it with shellac to ensure an oil-tight joint.

Note: Camshaft bearing liners are available from the manufacturers in two sizes:

(i) Standard   (ii) .015 inch under size.

2 Replace valve guides.

3 When replacing the valve seat inserts, suitable drifts should be fabricated. Valve seat inserts are serviced for both inlet and exhaust valves, oversizes for both the outside diameter and depth being available.

The best way of removing the valve seat inserts is to place a chisel at the joint of the insert and the cylinder block, strike the chisel sharply with a hammer and the insert will be forced upwards out of the block.

The recess in the cylinder block face should be cut to the dimensions shown below, and it is not necessary to freeze the inserts before fitting.

Inlet valve insert—standard:

Dia. of recess in block 1.1820–1.1825 inches.

Depth of recess in block 2.28–2.30 inches.

Exhaust valve insert—standard:

Dia. of recess in block 1.0820–1.0825 inches.

Depth of recess in block 2.28–2.30 inches.

Inserts for both inlet and exhaust valves are also available in the following oversizes:

+ .015 inch O.D. standard depth
+ .015 inch O.D. and depth
+ .030 inch O.D. standard depth
+ .030 inch O.D. and depth

In each case the oversize should be added to the block recess dimensions quoted above.

Angle of seat on valve head 45¼ deg.

Angle of seat in cylinder block 45 deg.

Enter the insert into the recess with the chamfered outer edge first, and drive into position with a drift, as it is important that the insert is driven squarely it may be found advantageous to extend the end of the drift into the valve guide bore. The dia. of the drift pilot should be just under a third of an inch.

4 Fit the tappets and replace camshaft. If possible the bottom of the crankcase should be facing upwards, this is to enable the tappet feet to clear the cams. Inspect the brass thrust washer behind the camshaft for wear and if necessary replace. Be careful not to damage the edges of the journals and liners as the camshaft is inserted. Check to see if the camshaft revolves freely in its bearings.

5 Refit the crankshaft.
(a) Replace the top halves of the bearing liners in their locations in the block making sure that the keys fit snugly in the keyways.
(b) Fit new crankshaft thrust washers, of the same thickness as those removed from the engine. Now fit the upper halves of the thrust washers on either side of the rear main bearing with the oil grooves facing the crankshaft flanges. Hold the washers in place by a smear of oil whilst the crankshaft is being fitted. Check that the end of the thrust washers are level with the cylinder block face, otherwise they may be distorted when the bearing cap is tightened down.
(c) The oil seal ends when fitted should stand about $\frac{1}{16}$ inch proud of the block and sump faces.
(d) Lightly lubricate the main bearing liners and make sure that the oil holes in the liners and the block are in line.
(e) Lower the crankshaft into position taking care not to damage the bearings or move the end-float thrust washers out of place.

6 Fit the lower halves of the main bearing liners in the main bearing caps, (FIG 1C : 9) again holding them in position with a smear of oil. In the case of the rear main bearing cap locate the lower halves of the thrust washers in the groove on each side of the bearing cap with their tongues fitting in the machined slots in the cap.

7 Locate the bearing caps in position with the arrows pointing towards the front of the engine and tighten the bolts to about 55 to 60 lb ft.

8 The end float on the crankshaft should be between .002 and .011 inch. If it is more than this, fit oversize thrust washers; the following oversizes are available from the manufacturers, .0025, .005, .007 and .010 inch.

9 Assemble the piston and connecting rod assemblies.
(a) Test connecting rod for alignment before refitting them to the piston. Any twist or bend in the rods may lead to excessive cylinder bore wear in the line of the crankshaft.
(b) Heat the piston in boiling water for a few minutes.
(c) Insert gudgeon pin, this should now press in with a little persuasion.
(d) Replace circlips at each end of gudgeon pin, ensuring that they fit snugly in the groove.
Note: The piston is marked with an arrow which should face the front of the engine, when the numbers stamped on the conrods face the camshaft side of the engine.

10 Check the fit of the pistons on the cylinder bores.
(a) Insert piston (with arrow on top pointing forward) and the special 9 x ½ inch feeler blade in bore (F.B. on thrust side of engine).
(b) With the aid of a 'pull scale' (FIG 1C : 10) remove feeler blade and note reading. Pistons should be selected to give a pull of between 6 lb and 12 lb when withdrawn from cylinder bore.

11 Fitting new piston rings.
(a) Thoroughly clean piston and bore.
(b) Place each ring in turn at the bottom of the piston ring travel (making sure that it is the appropriate bore) squaring it up by inserting the piston.
(c) By means of a feeler gauge, check the gap between the ends of each ring. These should be within the following limits.
1st compression oil control .007–.012 inch.
2nd compression   .008–.014 inch.
Note: If the bores are worn the gaps should be measured with the rings located in the unworn portion of the bore.
(d) Place each ring in the appropriate groove noting that the compression rings are marked 'top' and the top compression ring is chrome plated on outer face. The 2nd compression ring is externally recessed, one edge being relieved, and this edge should face downwards. The oil control ring fits in the lower piston groove.
(e) Check piston groove clearances (FIG 1C : 11) which should read:
1st compression ring .0015–.003 inch.
2nd compression ring .001–.0025 inch.
Oil control ring .001–.0025 inch.

12 Fit each piston and conrod into its appropriate bore, being careful not to snap the rings as they enter the bore. There are a number of good proprietary clamps on the market which may help you with this task.

Revolve the crankshaft until the big-end fits the appropriate crank pin. Fit the big-end cap to the conrod with the stamped numbers together, making sure that the numbers are on the camshaft side of the engine, when the arrow marked on the piston will point to the front of the engine.

Screw the conrod cap nuts on to the big-end studs and tighten them up to a torque of 20 to 25 lb ft. Fit a small locking nut to each stud and screw up to approx. a third of a turn beyond finger tight (2¼ to 3 lb ft.)

13 The end float of each conrod big-end should be between .004 and .010 inches. Check with feeler blade.

14 Replace the timing chain oil pipe. The upper end fits into a passage by the front camshaft bearing, and the

pipe is supported by a clip which should be securely screwed to the block with a locking washer under the screw.

15 Replace the crankshaft sprocket and key on the front end of the crankshaft pressing the sprocket into position with the marked face to the front.

(a) Fit camshaft sprocket temporarily on camshaft flange, locating it on the dowel.

(b) Revolve the crankshaft and camshaft until the timing marks on the sprocket line up on the centre line between the crankshaft and camshaft (FIG 1C : 12).

(c) Detach the camshaft sprocket from its flange, and fit the chain around both sprockets and refit the camshaft sprocket, making sure that the timing marks are still in line.

(d) Replace the locking plate and 3 bolts and tighten down same.

(e) Lock bolts with soft wire through the holes drilled in the bolt heads.

17 Install the oil pump and distributor drive gear.

(a) Engage the distributor drive coupling shaft temporarily with the tongued end of the drive gear.

(b) Install the gear so that when it is fully engaged with the camshaft gear the tongue of the drive is visible at the end of the coupling shaft and points towards No. 3 cylinder with the large 'D' towards No. 2 cylinder.

(c) Refit the retainer dowel, tapping it into position until it is flush with the block face.

(d) The timing marks on the sprockets should be in line when the distributor drive gear is installed.

18 Place the oil slinger on the front end of the crankshaft, and fit the cylinder front and side covers, making sure that the camshaft thrust plunger and spring are located in the end of the camshaft. The side cover

should be fitted first using a new gasket. Smear white lead on the centre bolt of the three side cover bolts when fitting. The side cover should fit flush with the front face of the cylinder block and also the face of the crankcase. Fit a new oil seal in the groove in the front cover.

Note: The oil seal should be soaked in clean engine oil for at least 3 hours before fitting.

Next fit the cylinder front cover using a new gasket.

19 Check the clutch pilot bearing and if necessary renew. When replacing remember the flat face of the bearing should face towards the clutch disc, and the shouldered side the crankshaft.

20 Check the flywheel ring gear and renew if necessary.

(a) Place the flywheel on a flat surface, so that the tapped holes for the clutch pressure plate bolts face downwards.

(b) Place the flywheel ring gear on a metal plate and heat.

(c) The ring gear should be heated to approximately 600°F. (An easy way to check that the ring is the right temperature is to place a little lead round the diameter of the ring, as lead melts at 600°F).

(d) Place the ring gear in position on the flywheel with the chamfered edge of the teeth downwards and tap it lightly until it is up against the shoulder of the flywheel.

(e) Hold the ring firmly as it cools so as to make sure that it does not spring away from the shoulder while cooling.

Note: No attempt should be made to fit the ring gear when it is cold.

21 Refit the flywheel.

(a) Check that the flywheel and crankshaft flanges are clean and free from burrs.

(b) Turn the crankshaft over so that the dowel in the flange is uppermost.

(c) Slide the flywheel down into its housing, locating it on the crankshaft flange and dowel. Fit a new locking plate and evenly tighten the four bolts to a torque of 21/23 lb ft.

FIG 1C : 12 Camshaft and crankshaft timing marks

FIG 1C : 13 Checking valve clearance

(d) Check the flywheel is true (the run out should not exceed .006 inch axially or radially.)

(e) Lock the flywheel bolts by means of the locking plates.

22 Re-assemble the valve mechanism.

(a) After replacing valve guides and valve seat inserts recut or regrind the valve seats concentric with the guides.

(b) Fit the valves after grinding-in the valve seats making sure that each valve is well lubricated.

(c) Place a valve spring and spring seat over each valve stem and compress them with the valve spring compressor or other suitable device.

(d) Insert the valve spring cotters.

(e) Adjust the valve clearances (FIG 1C : 13). The valve clearance is set by turning the adjuster which screws into the tappet. As the adjusters are self-locking, no separate lock-nuts are needed.

(f) Make sure that the valve to be adjusted is fully closed and hold the tappet with spanner. With a second spanner turn the adjuster until a clearance of .0115 to .0135 inch is established between the adjuster and the valve foot.

23 Refit the valve chamber cover using a new gasket.
Note: Two of the nine bolts are somewhat shorter than the others and should be fitted one at the top centre of the cover plate and the other directly above the fuel pump location. The bracket at the upper end of the engine ventilation pipe fits under the second bolt from the rear along the bottom edge of the cover and at the lower end of the pipe under one of the sump bolts. Screw the oil pressure warning light switch into its location at the rear end of the valve chamber cover.

24 Refit the cylinder head.

25 Replace the oil pump which is secured by two bolts and spring washers to the crankshaft flange. The pump fits with the filter screen cover pointing towards the front of the engine and the slot in the end of the oil pump shaft is located on the driving tongue of the oil pump and distributor drive gear.

26 Replace the sump and gaskets. The crankshaft front and rear oil seals which are located in the front and rear walls of the sump should be renewed. The ends of these seals should stand $\frac{1}{32}$ inch proud of the block sump faces. The new seals should be soaked in clean engine oil for 3 hours before assembly.

27 Fit the crankshaft pulley, making sure that the pulley slot lines up with the crankshaft key. Replace the pulley securing bolt and flat washer and tighten securely.

28 Refit the water pump to the front face of the cylinder block, making sure that the machined surfaces of the block and pump are clean. Place a new gasket on the block and fit the pump, securing it with 5 bolts and spring washers.
Note: Smear the bolts with white lead.

Position the fan pulley and fan on the water pump flange and secure with two bolts and spring washers.

29 Replace the exhaust and inlet manifolds on the side of the cylinder block. Place the manifolds loosely on the studs, and slip the gasket into position. Tighten up the four nuts and flat washers to ensure a gas-tight joint.

30 Replace the clutch disc and pressure plate assembly on the flywheel, remembering that the clutch disc fits with the long boss away from the flywheel. Before replacing the engine in the chassis much time will be saved if it is known that the clutch disc is aligned accurately with the clutch pilot bearing. If a proper tool or another main drive shaft is not available carve a suitable piece of wood to shape. This locating rod or mandrel should then be inserted in the disc and lined up with the clutch pilot bearing. By tightening down the clutch pressure plate, the disc is secured. If this is not done, not only will it be impossible to locate engine correctly but damage to the clutch is probable.

31 Before refitting the engine to the chassis, replace the following components.

(a) Replace the oil filter tube and oil filter. A new rubber sealing ring should be fitted between the filter body and the cylinder front cover before the filter centre bolt is tightened.

(b) Replace the thermostat in its location in the cylinder head and refit the top and bottom radiator hoses.

(c) Replace the fuel pump on the two studs, using a new gasket and tighten the nuts.

(d) Replace the fuel pump to carburetter pipe.

(e) Replace the sparking plugs in Nos. 1, 2 and 4 cylinders and screw the engine eye-bolt into No. 3 cylinder.

(f) Replace the two engine support brackets and the lefthand side support insulator.

(g) Replace the generator and generator mounting brackets, using sealing compound around the bolts.

(h) Replace the starter motor.

(i) Replace the fan belt and adjust the free play to $\frac{1}{2}$ inch between the crankshaft and water pump pulleys and fit the bottom radiator hose.
The engine is now ready for fitting to the chassis.

1C : 17 Replacing the distributor

1 Drop the distributor drive coupling shaft into position with the shouldered end uppermost and revolve it until it engages with the driving dogs of the oil pump and distributor drive shaft.

2 Fit the distributor and replace the distributor index plate retaining screw in such a way that the '0' on the index scale is in line with the mark on the cylinder head. Now proceed to time engine as in Chapter 3. Ignition.

1C : 18 Fault diagnosis (see Section 1E : 20).

1D : 1   Engine type

The 4/4 Series III, IV, V, 1600 and Competition models are fitted with Ford overhead valve engines which are all based on the Anglia (105E) unit used in the Series III. The Series IV engine is similar to the Consul Classic and the Series V to the Cortina 1500. The Competition V is the Cortina GT engine. The 1600 engine is dealt with at the end of this section.

The text in this chapter is based on an Anglia (105E) engine and therefore an eye must be kept on the Technical Data tables at the rear of the book when dealing with the larger capacity models.

The Engine is a four cylinder unit with overhead valves.

The valves are mounted vertically in the cylinder head, the valve guides being cast integral. The heads of the inlet valves are of larger diameter than those of the exhaust valves.

Pistons are of the aluminium alloy solid skirt type, the piston pins being fully floating and retained by means of end circlips fitted in the piston pin bosses.

A single row chain drives the camshaft from the crankshaft and a mechanically operated timing chain tensioner is fitted.

The distributor, which incorporates both mechanical and vacuum advance, is mounted on the righthand side of the engine and is driven through skew gears by the engine camshaft which also operates the fuel pump located on the righthand side of the engine towards the rear, by an eccentric.

1D : 2   Removing the cylinder head

1 Drain coolant (two taps, one in centre of radiator and one on left side of engine).
2 Disconnect battery.
3 Disconnect plug leads and mark same.
4 Remove spark plugs, clean and reset to correct gap.
5 Disconnect top hose and heater outlet hose from cylinder head (where fitted).
6 Disconnect vacuum pipe at the connection to the carburetter and also the fuel pump to carburetter pipe at the union on the carburetter body.

7 Disconnect carburetter controls and vacuum pipe to the distributor; it is advisable to remove the carburetter assembly from the outlet manifold to avoid damage.
8 Unscrew clamp and disconnect the exhaust manifold from the silencer inlet pipe.
9 Remove rocker cover complete with gasket (4 screws).
10 Remove rocker shaft retaining bolts, and remove assembly. The pushrods can now be withdrawn.
11 Unscrew cylinder head bolts in order given in FIG 1D : 3.
12 The head is now free and can be removed. If difficulty is experienced tap head with wooden mallet.

1D : 3   Removing the valves

Using a valve spring compressor, compress the spring and remove the two valve spring retainer collets which rest in the taper of the circular valve spring retainer.

Release the spring compressor when the valve spring retainer and spring may be removed. Remove the 'umbrella' type oil seal, from the valve stem when the valve may be withdrawn from the cylinder head.

Repeat this procedure for the remaining valves.

The valves should be kept to their own seatings, either by keeping them in the same order in a suitable fixture when removed from the engine, or by numbering them.

Do not centre-punch the valve heads as this is liable to cause distortion of the valves.

It should be noted that inlet valve heads are larger in diameter than exhaust valve heads.

It is now possible to decarbonize the engine and grind the valves if necessary.

1D : 4   Re-assembling the valves

Re-assemble the valves by first placing them in their respective guides. Taking the first valve, hold the valve against its seating and press the oil seals down the valve stems. Fit the valve spring and spring retainer.

Fit the valve spring compressor squarely on the first valve, compress the spring and replace the two split taper collets.

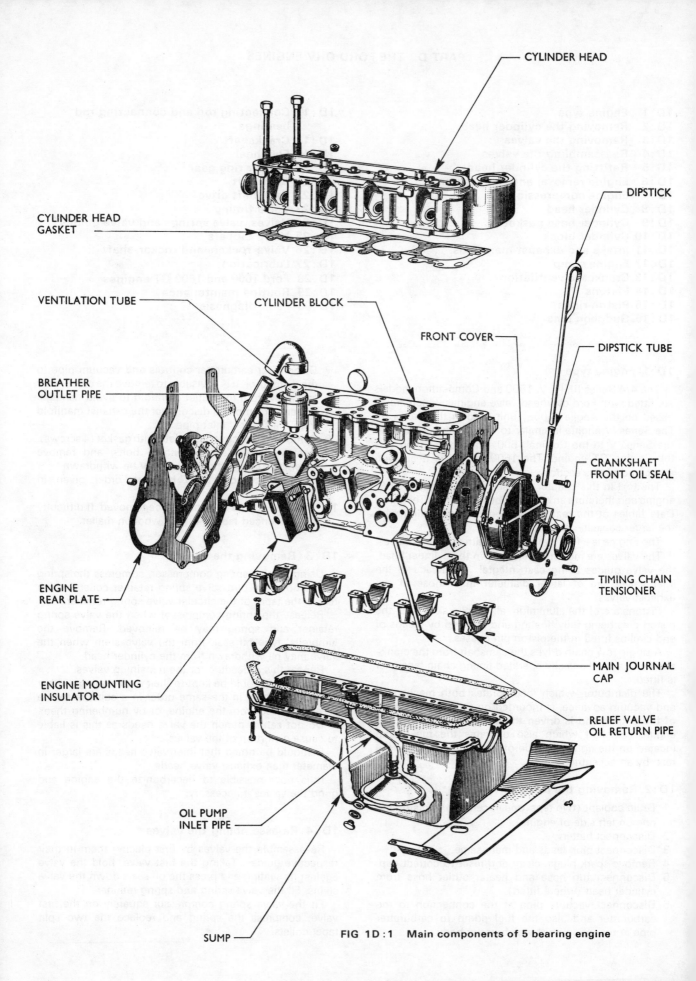

CYLINDER HEAD

CYLINDER HEAD GASKET

DIPSTICK

VENTILATION TUBE

CYLINDER BLOCK

FRONT COVER

DIPSTICK TUBE

BREATHER OUTLET PIPE

CRANKSHAFT FRONT OIL SEAL

ENGINE REAR PLATE

TIMING CHAIN TENSIONER

ENGINE MOUNTING INSULATOR

MAIN JOURNAL CAP

RELIEF VALVE OIL RETURN PIPE

OIL PUMP INLET PIPE

SUMP

FIG 1D:1   Main components of 5 bearing engine

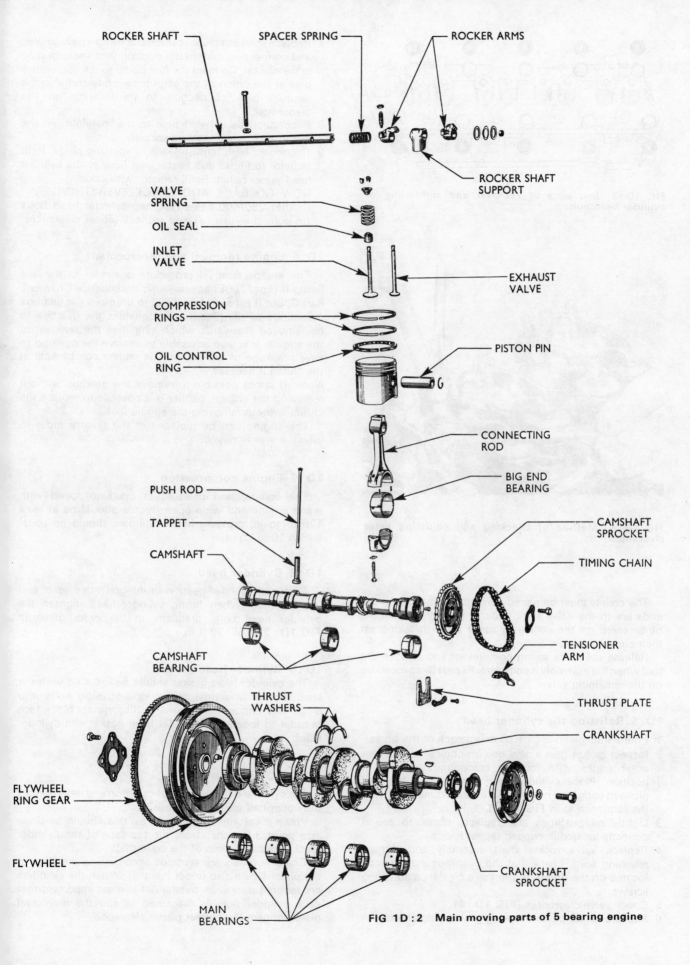

ROCKER SHAFT

SPACER SPRING

ROCKER ARMS

ROCKER SHAFT SUPPORT

VALVE SPRING

OIL SEAL

INLET VALVE

EXHAUST VALVE

COMPRESSION RINGS

OIL CONTROL RING

PISTON PIN

CONNECTING ROD

BIG END BEARING

PUSH ROD

TAPPET

CAMSHAFT

CAMSHAFT SPROCKET

TIMING CHAIN

TENSIONER ARM

CAMSHAFT BEARING

THRUST PLATE

THRUST WASHERS

CRANKSHAFT

FLYWHEEL RING GEAR

FLYWHEEL

CRANKSHAFT SPROCKET

MAIN BEARINGS

FIG 1D : 2   Main moving parts of 5 bearing engine

MAB1

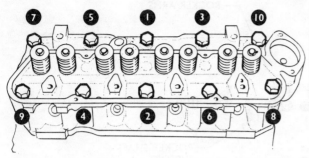

FIG 1D : 3 Sequence of removal and tightening of cylinder head bolts

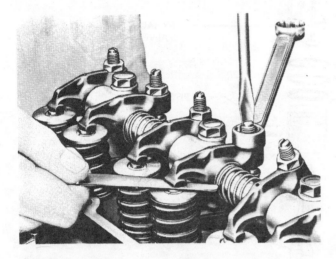

FIG 1D : 4 Method of checking and adjusting valve clearances

The collets must be paired correctly so that the wider ends are to the valve stem ends. A little grease should be smeared on the collets to assist them in taking up their correct position.

Release the valve spring compressor and remove the tool when the assembly is complete. Repeat this procedure on the remaining valves.

1.D : 5 Refitting the cylinder head

1 Pour a little clean engine oil down each of the bores.
2 Inspect gasket (use a new one for choice), and smear outer edges with jointing compound, and fit in position. Place cylinder head carefully on top and proceed to tighten head bolts a little at a time, following the sequence as in **FIG 1D : 3.**
3 Lightly oil pushrods and replace, check to see if correctly located in cupped tappet heads.
4 Replace valve rocker shaft assembly and tighten retaining bolts, check that the pushrods are correctly located on the domes of the valve clearance adjusting screws.
5 Check valve clearances (**FIG 1D : 4**).
6 Replace rocker cover checking gasket beforehand.

7 Replace sparking plugs, carburetter using a new gasket, and connect up carburetter controls and vacuum pipe to distributor. Connect the fuel pump to the carburetter pipe at the union of the carburetter body and also the vacuum pipe connection to its location on the carburetter.
8 Reconnect the exhaust pipe to the manifold. Fit the clamp and tighten screws securely.
9 Reconnect high tension leads to sparking plugs. Refit radiator top hose and heater inlet hose to the cylinder head water outlet. Refill radiator with coolant.
NOW GO BACK AND CHECK EVERYTHING.
After 250/500 miles retighten cylinder head bolts (in correct sequence) and recheck tappet clearances.

1D : 6 Engine removal and replacement

The engine removal procedure is similar to the 4/4 Series II (Ford 100E) as previously described in Chapter 1 Part C, but it is found beneficial to unfasten the gearbox mountings to the chassis. This enables the gearbox to be removed rearwards which simplifies the removal of the engine. It is also advisable to remove the dynamo to save breakage of the pulley. The engine can be split at the clutch if necessary.
Note: It is not possible to remove the gearbox without removing the engine, neither is it possible to replace the clutch without removing the engine.

The engine can be replaced in the reverse order to which it was removed.

1D : 7 Engine compression

The compression pressure at cranking speed with warm engine and wide open throttle should be at least 120 lb/sq in; pressure in all cylinders should be equal within 10 lb/sq in.

1D : 8 Cylinder head

Cast-iron cylinder head with integral valve seats and valve guides. When fitting cylinder head, tighten the cylinder head bolts gradually in the order given in **FIG 1D : 3** to 65–70 ft lb.

1D : 9 Cylinder head gasket

The cylinder head gasket should be installed with the steel face downwards; screw locating stud bolts into diagonally opposite bolt holes in the cylinder block face in order to locate the cylinder head gasket and cylinder head.

1D : 10 Cylinder block

The cylinder block is made of cast-iron and incorporates the upper half of the crankcase.

When measuring cylinder bores, this should be done at a point 3.5 inches from the top face of the cylinder block, across the axis of the crankshaft.

Grade numbers are stamped according to the sizes of the pistons (see also under Pistons). When the cylinders are rebored during an overhaul it is most important that each cylinder bore is machined to suit the individual piston to give the correct piston clearance.

1D : 11 Intake and exhaust manifolds

The intake and exhaust manifolds are joined together to form a 'hot-spot' for pre-heating of the mixture.

1D : 12 Engine sump

The removable engine sump is a steel pressing and can be lowered without hinderance.

1D : 13 Crankcase ventilation

The air for crankcase ventilation enters the engine via a steel wool filter in the oil filler cap. The outlet is fitted on the righthand side of the crankcase, on top of the fuel pump boss.

1D : 14 Pistons

Light alloy, solid skirt, cam ground pistons of the autothermic type, with two compression rings and one oil control ring above the gudgeon pin (piston pin) (FIG 1D : 5). Pistons are available in standard size and .030 inch oversize; each piston is marked with a grade number, which should correspond to the grade number of the cylinder in which the piston is to be fitted.

Piston clearance is measured by inserting the piston, together with a .0015 x .5 inch feeler gauge into the cylinder; a pull of 8–11 lb. should be required to remove the feeler gauge.

When the cylinders are rebored, it is most important that each cylinder bore is machined to suit the individual piston in order to give the correct piston clearance. The piston clearance should be measured at right angles to the gudgeon pin holes.

When installing pistons to connecting rods, the arrow mark on the piston head should coincide with the FRONT mark on the connecting rod; heat the pistons in oil or water prior to fitting the gudgeon pin.

Install the piston and connecting rod assembly in the engine with the arrow mark on the piston head toward the front of the cylinder block.

1D : 15 Piston rings

Each piston is equipped with two compression rings and one oil control ring, which are positioned above the gudgeon pin.

Ring clearance in groove, compression rings: .0016–.0036 inch.

Ring clearance in groove, oil control ring: .0018–.0038 inch.

Gap width, compression and oil rings: .009–.014 inch.

When installing piston rings, the word TOP on the compression ring should be facing upwards; the chromium-plated compression ring must be installed in the top groove.

Space the ring gaps at 120° before installing the piston in the cylinder.

1D : 16 Gudgeon pins

Hollow steel, fully floating gudgeon pins, retained in the piston by circlips.

Gudgeon pin clearance in connecting rod bush: .0001–.0003 inch (selective).

Heat pistons in water or oil when fitting gudgeon pins.

After the piston has cooled, the pin should be a tight fit in the piston.

FIG 1D : 5 A connecting rod and piston assembly (exploded)

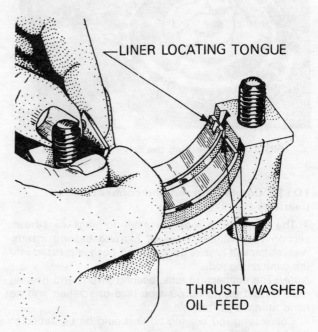

—LINER LOCATING TONGUE

THRUST WASHER OIL FEED

FIG 1D : 6 Main bearing cap and liner

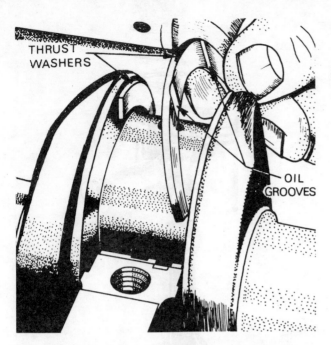

FIG 1D : 7   Replacing the crankshaft thrust washers

FIG 1D : 8   Checking the valve timing marks

1D : 17 Connecting rod and connecting rod bearings

The connecting rods are steel forgings of I-beam section with various types of big-end bearing inserts. A steel-backed bronze gudgeon pin bush is pressed into the connecting rod.

Note: The connecting rods, bearing inserts and bearing caps should on no account be filed or scraped and no hand fitting is permissible.

Connecting rod bearing bolts should be tightened to 20–25 lb ft.

1D : 18 Crankshaft

The crankshaft has three or five main bearings, (depending on the size and year of the engine) and runs in thin-wall, steel-backed bearing inserts with light metal linings. The crankshaft end-play is taken by semi-circular thrust washers which are fitted at either side of the centre main bearing **FIG 1D : 7**. The thrust washers should be fitted with the oil grooves facing the crankshaft flange.

In engines with numbers after approximately 105E–5200, an oil feed is provided to the rear crankshaft thrust washer. The centre main bearing cap is provided with a 30° chamfer .03–.04 inch wide between the bearing locating notch and the rear face of bearing cap. Oil is fed into the groove formed by this chamfer through a V-notch in the oilway at the locating tab end of the bearing insert.

Main bearing clearance: .0005–.002 inch.
Main bearing length: 1.00 inch.
Crankshaft end clearance: .003–.011 inch.
Main bearing bolts should be tightened to 55–60 lb ft. Check Technical Data Section for later engines.

1D : 19 Flywheel

The flywheel is fitted to the crankshaft by means of a locating sleeve, a dowel pin and four bolts.

Maximum allowable run-out, measured at the clutch surface is .004 inch.

Tighten flywheel bolts to 45–50 lb ft, and bend the tabs on the locking plate over the bolt heads.

1D : 20 Starter ring gear

Starter ring gear of special alloy steel, shrunk on to the flywheel.

1D : 21 Camshaft

The cast-iron camshaft is positioned in the righthand side of the engine crankcase and runs in three steel-backed babbit-lined bearing bushings. The end-play is taken by a thrust flange which is fitted between the front of the cylinder block and a collar on the camshaft front end. The camshaft sprocket is fitted to the camshaft by means of a dowel pin and two bolts.

1D : 22 Camshaft drive

Camshaft drive is by means of a single row roller chain with hydraulic tensioner.
Number of teeth on crankshaft sprocket, 17.
Number of teeth on camshaft sprocket, 34.

When fitting the camshaft sprocket and chain, the marked teeth on both sprockets should be on the centre line facing each other. **(FIG 1D : 8)**.

1D : 23 Valve timing

The valve timing should be checked with .015 inch inlet valve clearance and .027 inch exhaust valve clearance on cold engine. G.T. .016 inch and .026 inch respectively.

For valve clearances on all engines turn to Technical Data Section.

1D:24 Valves, valve springs and valve guides

Overhead valves, pushrod operated, with valve guides integral with the cylinder head, see Technical Data Section for clearances, etc. Single valve springs are used with a free length of 1.48 inch clearances.

1D:25 Valve tappets

Valve tappets of mushroom type. When removing valve tappets from the cylinder block, be sure to note the location of each tappet in order that it may be re-installed in the original bore.

1D:26 Valve-rockers and rocker-shaft

The valve-rockers are assembled on to the hollow steel rocker-shaft, which rests in four supports on the cylinder head. The seat of the front rocker-shaft support on the cylinder head is provided with an oil hole. When the valve-rockers and related parts are removed from the rocker-shaft, they should be reassembled in the following order: (FIG 1D:2).

Fit a new cotter pin in one end of the rocker-shaft, install a flat steel washer, a spring cup washer and a second flat washer on the shaft; slide a rocker on the shaft, followed by a rocker-shaft support. (The bolt holes in the rocker-shaft supports must be on the same side as the adjusting screw in the valve-rockers). Now install a rocker, a spring and a rocker, followed by a support and complete the assembly in this manner. After the last rocker arm has been fitted, install a flat washer, the steel spring cup washer and another flat washer on the shaft; secure all parts in place by fitting a cotter pin.

1D:27 Lubrication

Full pressure lubrication, by means of a bi-rotor or vane type oil pump which is situated at the righthand side of the crankcase. The oil pump is driven by the camshaft; oil enters the pump through a filter screen which is fitted to the pump suction pipe in the oil sump. Incorporated in the oil pump is a pressure relief valve, which, when open, allows the oil to return direct to the sump. This oil returns via a pipe to the base of the sump, thus preventing aeration of the oil. Oil from the pump is

FIG 1D:9 Bi-rotor oil pump completely dismantled

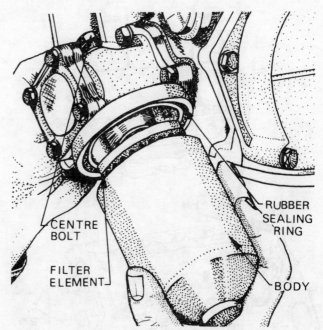

FIG 1D:10 Oil filter showing location of sealing arrangements

fed to the full-flow filter which is fitted to the pump housing. From the oil filter, the oil is fed through a cross-drilling above the centre main bearing to the main oil channel on the lefthand side of the engine. Oil is also fed via a short gallery to the oil pressure transmitter unit on the righthand side of the engine.

Separate oil channels feed oil from the main oil gallery to each main bearing; the connecting rod bearings are supplied with oil from the main bearings via drilled passages in the mainshaft.

A small oil hole is incorporated in each connecting-rod shoulder which allows a jet of oil to lubricate the non-thrust side of the cylinders at each revolution of the crankshaft.

The camshaft bearings are fed via channels in the cylinder block from the three main bearings.

A flat is machined on the front camshaft journal, allowing oil to be fed through channels in the cylinder block and cylinder head to the front rocker-shaft support from where the oil enters the hollow rocker-shaft to lubricate the valve-rockers. Each valve-rocker is drilled for lubrication of the valve stems and valve pushrods.

The oil feed to the rocker-shaft assembly is at a reduced pressure, the system being pressurised once per revolution of the camshaft.

The timing gears and chain are lubricated by a constant supply of oil from a drilling between the crankshaft and camshaft front bearings.

The normal oil pressure is 35–40 lb/sq inch; the oil pressure warning light remains on as long as the pressure is less than 5–7 lb/sq inch.

The oil pressure regulator valve (relief valve) is incorporated in the oil pump and is non-adjustable.

The oil pump is of the bi-rotor type and is installed at the righthand side of the crankcase (FIG 1D:9); the pump is driven by the camshaft.

The clearance between the lobes of the inner and outer rotors should not exceed .006 inch; the clearance

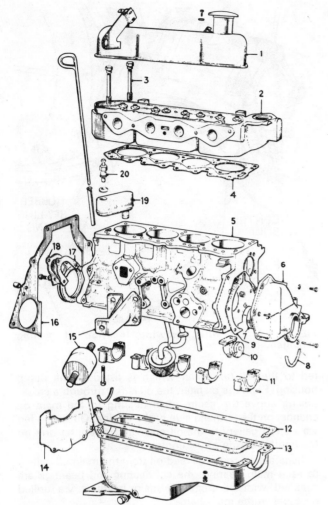

FIG 1D:11 The cylinder block and associated parts, 1600 engine

Key to Fig 1D:11   1 Rocker cover   2 Cylinder head
3 Head bolt   4 Head gasket   5 Cylinder block   6 Front
cover   7 Front seal   8 Cork packing strip   9 Cover gasket
10 Timing chain tensioner   11 Main bearing cap   12 Sump
gasket   13 Sump   14 Dust cover   15 Mounting bracket
16 Rear gasket   17 Carrier gasket   18 Rear oil seal carrier
19 Oil separator   20 Crankcase emission valve

between the outer rotor and the pump housing should
not exceed .0075 inch.

New rotors are avilable as a matched pair only.
The end-clearance of the rotors should not exceed .005
inch; if necessary, the face of the pump body can be
lapped on a flat surface. A sliding vane type pump is
fitted to some engines, and the end-clearance should be
.005 inch as previously.

Fullflow oil filter, positioned on oil pump housing.
When fitting the filter housing, always install a new filter
sealing ring in the groove in the pump body at four
diametrically opposite points.

Do not fit the sealing ring at one point and work it
around the groove, because the rubber will stretch, thus
leaving a surplus which could cause an oil leak.

The oil filter is equipped with a pressure relief valve
which is incorporated in the oil pump body.

1D:28 Ford 1600 and 1600 GT engines

The Morgan 4/4 1600 was first introduced in October
1967 and utilises the 1598 cc crossflow engine introduced
by Ford at the same time. The engine is available in
standard and GT form and has been used in Cortina,
Capri and most recently Escort Sport and Ghia models.

Compared with the previous 1500 cc unit the block
height of the 1600 engine has been increased by .44 inch
to allow for its longer stroke. The static parts of the engine
are illustrated in **FIG 1D:11**. The bottom end is virtually
unchanged except for the crankshaft where the balance
weights are arranged differently to take account of the
greater reciprocating weights of pistons and connecting
rods. Bearing shapes and sizes remain the same. The
H-section connecting rods are sturdier and measure
4.93 inches between centres. Big-end caps are still
located by spring dowels and retained by bolts, but these
are now of larger diameter. Because of the reduced space
between the top of the little end and the recessed piston
crown, the little end balance boss is placed on the thrust
side of the little end bearing. The oil pump, distributor,
water pump and camshaft are unchanged. The new crossflow cylinder head is the biggest point of difference from
the earlier versions. The inlet ports now curve in from the
right side of the engine between the pairs of pushrods.
The bolt spacings and the pushrod and rocker gear are
otherwise the same. The sparking plugs are positioned on
the left (**FIG 1D:12**), at a point intended to keep the
flame paths to a minimum. The valves and collets have
been re-designed with three grooves to allow the valves
to rotate slowly when in operation, thus preventing
uneven wear and extending the life of the valves. An
item which has been modified and made simpler is the
one-piece tappet adjuster (**FIG 1D:13**).

The engine is fitted with a new Weston-Thompson
graduated opening thermostat with a stepped seat. A
semi-closed ventilation system is fitted and consists of a
breather incorporated in the oil filler cap, an oil separator
located on the fuel pump mounting pad, an emission
valve which fits into a grommet on top of the oil
separator, and a connecting tube to the inlet manifold.

Other modifications include a new camshaft and
different inlet and exhaust manifolds. The exhaust mani-

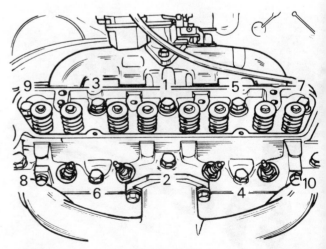

FIG 1D:12   1600 cylinder head showing bolt tightening
sequence

fold is of four-branch design special to Morgan cars. The GT version weighs slightly less than the standard version as the flywheel has been reduced by 7½ lb.

Overhaul of the 1600 standard and GT engines is generally as for the other Ford OHV engines but reference should be made to the **Technical Data** at the end of this manual for detailed variations.

1D:29 Routine maintenance

After the first 600 miles, especially after an overhaul, and ideally also from new, tighten the cylinder head bolts to 65 to 70 lb ft torque, using the sequence shown in **FIG 1D:12**. At the same time tighten the sump bolts to 6 to 8 lb ft. Check also manifold and exhaust outlet bolts, torque 15 to 20 lb ft. On GT engines the outlet bolts should be tightened to 6 to 8 lb ft. Check also valve clearances and adjust where necessary using a $\frac{7}{16}$ inch AF ring, tube or socket spanner in good condition. Do not use an open-ended spanner. Valve clearances with the engine hot should be as follows:

Standard engine: inlet, .010 inch; outlet, .017 inch.
GT engine: inlet, .012 inch; outlet, .022 inch.
Use the following sequence starting with No. 1 valve at the front:

Valves fully open (rockers right down)	Valves to adjust
1 and 6	3 and 8
3 and 8	1 and 6
2 and 4	5 and 7
5 and 7	2 and 4

After the first 2–3000 miles change the oil and filter element. After this the oil should be changed every 4–6000 miles and the filter element every 8–12,000 miles.

FIG 1D:13   Checking and adjusting valve clearances, Ford 1600 engines from 1970

Changes should take place more frequently where the vehicle is used predominantly for short journeys.

Clean and test the crankcase emission valve every 12,000 miles. Check regularly, especially after replacements of various components, all gaskets and joints for oil leaks and renew gaskets where necessary.

1D:30 Fault diagnosis (see Section 1E:20)

1E : 1   Engine type

The Plus Four, introduced in 1950 was fitted with a Standard Vanguard engine, with a few slight modifications:

1 A shorter water pump and pulley is used.
2 The centre springs on the clutch driven plate are different.
3 A double water outlet elbow is fitted as opposed to a single on the original.
4 The inlet manifold has a 3 degree cant for the carburetter (6 degree on the Vanguard).

Also a cover replaces the air cleaner on the carburetter air intake, in some instances.

Apart from this the engine is entirely Standard and all parts are interchangeable. **(FIG 1E : 1).**

The engine is mounted at the front on bonded rubber blocks which are bolted to lugs on the front engine plate and to cast light alloy brackets bolted to the chassis frame. The rear of the engine is mounted on Silentbloc rubber bush assemblies let into the top of the cross-member.

All mounting bolts should be fully tightened.

The TR engines are of the same basic design as the Vanguard but tuned and strengthened, etc. to give a higher performance. The details of the overhaul, etc. are very similar to the earlier engine and where they differ the TR figures are noted in brackets.

Note: It will be found advantageous if the starting handle guide fitted in front of the lower pulley is removed. **(FIG 1E : 2).** This funnel-shaped guide is not necessary

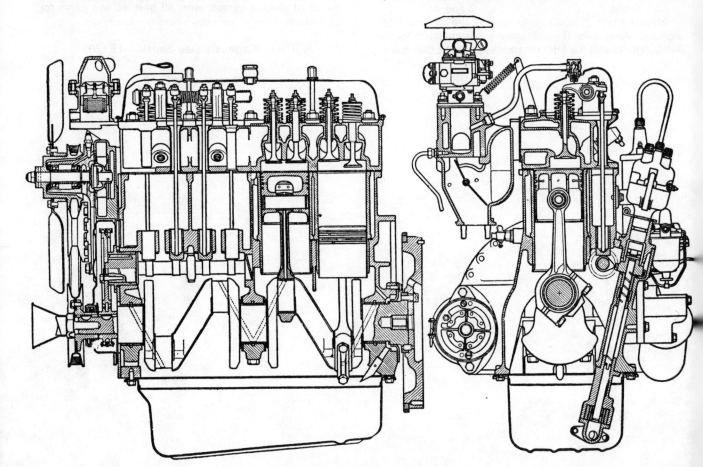

FIG 1E : 1   Longitudinal and transverse engine sections Plus/4 1952

on the Morgan and hinders work on the lower part of the engine. It is spot welded at three places and can be tapped off fairly easily.

1E : 2 General description

The engine, a four cylinder unit of 92 mm stroke and 85 mm bore (TR2 and TR3 83 mm TR4 86 mm) has a capacity of 2088 cc (TR2 and TR3 1991 cc, TR4 2138 cc). In main features, the engine is orthodox. The crankshaft is carried in three large-diameter main bearings, with the flywheel and clutch at the rear and the timing sprocket at the front driving the camshaft through a double-roller chain. Oil pump and distributor are in line at a slight angle to the vertical, the one deep in the sump, the other on the side of the engine, both driven from the one skew gear on the camshaft.

The connecting rods have angular-jointed big-ends, bushed small-ends, and gudgeon pins located by circlips. The pistons each have a slot in the non-pressure side of the skirt, though the slot does not extend right through to the bottom. Valves are overhead type, operated by rockers and pushrods, through tappets from the camshaft. Adjustment of valve clearances is made by removing the cover on the cylinder head.

The engine incorporates a special feature in the cylinder sleeves employed in manufacture. These are of the 'wet' type and can be removed and fitted as a servicing operation without the need for special equipment such as an hydraulic press or ram. Employing sleeves, it is possible to select a special material for the bores in relation to the rest of the cylinder block—thus tending to increase cylinder life. With this engine it may be further extended as the sleeves can be lifted and rotated through 90 deg., to present less worn faces to the thrust of the pistons. When it is necessary to renew pistons and cylinders, this can be done with standard components, maintaining the bores the original size. With a 'wet' type liner or sleeve in direct contact with the water or coolant, the cylinder is completely concentric being machined inside and out. Cooling is improved as a consequence, and expansion is uniform. Finally, the water jacket can be properly cleaned out during an overhaul.

The ventilating system depends for its function on the engine being sealed. Seals fitted in the timing cover and at the rear of the crankshaft must be in good condition, and all joints and unions airtight to maintain the depression in the crankcase. From this it will be seen that the engine should be particularly clean and certain troubles non-existent.

1E : 3 Service adjustments

Adjust sparking plug gaps to correct settings. The crankshaft pulley is drilled with a small hole which aligns to a pointer on the timing cover at t d c. (FIG 1E : 2). This point for No. 1 cylinder firing stroke can be obtained by removing No. 1 sparking plug, placing a thumb in the hole to feel pressure as the engine is rotated, and stopping when the hole in the pulley is against the pointer.

The ignition timing at full retard, should be 4 deg. before t d c, or slightly earlier with high octane fuels. The distributor setting is provided with Advance—Retard adjustment, by means of which slight regulation or correction can be made in conjunction with road testing.

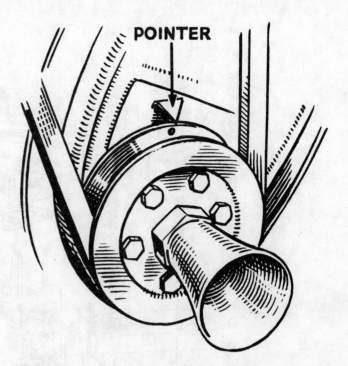

FIG 1E : 2 Starting handle guide and t d c indicating device (Standard Vanguard)

Advance must be kept below the point where pinking occurs when the engine is clean and in good condition. If the distributor is removed, the clamping bolt should not be slackened, otherwise the head can turn and the timing will require resetting. See Chapter 3—Ignition.

FIG 1E : 5 illustrates the Vanguard arrangement of valve-rocker and springs, with the positions where clearance is tested and adjustment made. The valves in the TR engines (FIG 1E : 6) are secured by cotters, etc. Proceed to check tappet clearances as follows. The engine should be turned until the valve whose clearance is to be checked or set, has just closed, then rotation should be continued a further halfturn. Cam and tappet will then be in correct relationship. The rocker-cover must, of course, be removed. Dynamo belt adjustment can be made by slackening the two cradle bolts and the link, then moving the dynamo and tightening the link bolt, checking belt deflection with thumb pressure, and finally tightening all bolts. As fan and water pump are also driven by the belt, its adjustment should occasionally be checked. Normal running temperature of the radiator water is 60 to 70 degrees Centigrade, which would be likely to increase with a slipping belt.

1E : 4 Decarbonizing—valve servicing

Decarbonizing and valve grinding are recommended after the first 5,000 miles, and thereafter at such intervals as may be necessary, normally about 15,000 miles. A tendency to pinking as carbon accumulates can be rectified on the timing adjuster, though there is obviously a limit to what is possible in this respect. In addition, loss of power and particularly compression due to valve and seat wear or burning indicate the need for decarbonizing and valve servicing.

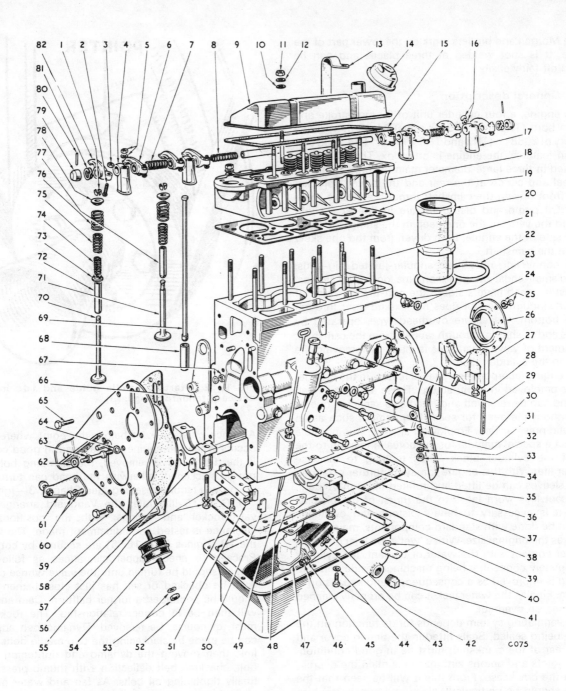

FIG 1E:3   TR4 engine fixed parts (exploded)

Key to Fig. 1E:3   1 Split collets   2 Adjusting screw   3 Nut   4 Rocker pedestal   5 Nut and spring washer   6 Rocker, R.H.
7 Spring   8 Spring—centre   9 Rocker cover   10 Fibre washer   1 Nyloc nut   12 Plain washer   13 Lifting eye   14 Filler cap
15 Rocker cover gasket   16 Screw and shakeproof washer   17 Rear rocker pedestal   18 Cylinder head   19 Cylinder head gasket
20 Cylinder liner   21 Cylinder head stud   22 Liner gasket   23 Drain tap and fibre washer   24 Stud   25 Setscrew and spring
washer   26 Rear oil seal   27 Rear main bearing cap   28 Sealing felt   29 Distributor drive gear bush   30 Oil gallery plug and
copper washer   31 Setscrew   32 Spring washer   33 Nut   34 Breather pipe   35 Oil filter attachment bolt and spring washer
36 Cylinder block   37 Sump gasket   38 Centre main bearing cap   39 Sump   40 Breather pipe bracket and distance piece
41 Sump plug   42 Oil pump filter gauze   43 Bolt   44 Setscrew and spring washer   45 Spring washer   46 Nut   47 Oil pump
48 Oil pump gasket   49 Dipstick   50 Sealing piece   51 Front sealing block   52 Screw   53 Nut and spring washer   54 Engine
mounting   55 Main bearing cap bolt and spring washer   56 Front main bearing cap   57 Gasket   58 Front bearer plate   59 Setscrew and spring washer   60 Setscrew and spring washer   61 Torque reaction arm and buffer   62 Fibre washer   63 Shouldered
stud   64 Spring washer   65 Bolt   66 Lifting eye   67 Nut and spring washer   68 Tappet   69 Pushrod   70 Exhaust valve
71 Inlet valve   72 Exhaust valve guide   73 Collar   74 Auxiliary valve spring   75 Inner valve spring   76 Outer valve spring
77 Inlet valve guide   78 Valve collar   79 Rocker shaft end cap   80 Mills pin   81 Spring   82 Rocker, L.H.

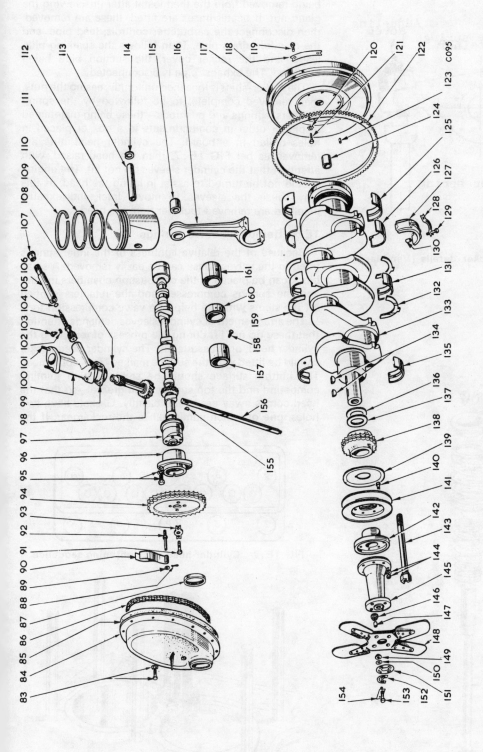

FIG 1E:4   TR4 engine moving parts (exploded)

Key to Fig 1E:4   83 Bolt and spring washer   84 Timing cover   85 Gasket   86 Timing chain   87 Oil seal   88 Split pin   89 Washer   90 Tensioner blade   91 Bolt
92 Tensioner pin   93 Lockplate   94 Camshaft sprocket   95 Bolt and spring washer   96 Front camshaft bearing   97 Camshaft   98 Distributor drive gear   99 Gasket
100 Distributor pedestal   101 Stud   102 Spring washer   103 Peg bolt   104 Tachometer drive gear   105 Rubber 'O' ring   106 Drive gear housing   107 Cap
bush   116 Connecting rod   117 Flywheel   118 Lockplate   119 Bolt   121 Con-rod bolt   122 Starter ring gear   123 Dowel   124 Spigot bearing
108 Mills pin   109 Compression ring (taper)   110 Compression ring (parallel)   111 Oil control ring   112 Piston   113 Gudgeon pin   114 Circlip   115 Gudgeon pin
125 Rear main bearing shell   126 Con-rod bearing shell   127 Con-rod cap   128 Lockplate   129 Con-rod cap   130 Dowel   131 Centre main bearing shell   132 Lower thrust
washer   133 Crankshaft   134 Woodruff keys   135 Front main bearing shell   136 Shim washer .004 inch (.1 mm)   137 Shim washer .006 (.15 mm)   138 Crankshaft
139 Oil thrower disc   140 Bolt   141 Pulley   142 Pulley hub   143 Starting handle dog bolt   144 Washer and nut   145 Fan extension   146 Rubber bush
sprocket   147 Distance tube   148 Fan   149 Rubber bush   150 Plain washer   151 Plate   152 Balancer   153 Bolt   154 Lockplate   155 Woodruff key   156 Oil pump drive
shaft   157 Intermediate front camshaft bearing   158 Peg bolt   159 Upper thrust washer   160 Intermediate rear camshaft bearing   161 Rear camshaft bearing

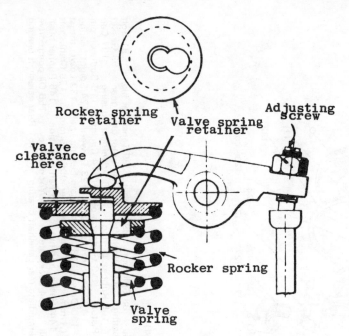

FIG 1E:5   Spring-valve and rocker details (Vanguard only)

Dismantling procedure is as follows. The battery is disconnected and the cooling system drained. The carburetter air cover is removed, detaching the crankcase ventilating pipe. The top water hosepipe is disconnected and the bypass on the thermostat, the thermometer bulb being removed from the thermostat after unscrewing the gland nut. If heater hoses are fitted, these are removed, then disconnect the carburetter controls, feed pipe, and the manifold drain pipe. Then follows the sparking plug leads, and the rocker cover, the suction pipe being detached. The exhaust pipe is disconnected.

The rocker-shaft is loosened uniformly, easing the nuts, then removed complete, to be followed by the spring retainers, springs and pushrods—these being maintained in proper order in compartments in a box or placed in holes drilled in a board. The cylinder head nuts are removed as per FIG 1E:7, then the head raised, with attention that the cylinder sleeves do not lift. The engine should not be turned to assist in lifting the head, as this may cause the sleeves to move. Inlet and exhaust manifold are removed together from the head.

1E:5 Removing valve springs

Because of the relative lightness of the inner springs fitted to the valves, these can be easily removed. A small block can be placed in the combustion chambers in turn, and the springs compressed and the retainers slipped off the stems with the help of a valve compression tool.

The arrangement of cylinder sleeves demands attention that these do not lift during the process of removing the cylinder head, or subsequently. The cylinder head gasket should be fitted with the surface marked 'Top' uppermost. The bottom surface should be smeared with jointing compound and the top surface with grease—so that the head comes away easily and cleanly. Gaskets have two holes, one of which admits oil to the rockergear. If the

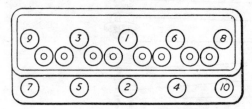

FIG 1E:7   Cylinder head nut tightening sequence

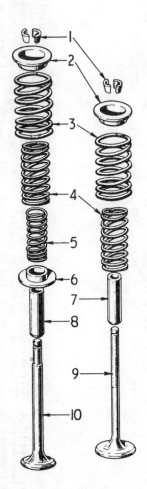

FIG 1E:6   Valve details (TR4)

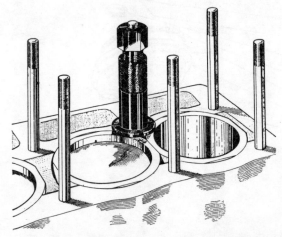

FIG 1E:8   Cylinder liner retainer in position

gasket is in good condition it can be used again, being left in position while the pistons are cleaned. In this case, retainers for holding the cylinder sleeves are placed on top of the gasket.

The sleeve retainers—of which two are required, each holding two sleeves—are fitted over cylinder head studs and tightened down just firm with a nut (FIG 1E : 8). They have a large flat-flanged head which overlaps the flanges of two sleeves. A suitable substitute for each consists of a large washer and a piece of tubing. Devices of this sort must be fitted before the engine is rotated.

1E : 6 Decarbonizing the pistons, etc.

In cleaning carbon from the pistons, two should be near t d c, and the other bores and openings to the pushrod chambers plugged with clean rag—likewise waterways at the sides of the sleeves. As usual, a small ring of carbon should be left round each piston perimeter—for guidance, to which an old piston ring can be used. The gasket should then be removed, its faces carefully scraped, together with those of the cylinder block.

The cylinder head having been cleaned, valve seating faces can be examined. Tools as depicted in FIG 1E : 9 are employed for truing pitted or burnt seatings and for chamfering the edges where—after a considerable period of running and several regrindings—seatings are becoming pocketed. The included angle of the valve seating is 89 deg., while the standard valve angle is 90 deg. These together produce a correct seating effect.

Valves should be trued on their seating faces either in a lathe or on valve face-grinding equipment. Good seatings will not normally be obtained by merely regrinding the valves, and the seatings in the head will be altered, so that when truing is done more metal than would otherwise be the case will need to be removed.

1E : 7 Valves and valve guides

The valve guides must be in good condition for the pilots of the cutters to be located truly; these pilots are $\frac{5}{16}$ inch diameter.

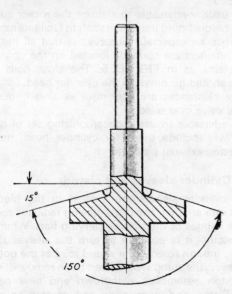

FIG 1E : 9   Valve seat cutter and chamfering tool for truing pitted and burnt valve seatings and chamfering the edges where seatings have become pocketed.

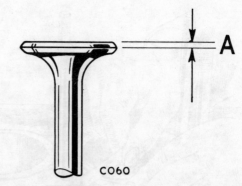

FIG 1E : 10   Minimum thickness at 'A' $\frac{1}{32}$ inch

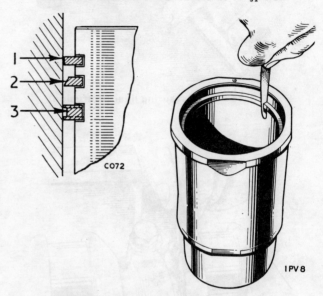

FIG 1E : 11   Measuring ring gaps

Key to Fig 1E : 11   1 Plain compression ring   2 Taper faced compression ring   3 Oil control ring

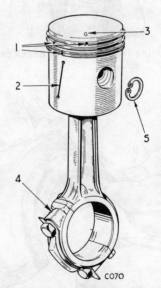

FIG 1E : 12   Disposition of piston slot relative to the bearing cap

Key to Fig 1E : 12   1 Piston rings   2 Slot in piston
3 Identification symbol   4 Cap   5 Circlip

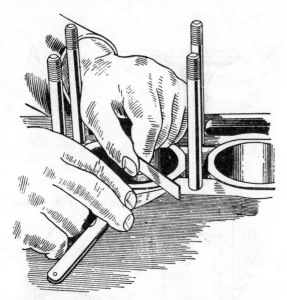

FIG 1E:13   Measuring liner protrusion

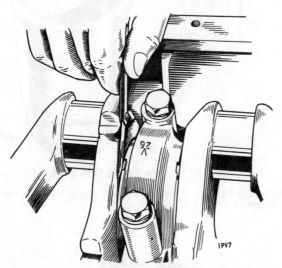

FIG 1E:14   Using feeler gauges to check crankshaft end float

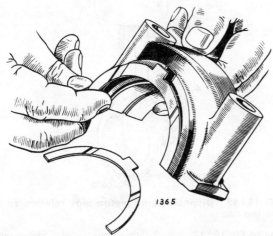

FIG 1E:15   Fitting thrust washers to main bearing cap

New clearances between inlet valves and guides are from .001 to .003 inch, while for exhaust valves and guides new clearances are from .003 to .005 inch. Permissible worn dimensions for inlet valve stems are $\frac{5}{16}$ inch minus .006 inch, and for exhaust valve stems minus .007 inch. For both inlet and exhaust valve guides permissible worn dimensions are $\frac{5}{16}$ inch plus .003 inch. Guides are removable by means of well-fitting drifts or extractor tools. In refitting, the distance from the tops of the guides to the upper face of the cylinder head should be $\frac{25}{32}$ inch.

Inlet valve heads are 1.50 inch. (TR 1.56 inch) diameter, exhaust valve heads 1.28 inch (TR 1.3 inch) diameter. The valve seating faces should be approximately .440 inch (TR .0469 inch) wide. Where valves are faced or ground to true the seatings prior to grinding-in the cylinder head, the edge of the head above the seating must not be less than a full $\frac{1}{32}$ inch, or there will be danger of the edge curling or burning, see **FIG 1E:10**.

Vanguard valve springs should be as follows: inner spring, fitted length 1.31 inch, free length 1.81 inch (approx.); outer spring, fitted length 1.63 inch, free length 1.97 inch (approx.). The fitted load of both springs is 28 lb, plus 2 lb, minus 1 lb.

TR valve springs:

	Inlet Inner	Inlet Outer	Exhaust Inner	Exhaust Outer
Free length (inches)	2.080	1.980	2.080	1.980
Fitted length (inches)	1.500	1.560	1.450	1.560
Fitted load (lb.)	33	38	36.5	38

All but earliest Vanguard engines have 2 inlet springs and 3 exhaust springs.

1E:8 Assembling head and valve gear

Valve stems should be smeared with oil during assembly, and the walls of the cylinder sleeves can be lightly oiled, the engine rotated (sleeve retainers in position), and surplus oil wiped off the pistons at tdc. The tightening order for the head nuts is shown in **FIG 1E:7**.

It is usually advisable to slacken the rocker adjusting screws before fitting the rocker shaft to facilitate assembly. A point to be especially observed is that all the rocker spring retainers are correctly located on the ends of the valve stems as in **FIG 1E:5**. The close coils of the springs should go down to the cylinder head.

Valve clearances are later reset as already described and the valve gear oiled.

It is advisable to use a decarbonizing set of gaskets, which will include those for cylinder head, manifold, carburetter, exhaust pipe, etc.

1E:9 Cylinder sleeves and pistons

The cylinder sleeves are located in the block and against one another, the block having radiused recesses, and the flanges of the sleeves carrying flats. When slight wear occurs, it is possible to turn the sleeves through 90 deg., though to ensure a sound joint at the bottom of the sleeves, the sump would need to be removed, sleeves and piston assemblies withdrawn and new packings fitted. Piston and connecting rod assemblies can be removed from the sleeves, maintaining these in position with retainers, if it is only desired to examine pistons and rings—and possibly renew the rings. Alternatively, sleeves, pistons and connecting rods can be withdrawn together.

There are three grades of cylinders and pistons, designated F, G and H, the sleeves and pistons being marked respectively.

1E:10 Piston rings

Piston ring gaps in the sleeves should be .003 to .007 inch (TR2 .010 inch TR3 & 4 .015 inch), tested with a feeler gauge and lined up by means of entering the piston behind the ring. (FIG 1E:11). Side clearances of rings in grooves when new are from .001 to .003 inch for compression and scraper rings (TR .001—.0035 inch compression ring only). Permissible worn clearances are .005 inch. Permissible worn ring widths are; compression .075 inch, scraper .154 inch. These can be checked with a micrometer. Groove widths should not exceed the following: compression rings .081 inch, (TR .065 inch), scraper rings .159 inch.

Ring groove widths in pistons can be checked by entering rings with feeler gauges—the rings having been checked for width with a micrometer. Alternatively, a small piece of strip metal, or the shank of a small drill, carefully filed with flats to size, can be used as a gauge. Pistons can be entered in the sleeves using a piston ring compressor. The ring gaps should be spaced round the pistons, and it should be observed that the pistons and connecting rods are fitted in correct relationship, and the sleeves likewise where these have been removed, so that the assemblies will be in the proper fitting attitude— the sleeves in the block, and the big-ends for the crank-shaft.

The open side of the big-end bearing should be on the same side as the slit in the Aeroflex compensating piston, and both should face the camshaft (FIG 1E:12). In this way, maximum thrust will be taken on the solid portion of the piston skirt, and on the connecting rod half of the big-end. Piston rings, pistons and bearings should be smeared with engine oil during assembly.

1E:11 Cylinder sleeve fitting

Before fitting new 'figure of eight' packings to the sleeves, any roughness should be removed from the cylinder block recesses, and all faces wiped clean. As for the cylinder head gasket, it is recommended that the packings be smeared with jointing compound on their undersides and with grease on their top sides.

When sleeves are in position, their upper faces should stand proud of the cylinder block as shown in FIG 1E:13, a distance of from .003 to .005 inch. This is tested by placing a small straightedge across the top of each sleeve in turn, and checking under the ends with feeler gauges.

The big-end bearings are of the thinwall, shell or precision type, and the caps or connecting rods should not be filed to effect bearing adjustments.

Small-end bushes are a press fit in the connecting rods, and the new clearance for the gudgeon pins should be .0002 inch at 68 deg. F.

The bushes are reamed to .875 inch, plus or minus .0005 inch, and the gudgeon pins selected to provide the appropriate clearance. This procedure might, how-ever, have to be reversed in repair work; that is, the bushes

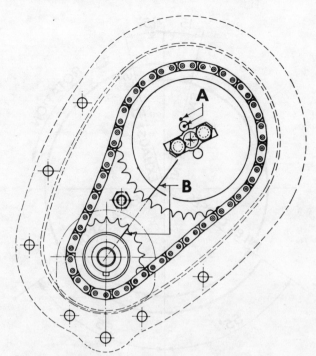

FIG 1E:16 Relative position of timing marks when No. 1 Piston is at t d c (compression stroke)

Key to Fig 1E:16   A Punch marks   B Scribed lines

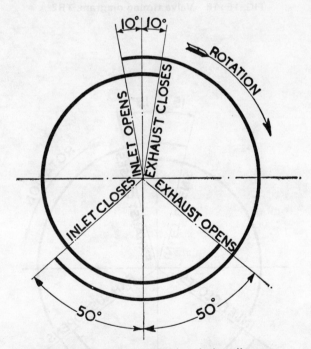

FIG 1E:17   Vanguard valve timing diagram

reamed with an expanding reamer to provide the working clearance for given gudgeon pins. New dimensions for gudgeon pins are .875 inch plus .0001 inch, minus .00025 inch. Permissible worn dimensions for small-end bushes are .876 inch and for gudgeon pins .874 inch. Alignment of connecting rods can be tested with mandrels on a surface plate, or on an alignment gauge.

For the big-end bearings new clearances are .0006 to .0025 inch (TR2 and TR3 .0016 to .0035 inch. TR4

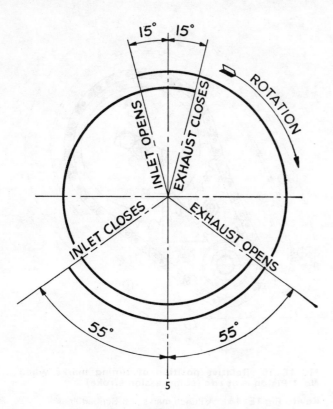

FIG 1E:18 Valve timing diagram, TR2

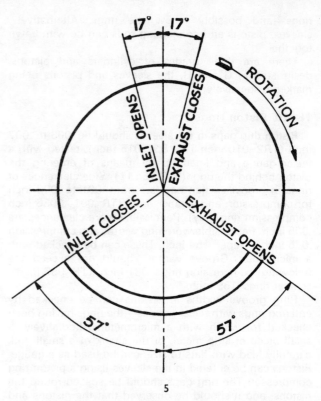

FIG 1E:20 Valve timing diagram, TR4

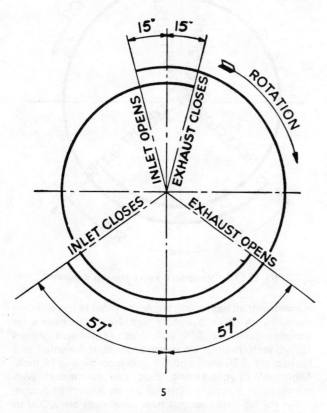

FIG 1E:19 Valve timing diagram, TR3

.0028 to .0040 inch) and permissible worn clearances .006 inch. End float or clearances on the big-ends should be between .0075 and .0105 inch (TR .007 and .014 inch). These can be checked with feeler gauges. The new crankpin diameter is 2.0866 inches plus or minus .0005 inch. Should crankpins be below 2.084 inch, when checked with an accurate micrometer, regrinding and the fitting of undersize bearings is necessary. Ovality and taper are acceptable as wear to the extent of .002 inch on crankpins and main journals. Thrust on the crankshaft is taken on steel-backed thrust washers fitted in halves either side of the centre main bearing (**FIG 1E:14 & 15**). Float here when new should be from .004 to .006 inch. Float up to .010 inch (dry) is permissible when worn.

1E:12 Engine removal

The engine can be removed from the car with the gearbox, or the gearbox can be removed first, but the unit should never be split at the bellhousing flange until the gearbox has been removed.

1 Disconnect headlamp wires (early type only).
2 Detach headlamp bar and brackets (external radiator models only).
3 Remove bonnet, and disconnect the radiator stay rods at the front ends.
4 Slacken hoses and undo the bolts (one each side) at the bottom of the radiator—this can now be removed.
   Note: The cowl must also be removed on cars with an internal radiator.
5 Disconnect all pipes, wires and controls including dipper switch and the four pipes connected to the suspension lubrication valve on the dash.

6 Detach centre dash panel over bellhousing, gearbox cowl and propeller shaft tunnel (wood screws).

7 Disconnect handbrake cable at the front end, and the propeller shaft at the front end. Undo speedo drive and the clutch linkage.

8 If the gearbox is to be removed separately, take out the rear mounting bolts, leaving the Silentbloc bushes *in situ*, place jack under centre tube.

9 Disconnect rear brake cable at hand lever also removing dowel pin off rear end.

10 Remove the setscrews holding the gearbox to clutch shaft housing, and draw gearbox back, bringing with it the long clutch shaft and muff coupling.

11 If the engine and gearbox are to be moved as one, detach gearbox cover with lever and selector forks.

12 Remove tie bar between valances on later models.

13 Take out front mounting set screws to brackets. Fit slings round front and rear of sump and lift the engine tilting to clear front suspension cross bar.

When reassembling the engine remember to replace the sponge rubber ring which fits around the clutch shaft housing behind the bellhousing, and seals against the dash panel.

1E : 13 Engine dismantling

With the engine out of the chassis and the gearbox and bellhousing removed, the clutch can be removed, then the flywheel, slackening two of the setscrews, removing the others, and employing a lever each side to free the wheel evenly, finally removing the two slack setscrews.

The engine should be cleared of accessories—carburetter, fuel pump, rocker cover, distributor, distributor driving shaft, water pump, manifolds, oil filter assembly, dynamo, etc. At the front of the engine the starter dog nut can be loosened (this can well be done before the flywheel is removed, or the latter can be held to prevent the crankshaft turning), then the nut removed, followed by the guide. The pulley requires an extractor. Shims as fitted should be noted, these being to set the starter handle for correct position in relation to compression.

Timing cover and chain tensioner can then be removed, and should it be necessary the oil seal can be extracted from the timing cover, observing the inside position of the lip.

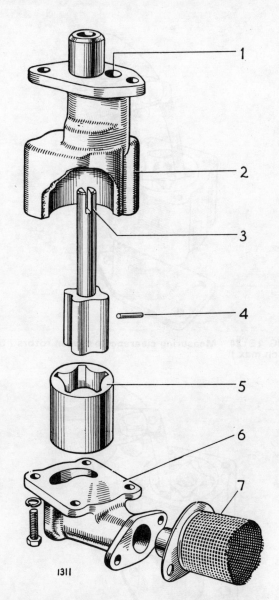

1311

FIG 1E : 22   Arrangement of oil pump components

Key to Fig 1E : 22   1 Oil pump outlet   2 Oil pump body
3 Shaft and inner rotor   4 Securing pin   5 Outer rotor
6 End plate   7 filter

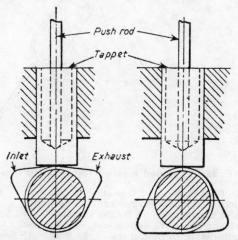

FIG 1E : 21   Tappets 'rocking' (left). Tappets on base or backs of cams (right)

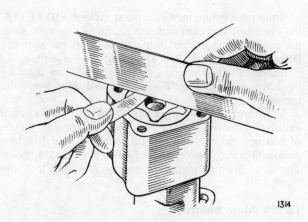

1314

FIG 1E : 23   Measuring rotor end clearance (.004 inch max.)

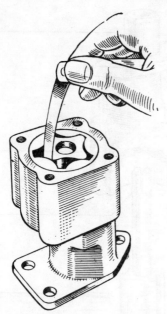

FIG 1E : 24 Measuring clearance between rotors (.010 inch max.)

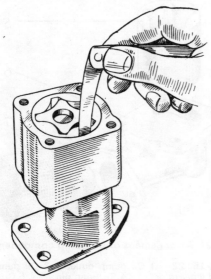

FIG 1E : 25 Measuring clearance between outer rotor and body (.010 inch max.)

Noting the timing marks on the sprockets, **FIG 1E : 16,** the camshaft sprocket and chain can be removed, then the crankshaft sprocket, retaining any shims with the latter sprocket to duplicate alignment on reassembly.

Rocker shaft, pushrods, cylinder head can then be removed, and cylinder head studs, and after these the tappets.

Sump and oil pump can be removed, and the camshaft extracted after the flanged front bearing. The two halves of the rear oil retainer can be removed, and the four connecting rod, piston and cylinder sleeve assemblies. The three main bearing caps can be removed, then the crankshaft.

1E : 14 Main bearings

Crankshaft main journal diameters are 2.479 to 2.4795 inches. New clearances are from .001 to .002 inches

(TR .0015 to .0025 inch). Should taper, ovality, or scoring be in excess of .002 inch (TR .0025 inch), the shaft should be ground and new undersize bearings fitted. Regrind dimensions are minus .020, .030, .040 inch below new dimensions. The dimension for a crankshaft not previously ground is 2.479 inches.

Oversize thrust washers (plus .005 inch) are available for when wear occurs on the crankshaft thrust face.

1E : 15 Camshaft bearings

The camshaft is fitted with a cast iron flanged front bearing, and the others are formed in the cylinder block.

On TR3 engines after No. TS9095E four Vandervell bi-metal bearings are used to accommodate the camshaft. A recognition feature of engines so fitted with these bearings will be that three setscrews retaining the three rearmost bearings will clearly be seen on the lefthand side of the cylinder block. The front bearing is pressed into the front bearing sleeve. End play is controlled by the front bearing, between a flange on the camshaft and the inside face of the timing sprocket. End play can be from .003 to .0075 inch (TR .004 to .0075 inch). New clearances for the camshaft bearings are .00275 to .00475 inch for the front bearing and .0025 to .0045 inch

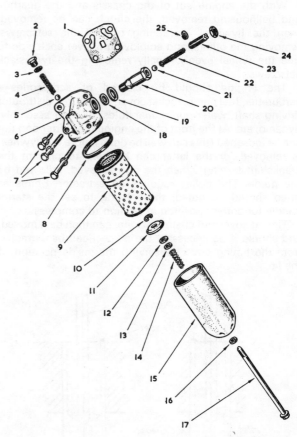

FIG 1E : 26 Exploded view of full flow oil filter (TR4)

Key to Fig 1E : 26 1 Gasket 2 Cap nut 3 Washer 4 Spring 5 Bypass valve ball 6 Body 7 Bolts 8 Rubber sealing ring 9 Filter element 10 Spring clip 11 Locating disc 12 Rubber seal 13 Washer 14 Spring 15 Container 16 Rubber seal 17 Bolt 18 Sealing ring 19 Washer 20 Valve body 21 Ball—relief valve 22 Spring 23 Adjusting screw 24 Locknut 25 Lead wire

(TR4 .0015 to .0029 inch) for the others. Maximum wear on the camshaft journals can be .003 inch, while in the bearings it can be .0035 inch.

1E:16 Timing

Valve timing for the various engines is shown in **FIGS 1E:17, 18, 19** and **20**, while **FIG 1E:16** depicts the timing marks on the sprockets and the end of the camshaft. With these markings, retiming the camshaft is quite straightforward.

Pistons Nos. 1 and 4 are set to tdc, at which position the keyways in the crankshaft will be underneath, the crankshaft sprocket being fitted. The camshaft sprocket is set with its scribed line in line with the line on the crankshaft sprocket and the camshaft with the punch mark in the hole adjacent to the punch mark; in this position, the camshaft sprocket is eased off, and the chain fitted with the driving side tight, then the timing is checked and, if correct, the setscrews are tightened and locked with the tab washer. Should there be no markings on the timing wheels (as when new ones are fitted) the procedure is as follows, it being assumed that camshaft, cylinder head and valve gear are fitted.

The rocker shaft is removed, and rocker springs extracted from the valves of Nos. 1 and 4 cylinders, the retainers be replaced, and the rocker shaft tightened down—with the precautions already mentioned. Clearances of the valves of Nos. 1 and 4 cylinders are set to .014 inch, (TR2 .015, TR4 .010 inch), the timing clearance. The engine is set at Nos. 1 and 4 tdc, and the camshaft turned so that the valves of No. 1 cylinder are in the 'rocking' position, with the cams as at **FIG 1E:21**, the exhaust just closing and the inlet just opening.
Note: Valve clearances are normally set with cams as in **FIG 1E:21** right.

1E:17 Oil pump

Main components of the Hoburn-Eaton double-rotor oil pump are shown in **FIG 1E:22**. The small centre rotor is pressed and pinned on the driving shaft, which is off-set from the centre of the other rotor. Both rotors turn in the casing, the outer one at a slower speed.

Because of the construction, the pump should operate satisfactorily for a very large mileage before attention is required. Clearance between rotors and cover should not exceed .004 inch **(FIG 1E:23)**. Oil pressure should be 40 to 60 lb (TR 60 to 70 lb) at normal speeds.

Filter elements should be renewed at intervals of about 8,000 miles **(FIG 1E:26)**. When fitting the oil pump and distributor driving shaft, the engine should be at No. 1 cylinder tdc, firing stroke, and the gear should be engaged with the offset slot for the distributor drive at approximately 5 minutes to 5 o'clock, the smaller portion of the circle to the rear of the engine, as in **FIG 1E:27**.

1E:18 Engine sealing

Attention should be given to ensuring sound seals and joints in assembling the engine.

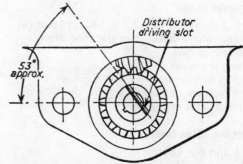

1E:27 Position of slot in distributor driving gear for ignition timing

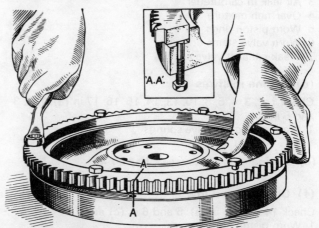

1E:28 Fitting ring gear to flywheel. Inset shows method of removing ring gear

1E:19 Starter gear ring

The method of fitting a new starter gear ring on early engines is to warm the ring in boiling water for several minutes (in a large flat pan) and start it on the flywheel spigot. Four clamps are then fitted, and tightened evenly, until in correct position. Should facilities for heating the ring be lacking, installation can be carried out cold in this manner. On later engines this can be simplified by the use of bolts as in **FIG 1E:28**.

1E:20 Fault diagnosis

(a) Engine will not start

1 Defective coil
2 Faulty distributor capacitor (condenser)
3 Dirty, pitted or incorrectly set contact breaker points
4 Ignition wires loose or insulation faulty.
5 Water on sparking plug leads
6 Corrosion of battery terminals or battery discharged
7 Faulty or jammed starter
8 Sparking plug leads wrongly connected
9 Vapour lock in fuel pipes
10 Defective fuel pump
11 Overchoking
12 Underchoking
13 Blocked petrol filter or carburetter jets
14 Leaking valves
15 Sticking valves
16 Valve timing incorrect
17 Ignition timing incorrect

(b) Engine stalls

Check 1, 2, 3, 4, 10, 11, 12, 13, 14 and 15 in (a)
1 Sparking plugs defective or gaps incorrect
2 Retarded ignition
3 Mixture too weak
4 Water in fuel system
5 Petrol tank vent blocked
6 Incorrect valve clearance

(c) Engine idles badly

Check 1 and 6 in (b)
1 Air leak at manifold joints
2 Slow-running jet blocked or out of adjustment
3 Air leak in carburetter
4 Over-rich mixture
5 Worn piston rings
6 Worn valve stems or guides
7 Weak exhaust valve springs

(d) Engine misfires

Check 1, 2, 3, 4, 5, 8, 10, 13, 14, 15, 16, 17 in (a); 1, 2, 3 and 6 in (b)
1 Weak or broken valve springs

(e) Engine overheats (see Chapter 4)

(f) Compression low

Check 14 and 15 in (a), 5 and 6 in (c) and 1 in (d)
1 Worn piston ring grooves
2 Scored or worn cylinder bores

(g) Engine lacks power

Check 3, 10, 11, 13, 14, 15, 16 and 17 in (a), 1, 2, 3 and 6 in (b), 5 and 6 in (c) and 1 in (d). Also check (e) and (f)
1 Leaking joint washers
2 Fouled sparking plugs
3 Automatic advance not operating

(h) Burnt valves or seats

Check 14 and 15 in (a), 6 in (b) and 1 in (d). Also check (e).
1 Excessive carbon around valve seat and head

(j) Sticking valves

Check 1 in (d)
1 Bent valve stem
2 Scored valve stem or guide
3 Incorrect valve clearance

(k) Excessive cylinder wear

Check 11 in (a) and see Chapter 4
1 Lack of oil
2 Dirty oil
3 Piston rings gummed up or broken
4 Badly fitting piston rings
5 Connecting rods bent

(l) Excessive oil consumption

Check 5 and 6 in (c) and check (k)
1 Ring gaps too wide
2 Oil return holes in piston choked with carbon
3 Scored cylinders
4 Oil level too high
5 External oil leaks
6 Ineffective valve stem oil seals

(m) Crankshaft and connecting rod bearing failure

Check 1 in (k)
1 Restricted oilways
2 Worn journals or crankpins
3 Loose bearing caps
4 Extremely low oil pressure
5 Bent connecting rod

(n) Internal water leakage (see Chapter 4)

(o) Poor circulation (see Chapter 4)

(p) Corrosion (see Chapter 4)

(q) High fuel consumption (see Chapter 2)

(r) Engine vibration

1 Loose generator bolts
2 Fan blades out of balance
3 Incorrect clearance for front engine mounting rubbers
4 Exhaust pipe mountings too tight

CHAPTER 2

CARBURETTERS & FUEL SYSTEMS

Five makes of carburetter have been fitted to the Morgan over the years, Solex, S.U., Stromberg, Zenith and Weber, the latter being fitted to the Super Sports Plus/4 and Four/4 Series V and 1600 Competition Models only. The carburetter was fed originally by an electric S.U. pump but has now been replaced by an A.C. mechanical unit on all models.

2 : 1 The S.U. fuel pump

Should pump trouble be suspected, first disconnect the pump union of the pipe from the pump to the carburetter and switch on the engine. If the pump functions the shortage is due either to blockage of the petrol pipe to the carburetter, or possibly to the carburetter float needle sticking up. If the pump will not function

after this has been done, first remove the filter which is held in position by the brass hexagon nut at the base of the pump and see if this is clear. Then disconnect the petrol pipe leading to the tank and blow down this with a tyre pump to ensure the pipe being absolutely clear, and reconnect the petrol pipe.

If the pump still does not function or only works slowly, the stoppage may be due to a bad earth return. To test for this, make definite metallic contact between the brass body of the pump and the car chassis with a short length of wire. If the pump then functions normally, the earth wire may be permanently connected. A bad connection in the pump itself may sometimes be traced to the nut on the terminal inside the cover not being screwed down firmly.

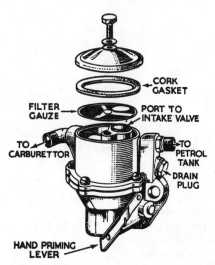

FIG 2:1 Early type of A.C. fuel pump (Four/4 Series I)

Should these points be found in order but the pump still does not work, the trouble is in the pump itself and the cause will be too much tension on the diaphragm or blackened contact points, the cause of which is the tensioning of the diaphragm. The remedy is to remove the cover from the contact points and pass a piece of thin card between the points when pressed together, so as to effect the necessary cleaning.

To release the tension on the diaphragm, remove the body from the base of the pump by undoing the small screws which hold these two parts together. The diaphragm itself will then be found to be adhered to the body of the pump from which it will have to be separated. A knife will help in this operation, care being taken to prevent the rollers which support the diaphragm, and act as a bearing, from falling out. The body should then be replaced on to the base, and the screws put in loosely, but before finally tightening up it is advisable to stretch the diaphragm to its highest possible position. This is effected by switching on the pump and holding the contact points together while tightening the screws well up. This will effect a permanent cure.

When releasing the tension of the diaphragm care should be taken not to alter the adjustment of the pump by unscrewing the armature, which is the steel plate fixed at the back of the diaphragm. Should the position of this be inadvertently altered it will have to be reset, which is done by screwing the diaphragm and armature into such a position that the contact breaker just throws over without the assistance of the contact blade, which should be held away when being set. When this position has been found, the armature will have to be unscrewed to the extent of two-thirds of a turn, when the cast iron pot may again be fixed to the base as per instructions.

Should a pump work intermittently or not start clicking when switched on in the morning, it is an indication that trouble is occuring, and it should be given immediate attention to obviate final stoppage on the road.

2:2 The A.C. fuel pump (early type)

The petrol pump is mounted on the side of the crankcase, and is operated by an eccentric cam.

Petrol flows through a strainer before passing through the non-return inlet valve (FIG 2:1). The pump chamber contains a non-return outlet valve and at the lower end a diaphragm operated by a pull-rod from the rocker arm which is in contact with the lever. The rocker arm constantly oscillates and if the pump chamber is full of petrol, causing the diaphragm to be depressed, the rocker arm works freely and does not operate the diaphragm. The spring behind the diaphragm provides a constant pressure of fuel to the carburetter float chamber, and thus the stroke of the diaphragm is automatically governed to meet the requirements of the carburetter. The rocker arm itself is spring loaded for the purpose of keeping the lever in contact with the cam and preventing noise. There is a drain plug fitted to the sediment chamber.

There are filters incorporated in the petrol pump and carburetter unions.

A hand primer is fitted to the pump so that it is unnecessary to turn the engine either by hand or by the starter if the tank has run dry and the pump becomes empty. A few strokes of the hand primer will soon fill the float chamber. It may be necessary to carry out this operation if the car has stood for several days without being used.

If the pump fails to supply petrol to the carburetter, attend to the following points.

Remove the filter cover and thoroughly clean away all deposits in the filter chamber. Here again dry deposits are comparatively harmless, but any gumminess, apart from being cleaned out of the filter chamber, must also as far as possible be washed out of the pump. The filter gauze should be cleaned either by rinsing it in petrol or blowing it on an airline, and then the gasket under the filter cover should be examined and if unduly compressed or cracked a new one fitted. Finally, the filter cover should be replaced and tightened, care being taken to ensure that apart from the gasket under the outer edge, the small washer employed under the head of the centre screw is also present. Next, reconnect the rear pipe to the pump but disconnect the delivery pipe up at the carburetter end, so that a delivery test can be made. To do this some fresh petrol should be put in the tank, and with the pipe up at the carburetter end disconnected, the pump should be operated either by the priming lever or by turning over the engine, and if everything is in sound condition there should be a positive delivery of petrol every working stroke of the pump. If as referred to earlier on there were any gummed deposits in the pump filter chamber, this testing process of the pump should be prolonged so as to thoroughly wash out its interior, as even a slight trace of gum can result in sticking, not only of fuel pump valves, but also the carburetter needle valve.

2:3 Fuel pump—Four/4 Series IV, V, 1600 and Competition models

This fuel pump is a self-priming unit operated through a spring-loaded arm from an eccentric on the camshaft (FIG 2:3). The filter screen, glass sediment bowl and the sediment chamber should be cleaned every 5,000 miles. Unscrew the sediment bowl retainer clamp screw and lift off the bowl and filter screen, carefully wash the screen in petrol and flush all traces of sediment from the sediment chamber. Refit all items in the reverse order to dismantling, but first check that the sediment bowl gasket is in good condition and that it will make an airtight joint.

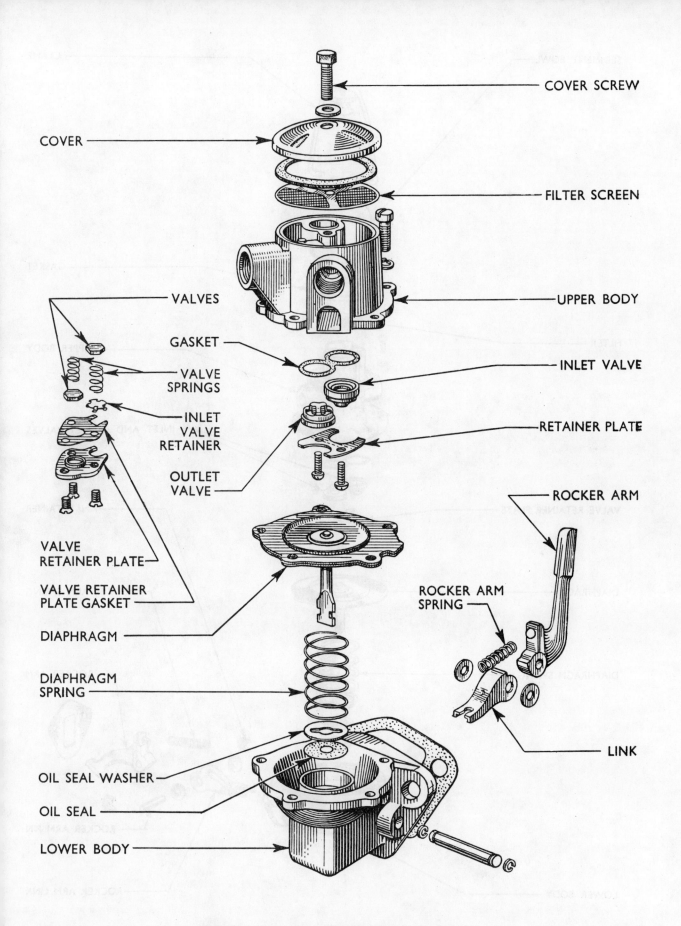

COVER SCREW

COVER

FILTER SCREEN

VALVES

UPPER BODY

GASKET

VALVE SPRINGS

INLET VALVE

INLET VALVE RETAINER

RETAINER PLATE

OUTLET VALVE

ROCKER ARM

VALVE RETAINER PLATE

ROCKER ARM SPRING

VALVE RETAINER PLATE GASKET

DIAPHRAGM

DIAPHRAGM SPRING

LINK

OIL SEAL WASHER

OIL SEAL

LOWER BODY

FIG 2:2   Fuel pump exploded (Four/4 Series II)

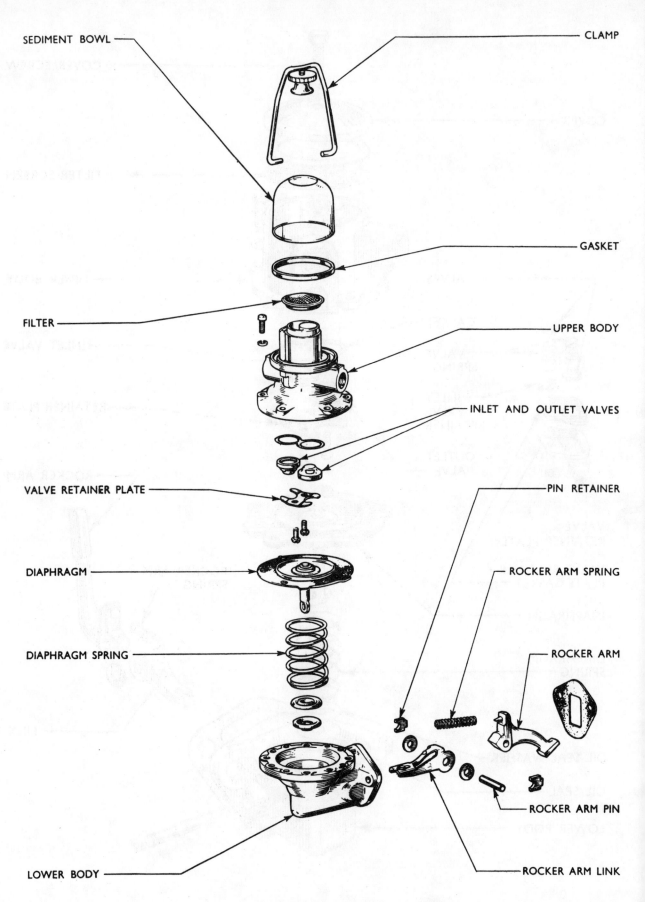

SEDIMENT BOWL

CLAMP

GASKET

FILTER

UPPER BODY

INLET AND OUTLET VALVES

VALVE RETAINER PLATE

PIN RETAINER

DIAPHRAGM

ROCKER ARM SPRING

DIAPHRAGM SPRING

ROCKER ARM

ROCKER ARM PIN

LOWER BODY

ROCKER ARM LINK

FIG 2:3   Fuel pump exploded (recent Four/4 models)

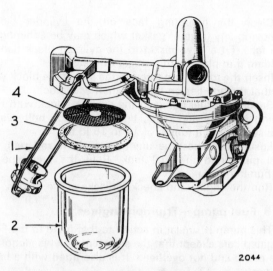

FIG 2:4   Fuel pump (Plus/4)

Key to Fig 2:4   1 Retaining stirrup   2 Glass sediment bowl   3 Cork seal   4 Gauze filter

2:4 Testing the fuel pump

Providing there are no leaks or obstructions in the fuel line, a quick check of the fuel pump efficiency can be made as follows:

Disconnect the fuel pump to carburetter pipe at the pump outlet.

Crank the engine by means of the starter motor, when a well-defined spurt of fuel should be apparent for each revolution of the camshaft. If the pump does not operate correctly, check the inlet depression and delivery pressure using suitable gauges.

OVERHAULING THE FUEL PUMP

2:5 To remove the fuel pump

Disconnect the fuel pump to carburetter pipe and remove the pipe.

Unscrew the union nut on the fuel line from the petrol tank. The pipe should be suitably plugged to prevent loss of fuel or the ingress of foreign matter.

Unscrew and remove the two bolts and spring washers securing the fuel pump to the cylinder block and detach the fuel pump, lifting the operating lever to clear the eccentric and the slotted hole in the block. Remove the gasket.

2:6 To dismantle the fuel pump

1 Mark the upper and lower bodies adjacent to the smaller tab on the diaphragm to ensure correct alignment on reassembly.
2 Unscrew the sediment bowl retainer clamp screw and lift off the bowl, filter screen and gasket.
3 Remove the six screws and spring washers securing the upper and lower fuel pump bodies, taking care when separating the flange joint to avoid damaging the diaphragm.
4 Turn the diaphragm, approximately a quarter turn (in either direction), to free the diaphragm rod from the rocker arm link, and detach the diaphragm.
5 Remove the diaphragm spring, oil seal retaining washer and rubber oil seal. The diaphragm and pull rod are riveted together and should not be dismantled.

6 The inlet and outlet valves are both retained by a spring steel plate secured by two screws. Remove the screws and plate, then the two valve assemblies together with the 'figure 8' gasket can be lifted from the upper body.
7 To dismantle the lower body, relieve the staking over the two pin retainers and withdraw these retainers from the casting. The pin, rocker arm, spring, link and two washers may then be removed as an assembly.

2:7 To reassemble the fuel pump

1 If the lower body has been completely dismantled, replace the rocker arm and link assembly as follows:

Position the rocker arm, with the boss between the flanges of the link, ensuring that the central web of the link and the spring seat location on the rocker arm are uppermost (See FIG 2:3). Align the holes in the link and rocker arm and insert the pivot pin.

Fit one thrust washer to each end of the pin, next to the link, and carefully insert the assembly into the lower pump body casting, with the spring seat on the rocker arm uppermost. Place the rocker arm spring in position so that the ends are located by the registers on the body and the rocker arm.

Insert two new pin retainers, one at each end of the pin, ensuring that these positively locate the pin in the casting. Stake over the casting to the pin retainers in two locations each side.

Note: New pin retainers should always be fitted after dismantling the lower pump body, as service replacement parts are supplied oversize with a shorter shoulder to enable the staking to be carried out satisfactorily. No attempt should be made to refit the old pin retainers.

Inspect the pin to make sure it is properly positioned and the rocker arm and link operate correctly. Test by moving the rocker arm toward the pump body, when the link is held downwards. If the link is held downwards, as will occur in operation when the carburetter float chamber is full, the rocker arm should be free to move without transmitting any movement to the diaphragm and link.
2 Assemble the spring, oil seal washer and oil seal to the diaphragm pull rod, in this order, taking care to avoid damage.
3 Insert the end of the diaphragm rod in the slotted end of the link, engaging the pull rod end by turning the diaphragm a quarter of a turn so that the SMALLER TAB on the diaphragm aligns with the mating mark on the lower body flange.
4 Hold the upper body with the valve locations uppermost. Fit the 'figure 8' gasket in the upper body, then fit the two valve assemblies as shown in FIG 2:3. Note that these will only seat properly when in their correct locations the right way up.

Assemble the retainer plate, securing it with the two screws.
5 Position the fuel pump upper body over the diaphragm on the lower body so that the inlet and outlet unions are at right angles to the mounting flange. Ensure that the mating mark made on the lower body is in line with the SMALLER TAB on the diaphragm. Depress the rocker arm until the diaphragm is level with the

flange, fit the six screws and spring washers and tighten them finger-tight.

6 Work the rocker arm several complete strokes to centralise the diaphragm and tighten the six screws evenly and securely, with the diaphragm in the 'down' position.

7 Refit the screen to the fuel pump body, ensure that the sediment bowl gasket is in good condition and then refit the sediment bowl. Tighten the clamp screw to retain the sediment bowl in position.

2:8 To refit the fuel pump

Ensure that the inlet and outlet port threads are perfectly clean.

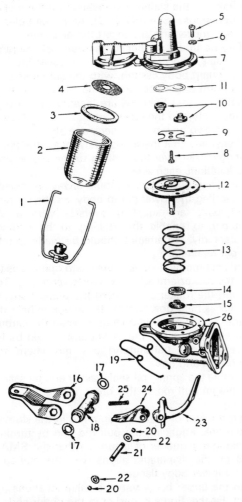

FIG 2:5 Fuel pump exploded (Plus/4)

Key to Fig 2:5 1 Stirrup 2 Glass sediment bowl 3 Cork seal 4 Gauze filter 5 Securing screw 6 Lock washer 7 Upper body 8 Screw for retaining plate 9 Valve retaining plate 10* Inlet and outlet valve assemblies 11 Valve gasket 12 Diaphragm assembly 13 Diaphragm spring 14 Oil seal retainer 15 Oil seal 16 Primer lever 17 Cork washer 18 Primer lever shaft 19 Hand primer spring 20 Circlip 21 Rocker arm pin 22 Washer 23 Rocker arm 24 Link lever 25 Rocker arm spring 26 Lower body
*These valves are identical, but on fitting them to the upper body the spring of the inlet valve is pointing towards the diaphragm and the spring of the outlet valve away from the diaphragm, as shown in the illustration.

Clean the mounting face on the cylinder block, removing any trace of gasket which may be adhering to the face. Fit a new gasket to the cylinder block flange, holding it in place with a smear of grease.

Insert the rocker arm through the slot in the block wall so that the arm lies on the camshaft eccentric.

Secure the fuel pump to the cylinder block with two spring washers and bolts, tightening each bolt evenly and securely to a torque of 12 to 15 lb ft.

Ensure that the pipe unions are clean and refit the fuel pipe from the fuel tank. Refit the fuel pipe to carburetter pipe.

Run the engine and check for leaks at the unions.

2:9 Fuel pump—Triumph engines

This pump is similar in action to that fitted to the Ford engined cars except that the sediment bowl is alongside the pump and not overhead. It is also fitted with a hand primer.

To clean the pump filter, loosen the thumb nut below the glass sediment bowl **(FIG 2:4)**. Swing the wire frame to one side and remove the sediment chamber, cork gasket and gauze filter for cleaning.

When reassembling, renew the cork washer if damaged.

Run the engine and check for leakage.

2:10 To dismantle fuel pump

1 Clean the exterior of the pump and file a mark across both flanges to facilitate reassembly.

2 Dismantle in the sequence given on **FIG 2:5**. Reassemble by reversing the sequence.

3 To remove the diaphragm assembly (12) first turn it through 90 deg. in an anti-clockwise direction and lift out of engagement with link lever (24).

2:11 Solex carburetters

All early Morgans were fitted with Solex carburetters, including the Standard Vanguard powered Plus/4 and the Ford powered Four/4 Series II and III. These instruments, whatever model you may have fitted to your engine are similar in design and the general information given applies to all types.

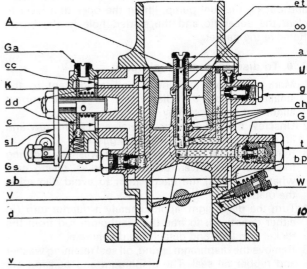

FIG 2:6 General layout of Solex carburetter

2:12 Slow running

Adjustment of the slow running should be made only when the engine is at normal running temperature (FIG 2:6). The output Pilot Jet (g) is mixed with air from Air Bleed (u) and fed into the channel terminating at (io) and finally controlled by Volume control screw (W).

It will then be seen that screwing in (W) reduces the volume of mixture and vice versa, offering a considerable latitude for adjustment of the volume and richness of mixture, to suit engine requirements.

2:13 Slow running adjustment

Satisfactory setting of the slow running is the result of combined adjustments to the brass volume control screw (W) and steel spring loaded slow running adjustment screw.

1 Screw in (W) until lightly seated, then unscrew one complete turn.
2 Start the engine and set slow running adjustment screw until the engine is running at about 500 rpm.
3 Unscrew (W) until the engine begins to 'hunt'.
4 Screw in (W) slowly until the 'hunting' just disappears.
5 If the engine speed is too high, reset the slow running adjustment screw, until the engine is running at 500 rpm.

6 This may cause a resumption of slight 'hunting'. If so turn (W) gently in a clockwise direction until the idling is perfect.

2:14 Adjustment of jets

Pilot Jet—A larger size pilot jet can be fitted to a worn engine if satisfactory slow running cannot be obtained with the original.

Main Jet—An engine will occasionally take a size smaller main jet in the carburetter without an appreciable loss of performance. If it is found that ample power is being obtained and there is no sympton of weak mixture, such as spitting back excessively in the carburetter during cold weather, when opening the throttle, it may be worth while to try a smaller main jet, for it is possible that in the summer, even if not all the year round, good results will be obtained from it with regard to better mpg.

2:15 S.U. Carburetters

All TR engined Plus/4s except the Super Sports model have been fitted with twin S.U. carburetters except for a short period when Stromberg-Zenith units were utilised.

The S.U. carburetter is of the air-valve type, simple in construction and relatively trouble-free in operation.

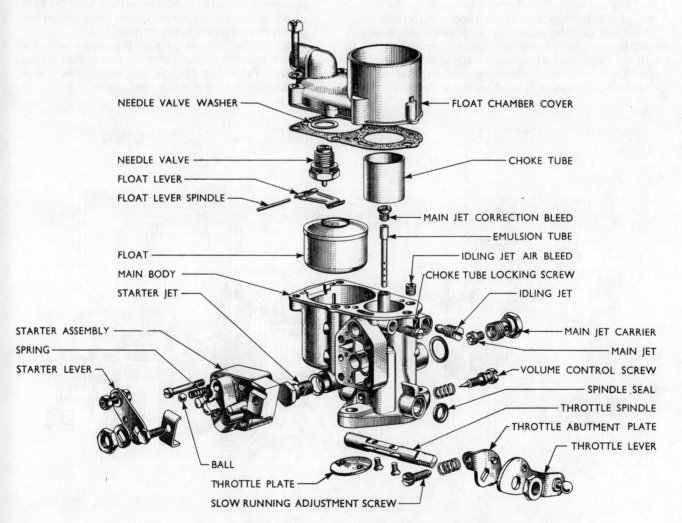

FIG 2:7 Exploded view of Solex B.26 ZIC-2 carburetter (Four/4 Series II)

An air valve piston moves a tapered needle in or out of a metering jet to provide the correct mixture, depending on the amount of air entering the carburetter. The throttle plate position determines the air velocity, which in turn determines the position of the air valve piston—and also the metering needle.

The TR2 engine is fitted with S.U. H4 carburetters whilst the TR3 has S.U. H6 units. These carburetters are identical except that the latter has a four-point mounting. TR4a engines are now fitted with S.U. HS6 carburetters, these follow the general principles of the earlier units, but dismantling, assembling and tuning details are dealt with later.

2:16 Effect of altitude and climate, etc.

The standard tuning employs a jet needle which is broadly suitable for temperate climates at sea level upwards to approximately 3,000 ft. Above this altitude it may be necessary, depending on the additional factors of extreme climatic heat and humidity, to use a weaker tuning than standard.

The factors of altitude, extreme climatic heat, each tend to demand a weaker tuning, and a combination of any of these factors would naturally emphasise this demand. This is a situation which cannot be met by a hard and fast factory recommendation owing to the wide variations in the condition existing and in such cases the owner will need to experiment with alternative weaker needles until one is found to be satisfactory.

If the carburetter is fitted with a spring loaded suction piston, the necessary weakening may be affected by changing to a weaker type of spring or by its removal.

2:17 Carburetter jet needles

Carburetter Type	No. of Carburetters	Standard Needle	Richer Version	Weaker Version
TR2 H4	2	FV	GE/R	CR
TR3 H6	2	SM	RH	SL

2:18 To remove jet needle

1 Remove the air-cleaner (if fitted).
2 Remove the damping piston from the top of the suction chamber.
3 Withdraw the three suction chamber securing screws and move the carburetter float chamber support arm to one side.
4 Lift the suction chamber and remove coil spring and washer from piston head.
5 Remove the piston with jet needle attached from the body of the carburetter and empty away oil in the reservoir.
6 Loosen screw in base of piston and withdraw jet needle.

2:19 To fit needle (Fig 2:11)

1 Ensure that the jet head is loose in the main body of the carburetter by loosening clamp ring.
2 Ascertain that the jet needle is perfectly straight and position it so that the shoulder is flush with the base of the piston, tighten screw to grip needle. Feed the needle into its recess in the jet head.
Note: On no account should the piston with the needle attached be laid down so that it rests on the needle. Failure to observe this point may cause carburation defects due to a bent needle.

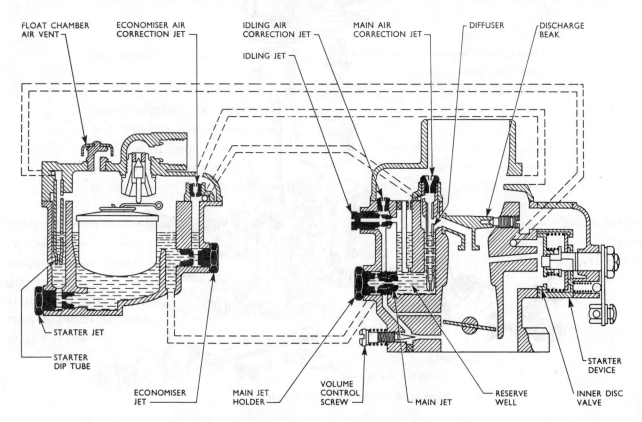

FIG 2:8   Operation of carburetter (Four/4 Series III)

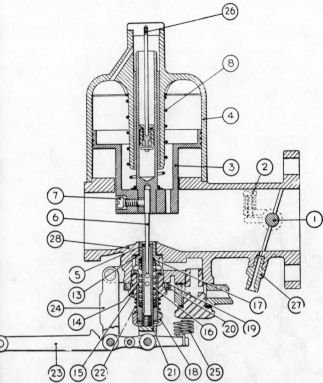

FIG 2:9 Sectional view of S.U. carburetter, for illustration purposes the jet lever and link have been turned 90 deg.

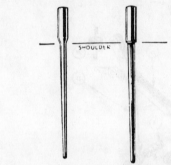

SHOULDER

FIG 2:10 Showing shoulder datum of the jet needles. The shoulder of the needle should be flush with the under face of the piston. Two types of shoulder are in use, and the correct datum point for each is shown

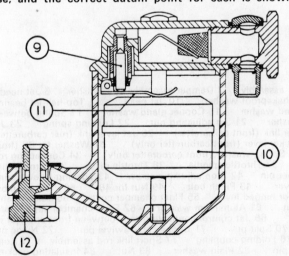

FIG 2:11 Section view of float chamber

3 Position the washer and the spring on top of the piston and the suction chamber over the piston.

4 Secure with the three attachment screws with the foremost accommodating the float chamber support arm.

5 Fill the piston reservoir with thin oil and fit the damper to the suction chamber.

6 Centralize the jet as described below.

7 Tune the carburetters as described in section headed 'carburetter tuning'.

2 : 20 Centralization of jet (Fig 2 : 9)

1 Disconnect the throttle linkage to gain access to the jet head (21) and remove damper (26).

2 Withdraw the jet head (21) and remove adjusting nut (18) and spring (22). Replace nut (18) and screw up to its fullest extent.

3 Slide the jet head (21) into position until its head rests against the base of the adjusting nut.

4 The jet locking nut (15) should be slackened to allow the jet head (21) and bearings (13 and 14) assembly to move laterally.

5 The piston (3) should be raised, access being gained through the air intake and allowing it to fall under its own weight. This should be repeated once or twice and the jet locking nut (15) tightened.

6 Check the piston by lifting to ascertain that there is complete freedom of movement. If 'sticking' is detected operation 4 and 5 will have to be repeated.

7 Withdraw jet head (21) and adjusting nut (18).

8 Replace nut (18) with spring (22) and insert the jet head (21).

9 Check oil reservoir and replace damper (26).

10 Tune the carburetters as described in section headed 'carburetter tuning'.

2 : 21 To assemble the carburetter(s)

Having ensured the cleanliness and serviceability of all component parts, it is suggested that the carburetter(s) are assembled in the following sequence.

The front carburetter differs from that of the rear insomuch that there are certain additions. As and when the additions occur they will be specifically mentioned.

1 Fit the ignition union to the front carburetter, this utilises the tapped bore which breaks through into the mixture passage.

2 Position the throttle spindle in the body in such a manner that the spindle protrudes less on the lefthand side looking at the air cleaner ends.

3 Feed the throttle disc into the slot of the spindle and secure with two countersunk screws. These screws have split shanks which are now opened by the insertion of the screwdriver blade.

4 Position the throttle stop with the two adjusting screws on the shorter end of the throttle spindle of the front carburetter body and secure with the taper pin; to the rear carburetter, fit the throttle stop with the single adjusting screw.

5 Feed the rocker lever bolt through the double coil washer and the rocker lever so that the platform of the lever is on the left viewing the bolt head. This assembly is fitted to the front carburetter with a plain washer between it and the carburetter. Ensure that the rocker lever moves freely.

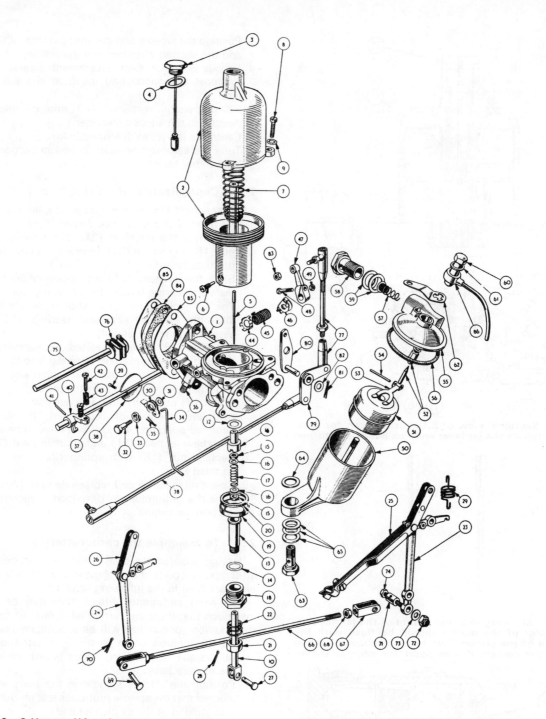

FIG 2:12   S.U. type H4 carburetter—exploded

Key to Fig 2:12   1 Body assembly   2 Suction chamber and piston assembly   3 Damper assembly   4 Washer   5 Jet needle
6 Needle locking screw   7 Piston spring   8 Securing screw   9 Shakeproof washer   10 Jet head   11 Top half jet bearing
12 Washer   13 Bottom half jet bearing   14 Washer   15 Cork gland washer   16 Copper gland washer   17 Spring between
gland washers   18 Jet locking nut   19 Sealing ring   20 Cork washer   21 Jet adjusting nut   22 Loading spring   23 Jet
lever (front carburetter)   24 Jet lever (rear carburetter)   25 Jet lever link (front carburetter)   26 Jet lever link (rear carburetter)
27 Clevis pin   28 Split pin   29 Jet lever return spring   30 Rocker lever (front carburetter only)   31 Washer for 30 (front
carburetter only)   32 Rocker lever bolt (front carburetter only)   33 Spring washer (front carburetter only)   34 Connecting rod
35 Split pin   36 Ignition connection union (front carburetter only)   37 Throttle spindle   38 Throttle disc   39 Throttle disc
attachment screws   40 Throttle stop (front carburetter only)   41 Taper pin   42 Stop adjusting screw   43 Locking screw spring
44 Anchor plate   45 Return spring   46 End clip   47 Throttle lever   48 Pinch bolt   49 Nut for 48   50 Float chamber
51 Float   52 Needle and seat assembly   53 Hinged lever   54 Pin for hinged lever   55 Float chamber cover   56 Joint washer
57 Petrol inlet filter   58 Banjo bolt   59 Fibre washer   60 Cap nut   61 Aluminium washer   62 Float chamber support arm
63 Float chamber attachment bolt   64 Fibre washer   65 Washer   66 Jet control connecting rod (between front and rear jet
levers)   67 Fork end   68 Nut on fork end   69 Clevis pin   70 Split pin   71 Choke cable swivel pin   72 Nyloc nut
73 Plain washer   74 Screw   75 Throttle spindle connecting rod   76 Folding coupling   77 Short link rod assembly   78 Long
link rod assembly   79 Bell crank lever   80 Pivot lever   81 Split pin   82 Plain washer   83 Nut   84 Insulating packing
85 Joint washer   86 Carburetter splash and overflow pipe

6 Fit the throttle spindle return spring anchor plate on the longer end of the spindle and anchor it on the web provided. Follow it with the spring and the end clip then adjust the tension and lock the end clip with the pinch bolt.

7 To the bottom half of the jet bearing position the copper washer followed by the jet adjusting sealing nut (threaded portion uppermost) spring and secure with the jet adjusting nut. Position the alloy sealing ring, flatter side downwards, and the cork washer over the thread of the jet adjusting nut.

8 Insert the jet assembly through the jet adjusting nut and bottom half of the jet bearing from below. Position the cork gland washer, the copper gland washer, spring, a second gland washer and cork gland washer on the head of the jet assembly.

9 Position a copper washer on the shoulders of the upper half jet bearing and, with the shoulder uppermost, balance the top half bearing on the cork gland washer of the jet assembly.

10 Feed the assembly mentioned in 8 and 9 into the carburetter body and secure with the sealing nut.

11 Fit the float to the pillar of the float chamber, this is symmetrical and can be fitted either way up.

12 The needle valve body is secured in the float chamber cover, position valve needle and hinge lever and insert pin. Adjust as described in next section.

13 Assemble the splash overflow pipe to the cap of carburetter float chamber with a washer interposed between.

14 Fit the float chamber cover to the float chamber and attach cap nut as assembled in operation 13. The nut is left loose at this juncture.

15 Fit the jet needle to the piston assembly and ensure that its lower shoulder is flush with that of the piston.

16 The piston and jet needle is now fitted to the body assembly so that the brass dowel in the carburetter body locates the longitudinal groove in the piston.

17 With the smaller diameter of the coil spring downwards, position the spring over the polished stem of the piston.

18 Fit the suction chamber over the spring and piston stem allowing the spring to position itself outside the suction chamber centre.

19 The suction chamber is secured to the carburetter body by three screws, these are fitted but left loose at this juncture.

20 The float chamber is now attached to the carburetter body by the float chamber attachment bolt. Two large bore fibre washers with a brass washer between are positioned between the bolt head and the float chamber and a small bore washer between the float chamber and the carburetter body. With the washers so placed the float chamber is attached to the carburetter body, the attachment bolt is left loose at this juncture.

21 Looking at the intake end of the carburetter body remove the righthand suction chamber securing screw (left loose in operation 19). With a shakeproof washer under its head feed the bolt through the float chamber steady bracket and replace to secure suction chamber. The three screws can now be fully tightened, the cap nut is, however, still left loose. The cap nut of the cover is tightened to secure the splash overflow

pipe for tuning purposes when fitted to the car. Attach the jet lever return spring to the position provided between jet assembly and float chamber.

22 The jet and jet needle are now centralized as described.

23 The damper assembly is fitted to the suction chamber dry. The oil reservoir is not filled until the carburetters are fitted to the car.

24 Select the jet lever of the front carburetter, identified by having two holes at the extremity of the longer arm. This is attached to the jet assembly by a clevis pin and split pin, position the second end of the lever return spring to the jet lever.

25 Feed the upper end of the tension link through the rocker lever of the front carburetter from behind and the second end through the jet lever. Secure both ends with split pins.

26 Select the front carburetter jet lever link, this is distinguished by the pinch bolt at one end. This is attached to the lug at the rear of the jet assembly and again to the elbow of the jet lever in such a manner that the pinch bolt end of this link points to the rear. Both attachments are made by clevis pins and splitpins.

The assembly of the jet lever and jet lever link to the rear carburetter is very similar. Both components are shorter than those fitted to the front carburetter.

2 : 22 To adjust the fuel level in the float chamber Fig 2 : 13

The level of the fuel in the float chamber is adjusted by setting the fork lever in the float chamber lid. It is suggested that the following procedure for its adjustment is adopted.

1 Remove the banjo bolt of the fuel connection and collect the two fibre washers and filter.

2 Loosen the screw securing the float chamber support arm to the carburetter body.

3 Withdraw the cap nut from the centre of the float chamber lid and remove washers and splash overflow pipe.

4 Swing the support arm clear to lift the lid of the float chamber and joint washer.

5 The set of the forked lever is correct when, with the lid of the float chamber inverted and the shank of the fork lever resting on the needle of the delivery valve, it is possible to pass a $\frac{7}{16}$ inch diameter rod between the inside radius of the forked lever and the flange of the lower face of the cover.

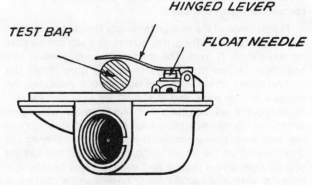

FIG 2 : 13   Adjusting the fuel level

2:23 Carburetter tuning Fig 2:9

This should be carried out without the Air Cleaners as it is found they have no effect on balance or performance but their removal considerably facilitates the operation. One clamping bolt of a throttle rod folding coupling should be loosened, the jet connecting rod should be disconnected at one of its fork end assemblies and the choke control cable released.

The rich mixture starting control linkage should also be disconnected by removing one of the clevis pins. This will enable each carburetter to be adjusted independently.

The suction chamber (4) and piston (3) should be removed and the jet needle (6) position checked. The needle shoulder, as shown in the illustration, should be flush with the base of the recess in the piston. The chamber and piston are now replaced.

The oil reservoir should be full and damping affect should be felt when replacing piston when securing nut is $\frac{1}{4}$ inch from the top of the suction chamber.

It is recommended that the adjusting nut (18) is screwed fully home and then slackened back two and a half turns (fifteen flats) as an initial setting.

The throttle adjusting screw (2) on each carburetter should be adjusted until it will just hold a thin piece of paper between the screw and the stop when the throttle is held in the closed position. The throttle butterfly (1) on each carburetter should then be opened by one complete turn of the adjusting screw.

The engine is now ready for starting and, after thoroughly warming up, the speed should be adjusted by turning each throttle adjusting screw an equal amount until the idling speed is approximately 500 rpm. The synchronization of the throttle setting should now be checked by listening to the hiss of each carburetter, either directly or by means of a piece of rubber tubing held near the intake.

The intensity of the noise should be equal and if one carburetter is louder than the other its throttle adjusting screw should be turned back until the intensity of hiss is equal.

After satisfactory setting of the throttle, the mixture should then be adjusted by screwing the jet adjusting nuts up or down on each carburetter until satisfactory running is obtained. The lever tension spring should be connected during this operation. This mixture adjusting may increase the engine idling speed and each throttle adjusting screw must be altered by the same amount in order to reduce speed to 500 rpm and the hiss of each carburetter again compared.

The balance of the mixture strength should be checked by independently lifting the piston of each carburetter no more than $\frac{5}{32}$ inch. The mixture is correct when this operation causes no change in engine rpm. When the engine slows down with this operation it indicates the mixture is too weak and it should be enriched by un-screwing the jet adjusting nut. An increase of engine speed during this operation indicates that the mixture is too rich and, consequently, it should be weakened off by screwing up the jet adjusting nut. The mixture setting should now give a regular and even exhaust beat, if it is irregular with a 'splashy' type of misfire and a colourless exhaust, the mixture is too weak. A regular or rhythmical type of misfire in the exhaust note, possibly with a blackish exhaust, indicates the mixture is too rich.

The jets of both carburetters should be held against the adjusting nuts before replacing the mixture control linkage, which should be adjusted as necessary, and similarly the throttles should be held tight against their respective idling stops before retightening the folding coupling clamp bolt.

2:24 Carburation defects

In the case of unsatisfactory behaviour of the engine, before proceeding to a detailed examination of the carburetter, it is advisable to carry out a general condition check of the engine, in respects other than those bearing upon the carburation.

Attention should, in particular, be directed towards the following:-

The ignition system.

Incorrectly adjusted contact breaker gap.

Dirty or pitted contact breaker points, or other ignition defects.

Loss of compression of one or more cylinders.

Incorrect plug gaps.

Oily or dirty plugs.

Sticking valves.

Badly worn inlet valve guides.

Defective fuel pump, or chocked fuel filter.

Leakage at joint between carburetters and induction manifold, or between induction manifold flanges and cylinder head.

If these defects are not present to a degree which is thought accountable for unsatisfactory engine performance, the carburetter should be investigated for the following possible faults.

1 Piston sticking. **FIG 2:9**. The symptoms are stalling and a refusal to run slowly, or lack of power and heavy fuel consumption.

The piston (3) is designed to lift the jet needle (6) by the depression transferred to the top side from the passage facing the butterfly. This depression overcomes the weight of the piston and spring (8). The piston should move freely over its entire range and rest on the bridge pieces (28) when the engine is not running.

This should be checked by gently lifting the piston with a small screwdriver and any tendency for binding generally indicates one of the following faults:-

(a) The damper rod may be bent causing binding and this can be checked by its removal. If the piston is now free the damper rod should be straightened and refitted.

(b) The piston is meant to be a fine clearance fit at its outer diameter in the suction chamber and a sliding fit in the central bush. The suction chamber should be removed complete with piston, and the freedom of movement checked after removal of the damper rod. The assembly should be washed clean and very lightly oiled where this slides in the bush and then checked for any tendency of binding. It is permissible to carefully remove, with a hand scraper, any high spots on the outer wall of the suction chamber, but no attempt should be made to increase the clearance by increasing the general bore of the suction chamber or decreasing the diameter of the piston. The fit of the piston in its central bush should be checked under both rotational and sliding movement.

2 Eccentricity of Jet and Needle. **FIG 2 : 9.** The jet (14) is a loose fit in its recess and must always be centred by the needle before locking up the clamping ring (15).

(a) The needle should be checked in the piston to see that it is not bent. It will be realized that it does not matter if it is eccentric as the adjustment of the jet allows for this, but a bent needle can never have the correct adjustment. See section on 'centralization of jet'.

3 Flooding from float chamber or mount of jet. **FIG 2 : 11.** This can be caused by a punctured float (10) or dirt on the needle valve (9) or its seat. These latter items can be readily cleaned after removal of the float chamber lid.

4 Leakage from bottom of jet adjacent to adjustment nut. Leakage in this vicinity is most likely due to defective sealing gland assemblies. There is no remedy other than removing the whole jet assembly after disconnecting the operating lever and cleaning or replacing the faulty parts. It is very important that all parts are replaced in their correct sequence, as shown in the illustration, and it must be realized that centralization of the jet and needle and retuning will be necessary after this operation.

5 Dirt in the Carburetter. This should be checked in the normal way by examining and cleaning the float chamber, but it may be necessary if excessive water or dirt is present to strip down and clean all parts of the carburetter with petrol.

6 Failure of fuel supply to float chamber. If the engine is found to stop under idling or light running conditions, notwithstanding the fact that a good supply of fuel is present at the float chamber inlet union (observable by momentarily disconnecting this), it is possible that the needle has become stuck to its seating. This possibility arises in the rare cases where some gummy substance is present in the fuel system. The most probable instance of this nature is the polymerized gum which sometimes results from the protracted storage of fuel in the tank. After removal of the float chamber lid and float lever, the needle may be withdrawn, and its point thoroughly cleaned by immersion in alcohol.

Similar treatment should also be applied to the needle seating, which can conveniently be cleaned by means of a matchstick dipped in alcohol. Persistent trouble of this nature can only be cured properly by complete mechanical cleansing of the tank and fuel system. If the engine is found to suffer from a serious lack of power which becomes evident at higher speeds and loads, this is probably due to an inadequately sustained fuel supply, and the fuel pump should be investigated for inadequate delivery, and any filters in the system inspected and cleaned.

7 Sticking jet. Should the jet and its operating mechanism become unduly resistant to the action of lowering and raising by means of the enrichment mechanism, the jet should be lowered to its fullest extent, and the lower part thus exposed should be smeared with petroleum jelly, or similar lubricant. Oil should be applied to the various linkage pins in the mechanism and the jet raised and lowered several times in order to promote the passage of the lubricant upwards between the jet and its surrounding parts.

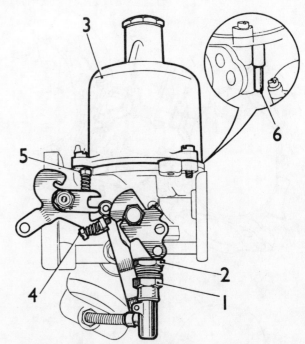

FIG 2 : 14   The S.U. type HS6 carburetter

Key to Fig 2 : 14   1 Jet adjusting nut   2 Jet locking nut
3 Piston/suction chamber   4 Fast-idle adjusting screw
5 Throttle adjusting screw   6 Piston lifting pin

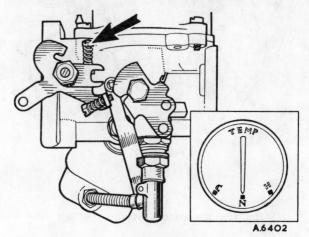

FIG 2 : 15

2 : 25 Tuning twin S.U. type H.S.6 carburetters

1 (a) Warm engine up to normal temperature.
   (b) Switch off engine.
   (c) Unscrew the throttle adjusting screw until it is just clear of its stop and the throttle is closed. **(FIG 2 : 15).**
   (d) Set throttle adjusting screw 1½ turns open.
2 (a) Slacken both of the clamping bolts (7) on the throttle spindle interconnections. **(FIG 2 : 16).**
   (b) Disconnect the jet control interconnection by slackening the clamping bolts (8).
   (c) Mark for reassembly and remove piston/suction chamber unit.
   (d) Disconnect mixture control wire.
   (e) Screw the jet adjusting nut (1) **(FIG 2 : 14)** until the jet is flush with the bridge of the carburetter or fully up if this position cannot be obtained.

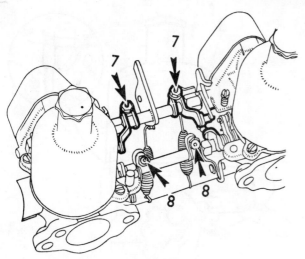

FIG 2:16

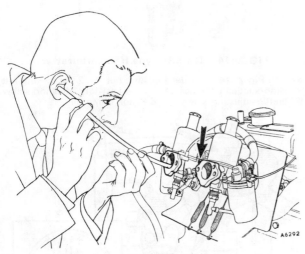

FIG 2:17

lifting pin of the front carburetter up $\frac{1}{32}$ inch (.8 mm) after free movement has been taken up. The graph illustrates the possible effect on engine rpm. **FIG 2:19**. Readjust the mixture strength if necessary.

(b) Repeat the operation on the other carburetters and after adjustment re-check since they are all inter-dependent.

(c) Check exhaust for regular even note.

6 (a) Set the throttle interconnection clamping levers (7) **(FIG 2:20)** so that the link pin is .006 inch (.15 mm) away from the lower edge of the fork (see inset). Tighten the clamp bolts.

(b) With both jet levers at their lowest position, set the jet interconnection lever clamp bolts (8) so that both jets commence to move simultaneously.

7 (a) Reconnect the mixture control wire with about $\frac{1}{16}$ inch (1.6 mm) free movement before it starts to pull on the jet levers **(FIG 2:21)**.

(b) Pull the mixture control knob until the linkage is about to move the carburetter jets, and adjust the fast idle screws, comparing the intensity of the air intake 'hiss' to give an engine speed of about 1,000 rpm when hot.

(c) Refit the air cleaners, if fitted.

2:26 Adjusting and servicing—jet centring

8 The piston should fall freely onto the carburetter bridge with a click when the lifting pin is released with the jet in the fully up position. If it will only do this with the jet lowered then the jet unit requires recentring. This is done as follows:

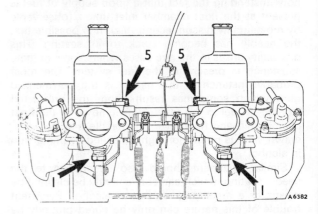

FIG 2:18

(f) Replace the piston/suction chamber unit as marked.

(g) Check that the piston falls freely onto the bridge when the lifting pin (6) is released **(FIG 2:14)**. If not, see items 8, 9 and 10.

(h) Turn down the jet adjusting nut (1) two complete turns.

3 (a) Restart the engine and adjust the throttle adjusting screws on each carburetter to give the desired idling speed as indicated by the glow of the ignition warning light.

(c) Compare the intensity of the intake 'hiss' on all carburetters and alter the throttle adjusting screws until the 'hiss' is the same **(FIG 2:17)**.

4 (a) Turn the jet adjusting nuts (1) on all carburetters up to weaken or down to richen the same amount until the fastest idling speed consistent with even running is obtained **(FIG 2:18)**.

(b) Readjust the throttle adjusting screws (5) to give correct idling if necessary.

5 (a) Check for correct mixture by gently pushing the

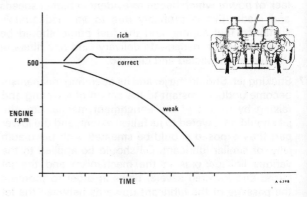

FIG 2:19

9 (a) Remove the jet head screw to release the control linkage.

(b) Withdraw the jet, disconnecting the fuel feed pipe union in the float chamber, and removing the rubber sealing washer. Remove the jet locking spring and adjusting nut **(FIG 2 : 22)**.

(c) Replace the jet and insert the fuel feed pipe connection into the float chamber.

(d) Slacken the jet locking nut until the assembly is free to rotate.

10 (a) Remove the piston damper and apply pressure to the top of the piston rod with a pencil **(FIG 2 : 23)**.

(b) Tighten the jet locking nut keeping the jet hard up against the jet bearing.

(c) Finally check again as in item 8.

(d) Refit the jet locking spring and adjusting nut. Before replacing the fuel feed pipe into the float chamber, fit the rubber sealing washer over the end of the plastic pipe so that at least $\frac{3}{16}$ inch (4.8 mm) of pipe protrudes (see inset). Reassemble the controls.

(e) Refill the piston dampers with the recommended engine oil, until the level is $\frac{1}{2}$ inch (13 mm) above the top of the hollow piston rod.

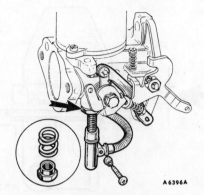

FIG 2 : 22

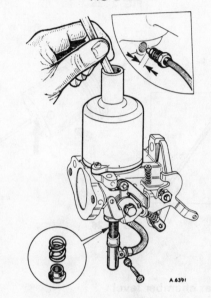

FIG 2 : 23

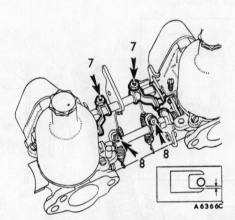

FIG 2 : 20

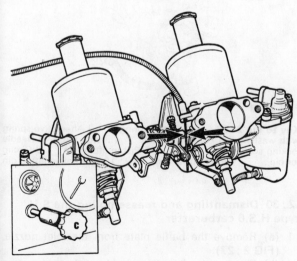

FIG 2 : 21

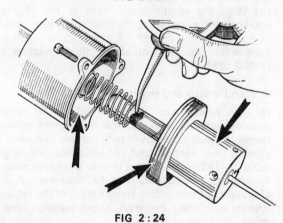

FIG 2 : 24

2 : 27 Cleaning

11 (a) At the recommended intervals mark for re-assembly and carefully remove the piston/suction chamber unit **(FIG 2 : 24)**.

(b) Using a petrol-moistened cloth, clean the inside bore of the suction chamber and the two diameters of the piston.

(c) Lightly oil the piston rod only and reassemble as marked.

(d) Refill piston damper.

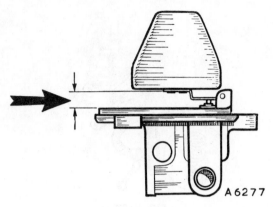

FIG 2 : 25

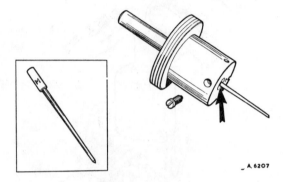

FIG 2 : 26

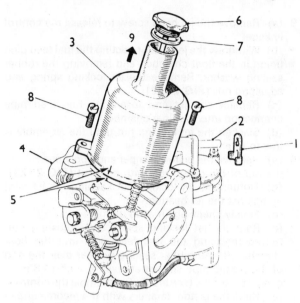

FIG 2 : 27

Key to Fig 2 : 27   1 Baffle plate   2 Inlet nozzle   3 Suction chamber   4 Carburetter body   5 Marks for replacement   6 Damper   7 Damper washer   8 Chamber retaining screws   9 Direction of removal

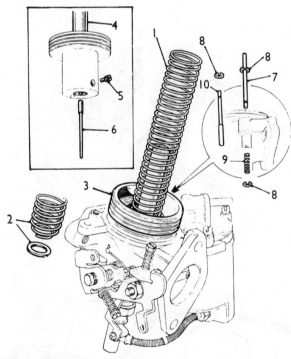

FIG 2 : 28

Key to Fig 2 : 28   1 Piston spring   2 Alternative spring with washer   3 Piston assembly   4 Piston rod   5 Needle locking screw   6 Needle   7 Piston lifting pin   8 Circlip for pin   9 Spring for pin   10 Alternative lifting pin

2 : 28 Float chamber level

12 (a) Remove and invert the float chamber lid.

(b) With the needle valve held in the shut-off position by the weight of the float only, there should be a $\frac{1}{8}$ to $\frac{3}{16}$ inch (3.2 to 4.8 mm) gap between the float lever and the rim of the float chamber lid **(FIG 2 : 25)**.

2 : 29 Needle size and position

13 (a) The needle size is determined during engine development and will provide the correct mixture strength unless extremes of temperature, humidity, or altitude are encountered. At altitudes exceeding 6,000 ft (1830 m) a weaker needle will be necessary. A different needle may also be necessary if any alteration to the standard specification of the exhaust system, air cleaner, camshaft, or compression ratio is made.

(b) To check that the correct needle is fitted: mark for reassembly and remove the piston/suction chamber unit **(FIG 2 : 26)**.

(c) Slacken the needle clamping screw, extract the needle, and check its identifying mark against the recommendation.

(d) Replace the correct needle and lock it in position so that the shoulder on the shank is flush with the piston base.

(e) Reassemble the piston/suction chamber unit as marked.

2 : 30 Dismantling and reassembling the S.U. type H.S.6 carburetter

1 (a) Remove the baffle plate from the inlet nozzle. **(FIG 2 : 27)**.

(b) Thoroughly clean the outside of the carburetter.

(c) Mark the relative positions of the suction chamber and the carburetter body.

(d) Remove the damper and its washer. Unscrew the chamber retaining screws.

(e) Lift off the chamber without tilting it.

2 (a) Remove the piston spring and washer (when fitted) **(FIG 2 : 28)**.

(b) Carefully lift out the piston assembly and empty the damper oil from the piston rod.

(c) Remove the needle locking screw and withdraw the needle. If it cannot easily be removed, tap the needle inwards first and then pull outwards. Do not bend the needle.

(d) If a piston lifting pin with an external spring is fitted, remove the spring retaining circlip and spring, then push the lifting pin upwards to remove it from its guide. With the concealed spring type, press the pin upwards, detach the circlip from its upper end, and withdraw the pin and spring downwards.

3 (a) Support the moulded base of the jet and slacken the screw retaining the jet pick-up link **(FIG 2 : 29)**.

(b) Relieve the tension of the pick-up lever return spring from the screw and remove screw and brass bush (when fitted).

(c) Unscrew the brass sleeve nut retaining the flexible jet tube to the float chamber and withdraw the jet assembly from the carburetter body. Note the gland, washer, and ferrule, at the end of the jet tube.

(d) Remove the jet adjusting nut and screw. Unscrew the jet locking nut and detach the nut and jet bearing. Withdraw the bearing from the nut, noting the brass washer under the shoulder of the bearing.

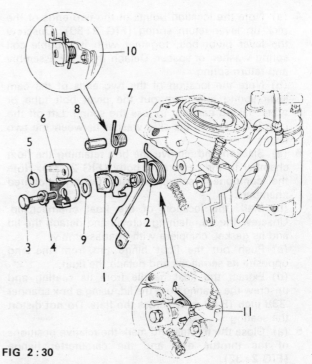

FIG 2 : 30

Key to Fig 2 : 30   1 Pick-up lever   2 Lever return spring
3 Lever pivot bolt   4 Double-coil spring washer   5 Spacer
(alternative)   6 cam lever   7 Lever spring   8 Pivot bolt
tube   9 Skid washer   10 Cam lever spring location
11 Pick-up lever spring location

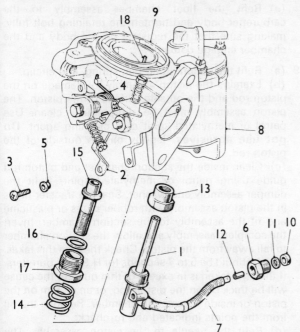

FIG 2 : 29

Key to Fig 2 : 29   1 Jet assembly   2 Pick-up link
3 Link retaining screw   4 Pick-up lever return spring
5 Brass bush   6 Sleeve nut   7 Flexible jet tube   8 Float-
chamber   9 Carburetter body   10 Gland   11 Washer
12 Ferrule   13 Jet adjusting nut   14 Spring for nut
15 Jet bearing   16 Brass washer   17 Jet locking nut
18 Piston key

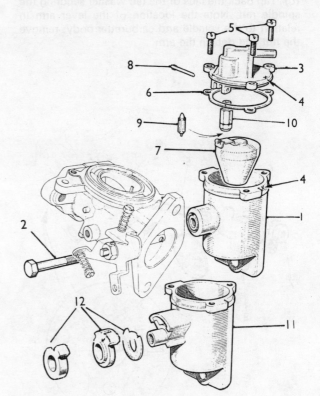

FIG 2 : 31

Key to Fig 2 : 31   1 Float chamber   2 Retaining bolt
3 Float chamber lid   4 Marks for replacement   5 Lid
retaining screws   6 Lid gasket   7 Float assembly   8 Float
hinge pin   9 Float needle   10 Needle seating   11 Alternative float chamber   12 Alternative spacers

4 (a) Note the location points of the two ends of the pick-up lever return spring **(FIG 2 : 30)**. Unscrew the lever pivot bolt, together with its double-coil spring washer, or spacer. Detach the lever assembly and return spring.

(b) Note the location of the two ends of the cam lever spring and push out the pivot bolt 'tube or tubes, taking care not to lose the spring. Lift off the cam lever, noting the skid washer between the two levers.

5 (a) Slacken and remove the bolt retaining the float chamber to the carburetter body **(FIG 2 : 31)**. Note the component sequence with flexibly mounted chambers.

(b) Mark the location of the float chamber lid. Unscrew the lid retaining screws and detach the lid and its gasket, complete with float assembly.

(c) Push out the float hinge pin from the end opposite its serrations and detach the float.

(d) Extract the float needle from its seating and unscrew the seating from the lid, using a box spanner .338 inch (8.58 mm) across the flats. Do not distort the seating.

6 (a) Close the throttle and mark the relative positions of the throttle disc and the carburetter flange **(FIG 2 : 32)**.

(b) Unscrew the two disc retaining screws. Open the throttle and ease out the disc from its slot in the throttle spindle. The disc is oval and will jam if care is not taken.

(c) Tap back the tabs of the tab washer securing the spindle nut. Note the location of the lever arm in relation to the spindle and carburetter body; remove the nut and detach the arm.

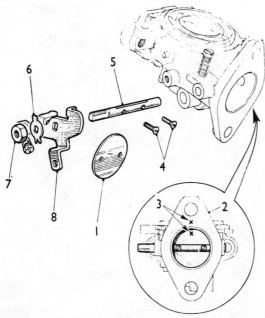

FIG 2 : 32

Key to Fig 2 : 32   1 Throttle disc   2 Carburetter flange
3 Marks for replacement   4 Disc retaining screws   5 Throttle spindle   6 Tab washer   7 Spindle nut   8 Lever arm

7 (a) Examine the throttle spindle and its bearings in the carburetter body. Check for excessive play. Renew parts as necessary.

(b) Refit the spindle to the body. Assemble the operating lever with tab washer and spindle nut, to the spindle. Ensure that when the stop on the lever is against the abutment on the carburetter body, i.e. throttle closed position, the countersunk ends of the holes in the spindle face outwards. Tighten the spindle nut and lock with the tab washer.

(c) Insert the throttle disc in the slot in the spindle in its original position as marked. Manoeuvre the disc in its slot until the throttle can be closed and fit two new retaining screws, but do not fully tighten.

Check visually that the disc closes fully, and adjust its position as necessary. With the throttle closed there must be clearance between the throttle lever and the carburetter body. Tighten the screws fully and spread their split ends just enough to prevent turning.

8 (a) Examine the float needle and seating for damage. Check that the spring-loaded plunger in the end of the plastic-bodied needle operates freely.

(b) Screw the seating into the float chamber carefully. Do not overtighten. Replace the needle in the seating, coned end first. Test the assembly for leakage with air pressure.

(c) Refit the float and lever to the lid and insert the hinge pin. Check the float level as previously described.

(d) Examine the lid gasket for re-use. Assemble the gasket on the lid and refit the lid to the float chamber in the position marked on dismantling. Tighten the securing screws evenly.

(e) Refit the float chamber assembly to the carburetter body and tighten the retaining bolt fully, making sure that the registers on the body and the chamber engage correctly.

9 (a) Refit the piston lifting pin, spring, and circlip.

(b) Examine the piston assembly for damage on the piston rod and the outside surface of the piston. The piston assembly must be scrupulously clean. Use petrol or methylated spirit as a cleaning agent. **Do not use abrasives.** Lightly oil the outside of the piston rod.

(c) Clean inside the suction chamber and piston rod guide using petrol or methylated spirit. Refit the damper assembly and washer. Seal the transfer holes in the piston assembly with rubber plugs or plasticine and fit the assembly to the suction chamber. Invert the complete assembly and allow the suction chamber to fall away from the piston. Check the time this takes, which should be 5 to 7 seconds for H.S.6 carburetters. If the time taken is in excess of that quoted, the cause will be thick oil on the piston rod, or an oil film on the piston or inside the suction chamber. Remove the oil from the points indicated and re-check.

(d) Refit the needle to the piston assembly. The shoulder or lower edge of the groove must be level with the bottom face of the piston rod. Fit a new needle locking screw and tighten. Invert the suction chamber and spin the piston assembly inside it to check for concentricity of the needle.

(e) Check the piston key for security in the carburetter body. Refit the piston assembly to the body and replace the piston spring over the piston rod. Fit the suction chamber and retaining screws. Tighten the screws evenly.

10 (a) Refit the jet bearing, washer, and locking nut; do not tighten the nut. Refit the jet in its bearing and the flexible tube to the base of the float chamber without the gland and washer.

(b) Centralize the jet as described previously.

(c) Withdraw the jet and tube; refit the spring and jet adjusting nut. Fit the gland washer and ferrule to the flexible tube. The end of the tube should project a minimum of $\frac{3}{16}$ inch (4.8 mm) beyond the gland. Refit the jet and tube. Tighten the sleeve nut until the neoprene gland is compressed. Overtightening can cause leakage.

(d) Refit the damper and washer.

11 (a) Reassemble the pickup lever, cam lever, cam lever spring, skid washer, and pivot bolt tube or tubes in the positions noted on dismantling.

(b) Place the pickup lever return spring in position over its boss and secure the lever assembly to the carburetter body with the pivot bolt. Ensure that the double-coil spring washer or spacer fits over the projecting end of the pivot bolt tube.

(c) Register the angled end of the return spring in the groove in the pickup lever, and hook the other end of the spring around the moulded peg on the carburetter body.

(d) Fit the brass ferrule to the hole in the end of the pickup link. Relieve the tension of the return spring and fit the link to the jet with its retaining screw. When finally tightening the screw, support the moulded end of the jet.

(e) Refit the baffle plate to the float chamber lid nozzle.

2:31 Zenith-Stromberg series 175 CD carburetters

This carburetter was fitted to Plus/4 models from 1964 to early 1967. The unit functions on the constant vacuum or variable choke principle. It is dust proof and compact and incorporates a float chamber which surrounds the jet orifice in place of the outrigged type of float chamber which is mounted away from the jet.

The float is manufactured of expanded synthetic material which eliminates the possibility of punctures. It is made in twin parts both being attached to the same lever to operate the fuel valve.

The float chamber can be removed from below, leaving the float and jet housing in position. This arrangement simplifies cleaning and float level adjustments.

The carburetter has a cold starting device in conjunction with the throttle which provides a specific degree of opening to give a fast idle.

2:32 Starting from cold (FIG 2:33)

The mixture is enriched for cold starting when the choke control is pulled. This operates a lever (6) which rotates the starter bar (20) to lift the air valve (18) and needle (29), thus increasing the area of the annulus between needle and jet orifice. Simultaneously, a cam on the lever (6) opens the throttle beyond its normal idle position to provide increased idling speed, according to the setting of the screw (4).

When the motor fires the increased depression will lift the air valve (18) to weaken the initial starting mixture and prevent the engine stalling through over richness.

While the choke remains in action the car may be driven away, but the control knob should be released or pushed in gradually as the engine attains normal working temperature. This will progressively decrease the extent of enrichment and the degree of throttle opening for fast–idle to the point where the screw (4) is out of contact with the cam on the choke lever, and the throttle is permitted to return to the normal idle position as determined by the setting of the throttle stop screw (3). *Note:* The accelerator pedal should not be depressed when starting from cold.

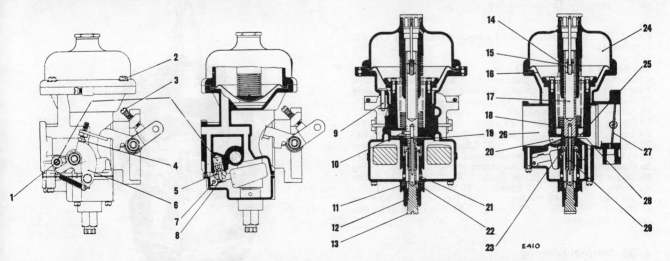

FIG 2:33 Functional diagram of Zenith-Stromberg 175 CD carburetter

Key to Fig 2:33 1 Petrol inlet 2 Screws 3 Throttle stop screw 4 Screw 5 Needle seating 6 Lever 7 Float arm 8 Needle 9 Spring-loaded pin 10 Locking screw 11 'O' ring 12 Jet assembly 13 Jet adjusting screw 14 Damper 15 Coil spring 16 Diaphragm 17 Guide rod 18 Air valve 19 Jet orifice 20 Starter bar 21 Inlet hole 22 Inlet hole 23 Orifice bush 24 Chamber 25 Air valve drilling 26 Bore 27 Throttle 28 Bridge 29 Metering needle

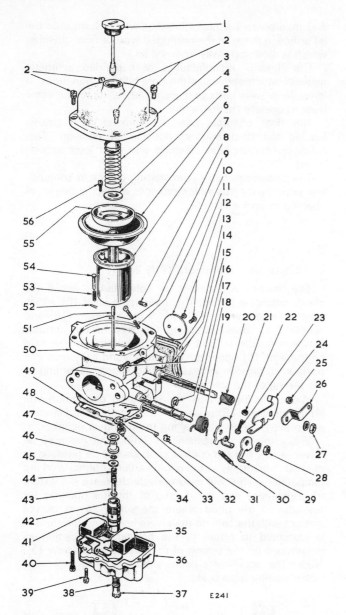

FIG 2:34 Exploded view of Zenith-Stromberg 175 CD carburetter

Key to Fig 2:34   1 Damper   2 Screw   3 Cover
4 Return spring   5 Washer   6 Diaphragm air valve
7 Air valve   8 Locking screw   9 Clamping screw   10 Spring
11 Butterfly   12 Screw   13 Insulating washer   14 Joint
15 Screw   16 Retaining ring   17 Starter bar   18 Spindle
19 Spring   20 Spring   21 Lever   22 Nut   23 Screw
24 Lever   25 Nut   26 Lever   27 Nut   28 Nut
29 Lever   30 Spring   31 Clip   32 Fulcrum pin
33 Washer seating   34 Needle valve   35 Float assembly
36 Float chamber   37 Adjusting screw   38 'O' ring
39 Screw (short)   40 Screw (long)   41 'O' ring   42 Bushing screw   43 Jet   44 Spring   45 Washer   46 'O' ring
47 Jet bush   48 Washer   49 Gasket   50 Body
51 Needle   52 Clip   53 Spring   54 Pin   55 Retaining ring   56 Screw

2:33 Normal running

With the opening of the butterfly throttle, manifold depression is transferred, via a drilling (25) in the air valve, to the chamber (24) which is sealed from the main body of the diaphragm (16).

The pressure difference between chamber (24) and that existing in the bore (26) causes the air valve to lift, thus any increase in engine speed or load will enlarge the effective choke area since the air valve lift is proportional to the weight of air passing the throttle (27). By this means, air velocity and pressure drop across the jet orifice remain approximately constant at all speeds.

As the air valve (18) rises it withdraws a tapered metering needle (29), held in the base of the air valve by the screw (10), from the jet orifice (19) so that fuel flow is increased relative to the greater air flow.

2:34 Acceleration

At any point in the throttle range a temporarily richer mixture is needed at the moment of further throttle opening. To provide this, a dashpot and hydraulic damper is arranged inside the hollow guide rod (17) of the air valve.

The rod is filled with S.A.E.20 oil to within a $\frac{1}{4}$ inch of the end of the rod in which the damper (14) operates, when the throttle is opened, the immediate upward motion of the air valve is resisted by the damper during which time the suction or depression at the jet orifice is increased to enrich the mixture.

The downward movement of the air valve (18) is assisted by the coil spring (15).

2:35 Dismantling carburetter assembly (FIG 2:34)

First clean off surfaces of carburetter with paraffin. Remove all connecting linkage and pipes from carburetter.

Unscrew damper (1) from suction chamber. Remove four screws from cover (3) and take cover from main body (50). Remove return spring (4), washer (5), diaphragm (6), retaining ring (55) and air valve (7).

If it is necessary to renew the diaphragm, remove four screws (56) securing diaphragm to air valve.

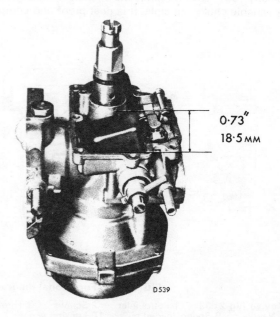

FIG 2:35 Checking float chamber

Take out adjusting screw (37), (a coin will suffice), and bushing screw (42) from base of carburetter. Remove eight screws (39) and (40), three short and five long (float chamber to main body), and take off base unit of carburetter (float chamber) (36), together with float gasket (49).

Take out jet (43) and spring (44), washer (45), 'O' ring (46). Remove needle valve (34).

Examine the butterfly assembly for wear.

Clean and check all dismantled components, and renew unserviceable items.

Reassemble the carburetter by reversing the above procedure.

2 : 36 Float chamber fuel level (FIG 2 : 35)

To check the float level, remove the carburetter from the engine and remove the float chamber. Invert the carburetter. Check that the highest point of the float, when the needle is against its seating, is .73 inch (18.5 mm) above the face of the main body. Reset the level by carefully bending the tag which contacts the end of the needle. The addition of a thin fibre washer under the needle valve seat will effectively lower the fuel level.

2 : 37 Jet centralization

Efficient operation of the carburetter depends upon a freely moving air valve and a correctly centred needle in the jet orifice. The air valve may be checked for freedom by lifting the valve with the spring-loaded pin (9) **(FIG 2 : 37)**. A valve failing to fall freely indicates a sticking valve, or an offcentred jet, and/or the needle (29) fouling the jet orifice. Rectify by removing and cleaning the valve and bore in paraffin, or by recentralizing the needle in the jet.

Note: When required, the jet needle must be renewed by one bearing the same code number. The shoulder of the needle must be fitted flush with the lower face of the air valve.

2 : 38 Procedure (FIG 2 : 33)

1 Lift the air valve (18) and fully tighten the jet assembly (12).
2 Screw up the orifice adjuster until the top of the orifice (19) is just above the bridge (28).
3 Slacken off the jet assembly (12) approximately one half turn to release the orifice bush (23).
4 Allow the air valve (18) to fall; the needle will then enter the orifice and thus centralize it.
5 Slowly tighten the assembly (12), checking frequently that the needle remains free in the orifice. Check by raising the air valve approximately $\frac{1}{4}$ inch (6.35 mm) and allowing it to fall freely. The piston should then stop firmly on the bridge.
6 Reset the engine idling.

2 : 39 Adjustment : setting the idle (FIG 2 : 38)

Two adjustment screws are used to regulate the idle speed mixture. The throttle stop screw (3) controls the speed, and the jet adjusting screw (13) determines the quality of air-fuel mixture entering the cylinders. Turning the jet adjusting screw **clockwise** decreases the mixture strength: **anticlockwise** will enrich.

FIG 2 : 36   Diaphragm location point

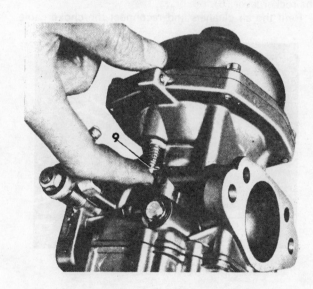

FIG 2 : 37   Checking air valve for freedom with spring-loaded pin (9)

FIG 2 : 38   Idle speed and mixture adjustment screw

With the engine at normal working temperature, remove the air cleaner and hold the air valve down on to the bridge in the throttle bore. Screw up the jet adjustment screw (13)—a coin is ideal for this purpose—until the jet contacts the underside of the air valve. From this position turn down the jet adjusting screw three turns. This establishes an approximate jet position from which to work.

Run the engine until it is thoroughly warm and adjust the stop screw (3) to give an idle speed of 600/650 rpm. The idle mixture is correct when the engine beat is smooth and regular and the air intake 'hiss' is equal on both carburetters (FIG 2 : 39).

As a check, lift the air valve a very small amount $\frac{1}{32}$ inch (.794 mm) with a long thin screwdriver and listen to the effect on the engine. If the engine speed rises appreciably, the mixture is too rich and, conversely, if the engine stops, the mixture is too weak. Properly adjusted, the engine speed will either remain constant or fall slightly on lifting the air valve.

Reset the screw (4) (FIG 2 : 40), to give .062 inch (1.587 mm) clearance between the end of the screw and the rocker lever (6).

Refit the air cleaners and reconnect the choke cable.

FIG 2 : 39 Checking 'hiss'

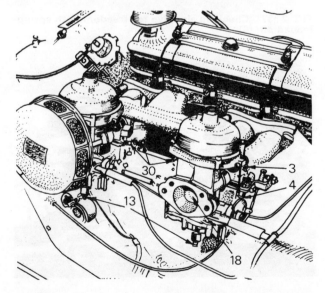

FIG 2 : 40 Twin carburetter installation as on TR4

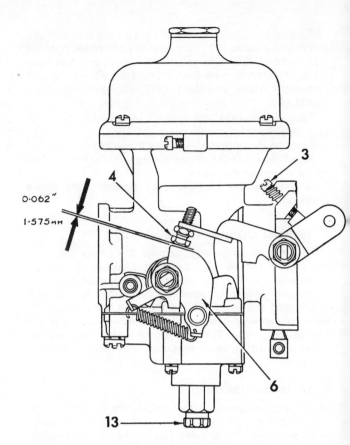

FIG 2 : 41 Stromberg-Zenith 175 CD carburetter linkage

Key to Fig 2 : 41   3 Throttle stop screw   4 Screw
6 Lever   13 Jet adjusting screw

2 : 40 Adjusting and synchronizing twin carburetter installation (FIG 2 : 41)

Loosen the clamping bolts (30) on the throttle spindle couplings between the two instruments. Next, unscrew the throttle stop screw (3) to permit the throttle in each carburetter to close completely, and tighten the clamping bolts on the couplings between the spindles of the two carburetters.

Screw in the throttle stop screws (3) to the point where the end of the screw is just contacting the stop lever attached to each throttle spindle. From this point, rotate the stop screw in each carburetter one complete turn to open the throttles an equal amount to provide a basis from which final speed of idle can be set.

Having reconnected the throttles and set each open an equal amount, regulate the jet adjusting screws (13) in the instruments as detailed under the heading 'setting the idle', i.e. three turns down from the point where the jet orifice comes into contact with the base of the air valve (18).

2 : 41 Jet and throttle interconnection adjustment (FIG 2 : 41)

With the choke control fully 'in', the engine warm and idling on a closed throttle, adjust the screw (4) to give a clearance of $\frac{1}{16}$ inch (1.587 mm) between the end of the screw and the rocker lever (6).

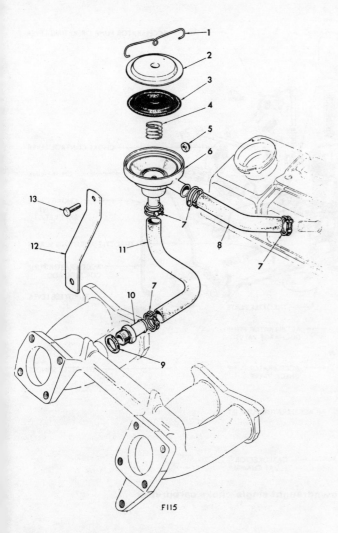

FIG 2 : 42   Crankcase breather regulator valve details (TR4)

Key to Fig 2 : 42   1 Clip   2 Cap   3 Diaphragm
4 Spring   5 Nut   6 Regulator valve body   7 Clip   8 Hose
9 Cork washer   10 Adaptor   11 Hose   12 Bracket   13 Bolt

Always check this adjustment when the throttle stop screw (3) is altered.

Note: Remember that the idle quality depends to a large extent upon the general engine condition, and such points as tappet adjustment, spark plugs, and ignition timing should be inspected if idling is not stable. It is also important to eliminate any leaks in the induction system.

2 : 42 Crankcase breather valve (FIG 2 : 42)

At 12,000 mile intervals, slacken the pipe clips (7) and remove the breather pipes (8) and (11). Remove the nut (5) and bolt (13) and lift off the valve assembly. Disengage the clip (1) from the valve body and lift out the diaphragm (3) and spring (4). Clean the components by swilling them in methylated spirits (denatured alcohol). Ensure that the breather pipes are clean and serviceable. Reverse the dismantling sequence to reassemble.

2 : 43 Zenith downdraught carburetters Four/4 Series IV and V.

This carburetter is of the single-venturi downdraught type. It incorporates an accelerator pump to ensure smooth and rapid acceleration, an economy device controlled by the manifold depression and a choke valve of the semi-automatic stranglar type.

2 : 44 Dismantling

The carburetter is quite readily dismantled for cleaning or rectification. After removing the air filter if fitted the control cable to the choke should be disconnected at the lever, along with its casing anchorage to the bracket. Disconnect the upper end of the throttle rod, and undo the fuel pipe union. The vacuum pipe of the distributor can be separated at the rubber connection. The carburetter is then removed from the induction manifold, after unscrewing its flange nuts.

The carburetter should not be dismantled unnecessarily. Although it is not difficult to strip completely, attention should normally be confined to periodic cleaning at long intervals, as the fuel and air filtration arrangements usually prevent foreign matter from entering in any significant quantity.

The float chamber is removed by unscrewing its four retaining bolts. The float arm and float are lifted out, when all sediment can then be removed by washing in petrol. The jet should not require removal, unless obstruction is suspected, but they can be blown. A wire probe must on no account be used.

For satisfactory operation all the controls should be in correct adjustment. The choke cable should have about $\frac{1}{8}$ inch freedom when the control on the dashboard is fully pushed home. In its closed position for starting, the edge of the throttle butterfly valve should clear the inside of the throughway by an amount which allows a $\frac{15}{64}$ inch or .914 mm (No. 64) drill to be inserted in the gap, at a position at right angles to the throttle spindle when looking down the bore. The same setting can be obtained by noting the position of the throttle-stop with the throttle fully closed, and then screw-in about six turns from this position. (The screw spring will have to be taken off to allow this positioning). The choke link to the throttle should then be adjusted in length so that the choke is fully closed with the throttle thus far open.

2 : 45 Slow running

The slow-running can be adjusted quite simply, with the engine at normal running temperature, by turning the throttle stop screw until the speed is a fast idle. The volume control screw is then adjusted in or out until firing is even. If the engine now runs too fast, alter the throttle stop to suit, following this if necessary by further adjustment of the volume control screw. Do not attempt to obtain too slow an idling speed, as there is no benefit thereby. The ignition timing should also be correct as detailed in Chapter 3. Alternatively a vacuum gauge can be used.

To adjust the accelerator pump stroke there is a stop fitted in the top of the float chamber under the operating arm. In a normal warm or temperate climate, the stop is set so that the arm contacts the large boss, giving a short pump stroke. In cold climates a longer stroke is necessary,

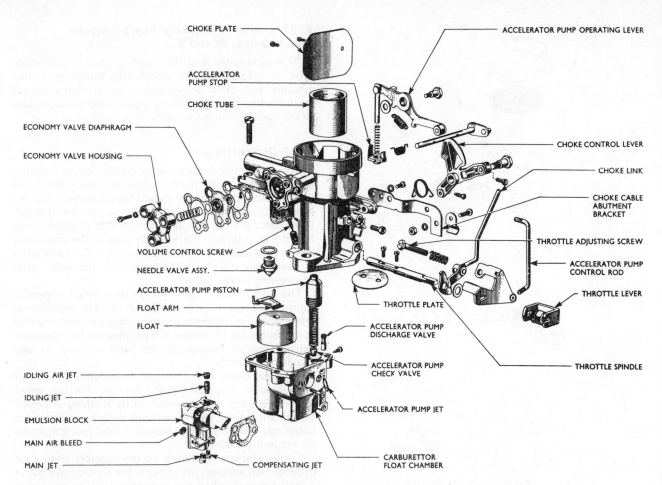

CHOKE PLATE

ACCELERATOR PUMP OPERATING LEVER

ACCELERATOR PUMP STOP

CHOKE TUBE

ECONOMY VALVE DIAPHRAGM

ECONOMY VALVE HOUSING

CHOKE CONTROL LEVER

CHOKE LINK

CHOKE CABLE ABUTMENT BRACKET

VOLUME CONTROL SCREW

THROTTLE ADJUSTING SCREW

NEEDLE VALVE ASSY.

ACCELERATOR PUMP CONTROL ROD

ACCELERATOR PUMP PISTON

FLOAT ARM

THROTTLE LEVER

FLOAT

THROTTLE PLATE

ACCELERATOR PUMP DISCHARGE VALVE

THROTTLE SPINDLE

IDLING AIR JET

IDLING JET

ACCELERATOR PUMP CHECK VALVE

EMULSION BLOCK

MAIN AIR BLEED

ACCELERATOR PUMP JET

MAIN JET

COMPENSATING JET

CARBURETTOR FLOAT CHAMBER

FIG 2:43 Exploded view of Zenith downdraught single-choke carburetter

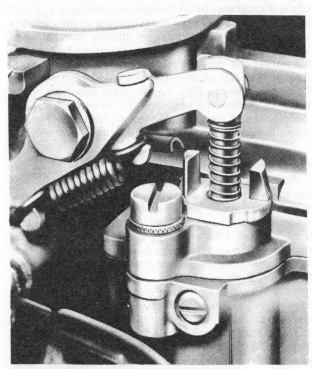

FIG 2:44 Accelerator pump in fully charged position. Note alternative stroke—adjustment stops

this being obtained by setting the stop to contact the small boss. The stop is altered to these positions by lifting it clear of the float chamber against its spring, and then turning it through a half-turn. The different stop heights are clearly shown in FIG 2:44.

To check the fuel level, the float chamber must first be filled with petrol to the correct level, by turning the engine over on the starter with the ignition switched off. The four securing bolts are then removed, and the chamber very carefully detached from the carburetter body. With the float in position, the level should be between $\frac{3}{4}$ inch and $\frac{53}{64}$ inch (19 to 21 mm) below the top face of the chamber. If the level is low, bend the float arm upwards; or downwards if the level is too high. Then drain off some of the fuel, refit the chamber, and repeat the process as before until the level is correct.

The carburetter is often blamed for many engine faults, but assuming that all other items are found correct in every detail, possible carburetter failures can be investigated methodically.

2:46 Defects

If starting from cold is difficult, assuming that the pump is supplying fuel make sure that the float needle valve is not sticking on its seating; the valve assembly can be

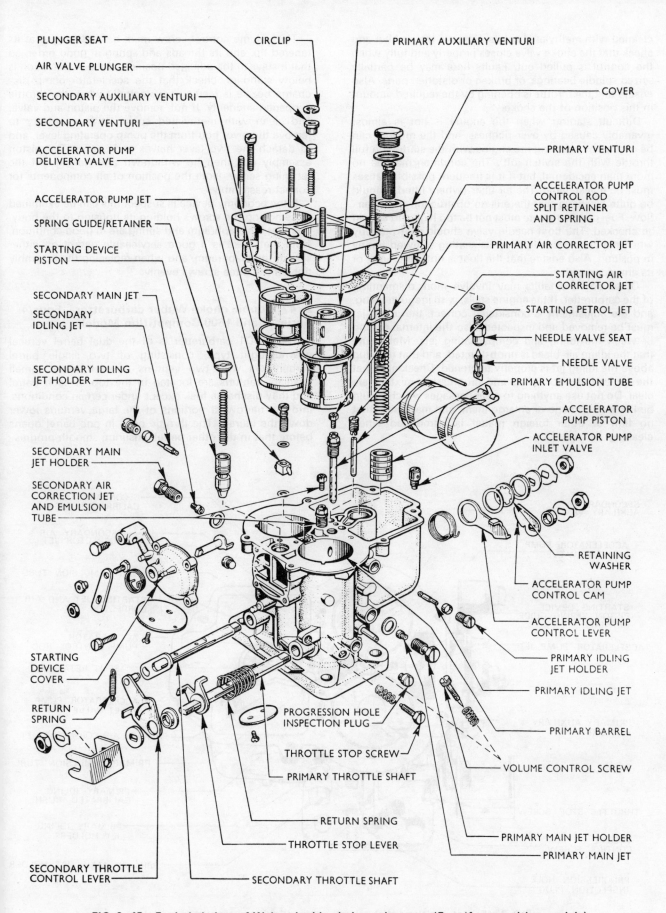

PLUNGER SEAT
AIR VALVE PLUNGER
SECONDARY AUXILIARY VENTURI
SECONDARY VENTURI
ACCELERATOR PUMP DELIVERY VALVE
ACCELERATOR PUMP JET
SPRING GUIDE/RETAINER
STARTING DEVICE PISTON
SECONDARY MAIN JET
SECONDARY IDLING JET
SECONDARY IDLING JET HOLDER
SECONDARY MAIN JET HOLDER
SECONDARY AIR CORRECTION JET AND EMULSION TUBE
STARTING DEVICE COVER
RETURN SPRING
SECONDARY THROTTLE CONTROL LEVER

CIRCLIP
PRIMARY AUXILIARY VENTURI
COVER
PRIMARY VENTURI
ACCELERATOR PUMP CONTROL ROD SPLIT RETAINER AND SPRING
PRIMARY AIR CORRECTOR JET
STARTING AIR CORRECTOR JET
STARTING PETROL JET
NEEDLE VALVE SEAT
NEEDLE VALVE
PRIMARY EMULSION TUBE
ACCELERATOR PUMP PISTON
ACCELERATOR PUMP INLET VALVE
RETAINING WASHER
ACCELERATOR PUMP CONTROL CAM
ACCELERATOR PUMP CONTROL LEVER
PRIMARY IDLING JET HOLDER
PRIMARY IDLING JET
PRIMARY BARREL
VOLUME CONTROL SCREW
PRIMARY MAIN JET HOLDER
PRIMARY MAIN JET

PROGRESSION HOLE INSPECTION PLUG
THROTTLE STOP SCREW
PRIMARY THROTTLE SHAFT
RETURN SPRING
THROTTLE STOP LEVER
SECONDARY THROTTLE SHAFT

FIG 2:45   Exploded view of Weber double choke carburetter (Four/4 competition models)

cleaned with methylated spirits. Remove the air filter and check that the choke valve closes properly and fully when the control is pulled out. Faults here may be partially seized spindle bearings, or broken or distorted parts. Also ensure that the throttle is opening by the required amount in this position of the choke.

Difficult starting when the engine is hot is almost invariably caused by over-richness, and the mixture can be cleared by spinning the engine with the starter, on full throttle with the switch 'off'. The condition may be no more than accidental, but if it is frequent possible causes must be investigated. The air filter (where fitted) should be quite clean, so that there is no obstruction to the air-flow. Fuel pump pressure must not be too high and should be checked. The float needle valve should seat properly when the chamber is full and its seating screwed tightly in position. Also ensure that the float is not punctured, or its arm damaged.

Other possible faults may involve more dismantling of the carburetter. If the engine stalls, with irregular idling, and the adjustment is considered correct, the idling jet must be removed and inspected, also the internal drilling between the idling and compensating jets. Make sure that the idling air-bleed is unobstructed, and that the plug above the idling jet is properly tightened. Check also that the outlet holes for idling and progression mixture are clear. Do not use anything to clear passages which would be liable to damage or enlarge them, and make sure that no fluff or other foreign matter is introduced when cleaning.

The volume control screw must be undamaged at its tapered tip, and its threads and spring in good order, so that it stays in the adjusted position. If the acceleration is below standard, check that the accelerator pump discharge nozzle is feeding satisfactorily when the throttle is opened suddenly. If not, remove the piston and valve, and clean with methylated spirits. It is necessary to remove the pivot bolt from the pump operating lever, and to detach the two lever halves and spring. The piston assembly can then be withdrawn after taking out the retaining screw. Note the position of all components for correct reassembly.

If the economy device is suspect this can be examined by removing the screws holding its housing to the body. See that the diaphragm and spring are in good condition. Note that there is a good serviceable gasket on either side of the diaphragm, and when replacing the assembly tighten the three screws evenly.

2 : 47 Double choke Weber carburetter—Four/4 Series V and 1600 Competition Models

The DCD1 carburetter is of the dual barrel vertical downdraught type, consisting of two single barrel carburetters with two venturis in each barrel. Small auxiliary venturis are located in the top of each barrel and they discharge fuel, except under certain conditions, into the narrowest portions of the large venturis lower down the barrels. The throttle plate in one barrel opens before that in the other barrel, ensuring smooth progres-

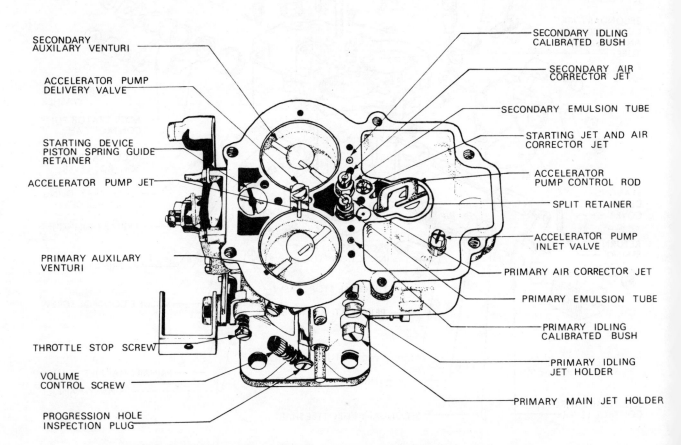

FIG 2 : 46   Jet positions Weber carburetter (Four/4 competition models)

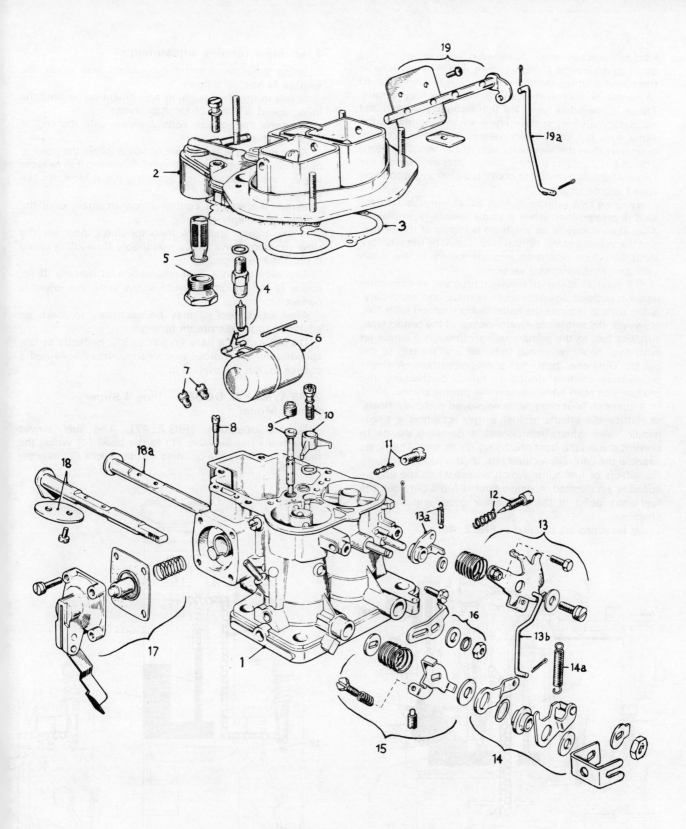

FIG 2:47 Components of later type Weber carburetter

Key to Fig 2:47 1 Lower body   2 Upper body   3 Gasket   4 Float needle valve   5 Filter and retainer   6 Float and pin   7 Primary and secondary main jets   8 Pump inlet valve stop   9 Air correction jet and emulsion tube   10 Accelerator pump discharge valve and jet   11 Idling jet and holder   12 Volume control screw and spring   13 Choke operating lever assembly   13a Choke relay lever and toggle spring   13b Fast-idle rod   14 Left to right, fast-idle lever, spacer, control lever for secondary throttle and primary throttle lever   14a Secondary throttle return spring   15 Idling stop lever and primary throttle return spring   16 Secondary throttle lever   17 Accelerator pump   18 Primary throttle shaft   18a Secondary throttle shaft   19 Choke spindle and plate   19a Choke connecting rod

sion as the accelerator is operated at low engine rpm, and good performance at high engine rpm. The venturis in the barrel with the throttle which opens first are referred to as the primary venturi and primary auxiliary venturi. Those in the other barrel are the secondary venturi and secondary auxiliary venturi. The auxiliary venturis are the same size, but the primary venturi is smaller (26 mm diameter) than the secondary venturi (27 mm diameter). The use of a smaller primary venturi operating before the larger secondary venturi or choke tube ensures good low speed engine torque.

By using two venturis in each barrel a greater depression is created than when a single venturi is employed. Also, the velocity of an airstream is higher at the centre, and the velocity of this central core is used by the auxiliary venturis, which discharge into the centre of the main venturis at the narrowest section.

The main jet, idling jet, emulsion tube and air correction jet are duplicated, again the terms 'primary' and 'secondary' being used to indicate the barrel being supplied with fuel. However, the single accelerator pump, of the piston type, supplies fuel to the primary venturi through a single jet with two 'beaks' mounted between and on top of the barrels. Only one 'beak' has a calibrated hole. A single progressive starting device is fitted, discharging the mixture into both barrels below the throttle plates.

A common float chamber is employed with twin floats, to reduce the effects of fuel surge, actuating a single needle valve which incorporates a damping device to prevent the needle from chattering on its seat. The floats straddle the centrally located jets, their position reducing the effects of fuel surge which occurs when the engine speed is accelerated. A gauze filter is fitted between the fuel entry point in the carburetter cover and the float chamber.

Jet locations are detailed in **FIG 2 : 46.**

2 : 48 Slow-running adjustment

Idling adjustment must be carried out when the **engine is hot,** as follows:

Screw in the slow-running adjustment screw until the idling speed is a little faster than normal.

Unscrew the volume control screw until the engine begins to 'hunt'.

Note that the volume control screw alters the volume of mixture passing into the engine. Screwing it in reduces the volume of mixture and screwing it out increases the volume.

Screw the volume control screw in again until the engine runs evenly.

If the engine speed is then too high, unscrew the slow-running screw until a reasonably slow idling speed is obtained.

This may cause a light resumption of hunting. If so, screw in the volume control screw until the idling is perfect.

After adjustment, it may be necessary to make an alteration to the distributor timing.

Do not expect a new engine to idle perfectly at low speeds until the various machined surfaces have had a chance to 'run themselves in'.

2 : 49 Weber 42 DCOE 8—Plus/4 Super Sports Model

Normal operation **(FIG 2 : 47).** The fuel arrives through the needle valve (1) to the bowl (4) where the float (3) controls the opening of the needle (2) in order

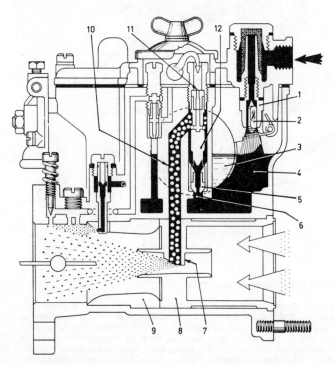

FIG 2 : 48   Weber 42 DCOE 8: normal operation

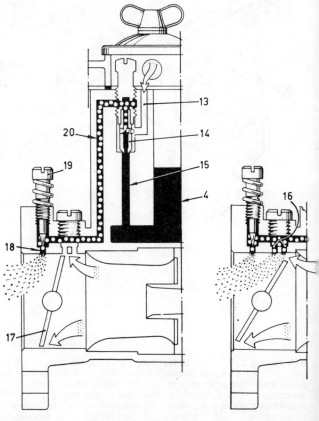

FIG 2 : 49   Weber 42 DCOE 8: idling and progression

to maintain a constant fuel level. Through the ducts (6) and the main jets (5). it reaches the emulsioning tubes (12), from which after having been mixed with the air coming from the air corrector jets (11), through the pipes (10) and the nozzles (7), it reaches the carburation area consisting of the auxiliary venturis (8) and chokes (9).

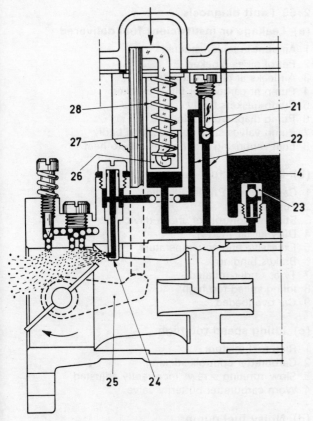

FIG 2:50   Weber 42 DCOE 8: acceleration

2:50 Idling operation and progressive action (FIG 2:49)

The fuel is carried from the bowl (4) to the Calibrated holes of the idling jets (14) through the ducts (15). Emulsified with the air coming from the ducts (13), through the ducts (20) and the idling feed holes (18), adjustable by means of screws (19), the fuel reaches the carburetter throats below the throttles (17). From the ducts (20) the mixture can reach the carburetter throats also through the progression holes (16).

2:51 Acceleration (FIG 2:50)

By closing the throttle valves, the lever (25), by means of the shaft (27), lifts the piston (26). The fuel is thus drawn from the bowl (4) into the pump cylinder through the suction valve (23). By opening the throttles, the shaft (27) is free and the piston (26) is pushed down under the action of the spring (28); by means of the ducts (22) the fuel is injected through the delivery valve (21) to the pump jets (24) into the carburetter throats. The inlet valve (23) is provided with a calibrated hole which discharges the excess fuel delivered by the accelerating pump into the float bowl.

2:52 Starting device (FIG 2:51)

The fuel flowing from the bowl (4) arrives at the starting device through the ducts (32) and the starting jets (30). Emulsified with the air coming from the hole (29) it reaches the valves opening (35) through the ducts (31) and thoroughly emulsified by air entering from orifices (34) is then carried by means of the ducts (33) to the carburetter throats below the throttles.

Engine cold starts—starting device inserted—position 'A'.

Engine half-warm starts—partial insertion of the device—Position 'B'

Engine warm up—during engine warming up, even if the vehicle is under way, the starting device must be gradually pushed into rest position.

Engine normal running—starting device must be pushed back as soon as the engine has reached the operative temperature—position 'C'.

2:53 Fuel tank removal

To remove fuel tank on coupe and four-seater, remove spare wheel and trim panel behind seats. Disconnect filler hose, pipe line and gauge wire. Take out two bolts at front, two at rear, and lift out. On two-seater, in addition unscrew filler cap assembly, take out four coach-bolts each side holding cradle to wheel arches, and two woodscrews each side to crossmember. Lower cradle until filler neck is clear of top of body.

On pre-war two seater models, to allow the neck of the petrol tank filler to clear the body, remove the two rearmost coach-bolts on each side of the wooden frame over the back axle. This will allow the frame to pivot slightly on the front bolts and drop the ½ inch necessary to clear.

2:54 Modification

Fuel filter:

On later cars a fuel filter has been incorporated into the fuel line between the pump and carburetter. Visual inspection will show if cleaning is necessary.

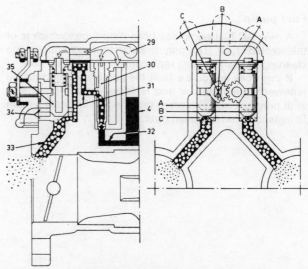

FIG 2:51   Weber 42 DCOE 8: starting device

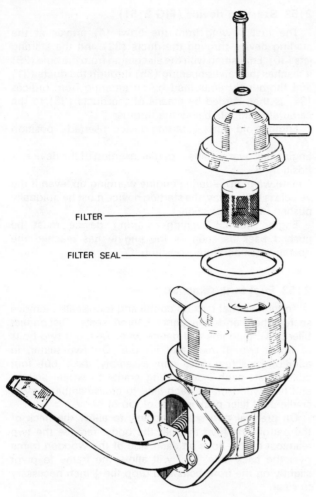

FILTER

FILTER SEAL

FIG 2:52 Exploded view of late type fuel pump

To clean the filter, remove it from the fuel line and blow through with compressed air in the reverse direction from the indicated flow. Refit in the fuel line with the arrow pointing towards the carburetter.

Fuel pump:

A new AC fuel pump has been introduced which is of the 'sealed' type. The only maintenance possible is the cleaning of the filter and replacement of the filter seal.

If this does not cure a fault the complete unit must be renewed. Pump removal and replacement is the same as with previous models except that the fuel lines are a push fit instead of having union nuts.

Fuel filter and seal (see FIG 2:52):

Pull the fuel pipe off the pump inlet tube, remove the securing screw as shown and lift off the sediment bowl.

Remove the filter and seal and clean as described in **Section 2:2**.

Refit in the reverse order.

2:55 Fault diagnosis

(a) Leakage or insufficient fuel delivered

1 Air vent in tank restricted
2 Petrol pipes blocked
3 Air leaks at pipe connections
4 Pump or carburetter filters blocked
5 Pump gaskets faulty
6 Pump diaphragm defective
7 Pump valves sticking or seating badly
8 Fuel vaporizing in pipelines due to heat

(b) Excessive fuel consumption

1 Carburetter(s) need adjusting
2 Fuel leakage
3 Sticking controls or choke device
4 Dirty air cleaner(s)
5 Excessive engine temperature
6 Brakes binding
7 Tyres under-inflated
8 Idling speed too high
9 Car overloaded

(c) Idling speed too high

1 Rich fuel mixture
2 Carburetter controls sticking
3 Slow-running screws incorrectly adjusted
4 Worn carburetter butterfly valve

(d) Noisy fuel pump

1 Loose mountings
2 Air leaks on suction side and at diaphragm
3 Obstruction in fuel pipe
4 Clogged pump filter

(e) No fuel delivery

1 Float needle stuck
2 Vent in tank blocked
3 Electric pump connections faulty
4 Electric pump contacts dirty
5 Pipeline obstructed
6 Pump diaphragm stiff or damaged
7 Inlet valve in pump stuck open
8 Bad air leak on suction side of pump

CHAPTER 3

IGNITION SYSTEM

All early model Morgan four wheel vehicles are fitted with Lucas coils and distributors and are all of a straight forward nature and typical for the period when they were fitted.

DISTRIBUTORS

3:1 Four/4 Series I

The Coventry Climax was fitted with a centrifugal advance and a Vernier timing adjustment which was located on the drive housing by a clamp plate. This was driven by a 'dog'. A two bolt cap at the bottom of the drive housing retains the skew gears. The range of the advance is 12 deg. and the points break at t d c. The location of ignition timing is by a line on the flywheel opposite a hole in the case which indicates t d c on No. 1 or No. 4 cylinder.

The Standard Special engine also has automatic advance and should be set to fire at t d c which means that when the engine is at rest the timing will be at full retard.

To time this engine turn the engine over until No. 1 piston reaches t d c. A mark on the flywheel indicates this position, but if the clutch housing is in position this mark will not be visible, in which case t d c for No. 1 cylinder is mid-way between the point of opening of the

inlet valve and the point of closing of the exhaust valve of No. 4 cylinder, when the engine is turned in a clockwise direction. *Note:* The cylinders are numbered in sequence from the back of the engine. Therefore No. 4 cylinder is nearest the radiator. A quick and simple method of

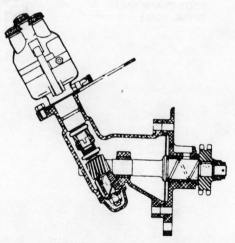

FIG 3:1 Section through Coventry Climax distributor Drive

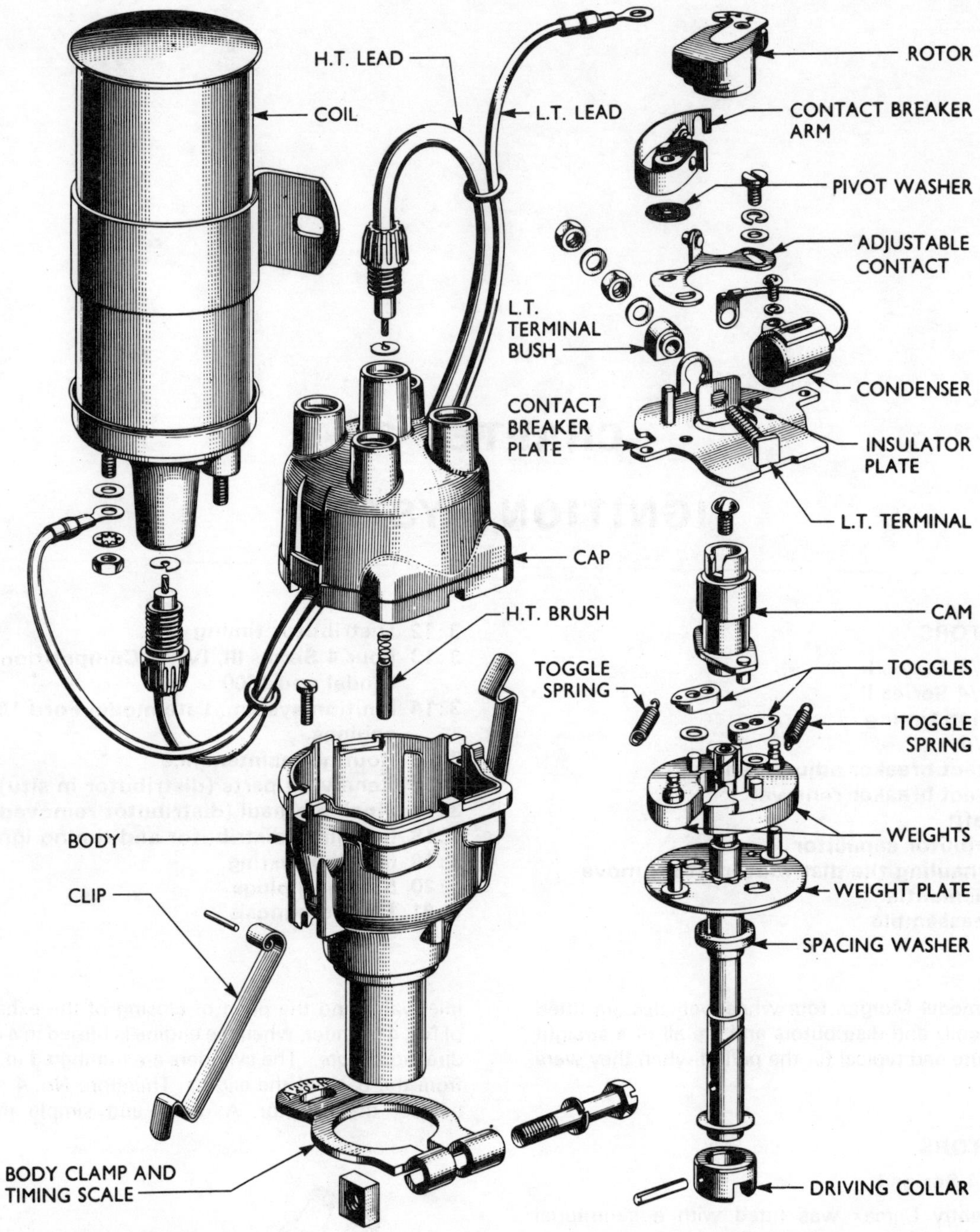
H.T. LEAD
COIL
L.T. LEAD
ROTOR
CONTACT BREAKER
ARM
PIVOT WASHER
ADJUSTABLE
CONTACT
L.T.
TERMINAL
BUSH
CONDENSER
CONTACT
BREAKER
PLATE
INSULATOR
PLATE
L.T. TERMINAL
CAP
CAM
H.T. BRUSH
TOGGLE
SPRING
TOGGLES
TOGGLE
SPRING
BODY
WEIGHTS
WEIGHT PLATE
CLIP
SPACING WASHER
BODY CLAMP AND
TIMING SCALE
DRIVING COLLAR

FIG 3:2 Exploded view of distributor Four/4 Series II

finding t d c is to remove the required spark plug, bend a piece of small diameter rod and insert it through the plug hole then revolve the engine slowly with the starting handle and t d c will then be felt. Slacken the clamp bolt, and turn the distributor body until the contact breaker points are just separating on the flank of the cam, when the distributor arm is opposite No. 1 segment in the cover, then retighten the bolt. The firing order is 1, 3, 4, 2. This setting should be regarded as a starting point, if the engine 'pinks' retard it one degree at a time. Alternatively advance it by the same amount until maximum performance is obtained without pinking.

3:2 Four/4 Series II

The distributor is located in a machined bore in the cylinder head and is driven by a vertical shaft geared to the centre of the camshaft. A tongue on the lower end of the same shaft engages with a slot in the oil pump shaft, and drives the oil pump which is located below the camshaft.

The distributor body is prevented from rotating by a screw passing into the cylinder head through an elongated hole in an index plate clamped to the distributor body. **(FIG 3:2)**. The ignition timing may be adjusted by slackening this screw and turning the distributor body to advance or retard the ignition, as required.

There is an automatic mechanical advance and retard control to vary the ignition timing to suit different engine speeds. This automatic control mechanism consists of a metal plate fixed to the distributor shaft on which are pivoted two weights. These weights move outwards under centrifugal force as engine speed increases, the amount of movement being controlled by the action of two small toggle springs.

3:3 Ignition timing

1 First check that the contact breaker points gap is correctly set to .014 to .016 inch.
2 Turn the engine so that No. 1 piston is coming up on its compression stroke, and align the notch on the crankshaft pulley with the timing mark on the cylinder front cover.

Slacken the screws securing the distributor index plate to the cylinder head and line up the '0' mark on the plate with the mark on the cylinder head. Tighten the screws to secure the plate in this position.

Apply a light pressure to the rotor arm in a clockwise direction, in order to take up any backlash in the drive. Slacken the distributor body clamp bolt and turn the distributor body anti-clockwise until the contact breaker points are closed. Next turn the distributor body clockwise until the points are just about to open, and tighten the body clamp bolt. The distributor body will then be positioned so the low tension terminal is directly above the index plate, which gives a static ignition setting of 5 deg. b t d c, and is suitable for regular fuels.

When premium fuels are used, set the timing as detailed above then slacken off the index scale screw and rotate the distributor body clockwise a further ¾ of a graduation. This gives a static setting of 8 deg. b t d c, which is more suited for premium grade fuels.

Replace the distributor cap and reconnect the leads to the sparking plugs and the ignition coil. No. 1 sparking plug should be connected to the contact on the distributor

cap adjacent to the rotor arm contact and the remaining plugs reconnected in the order 1, 2, 4, 3, working in an anti-clockwise direction.

Road test and make final adjustments.

Should the distributor be removed, it is essential to check that the distributor drive coupling is correctly positioned before replacing it.

The two driving dogs are offset leaving a large and small segment, the centre of the larger segment (or 'D') should point to No. 2 spark plug. Smear the distributor body shank with a high melting point water repellent grease before fitting.

3:4 Plus/4

The distributor is mounted on a pedestal at the L.H. side of the engine and driven by the camshaft, via a helical gear, which also drives the oil pump and tachometer. The degree of ignition advancement is controlled mechanically, according to engine speed, by two centrifugal weights mounted between a driving and driven plate within the body. Additional vacuum control, according to the effect of the load on manifold depression, is provided by a diaphragm acting directly on the contact breaker plate.

3:5 Contact breaker adjustment

Take off the distributor cap, remove the rotor arm and turn the engine until the contact breaker heel is on the highest point of the cam.

Slacken the screw **(FIG 3:3)** (28), insert the blade of a screwdriver into the slots (31), and twist the screwdriver to adjust the gap between the contact breaker points, which should be .014–.016 inch (.356–.406 mm) measured with a feeler gauge.

Tighten the locking screw, (28) recheck the gap and if satisfactory, refit the rotor arm and cap.

3:6 Contact breaker renewal

Slight pitting or discolouration of the points may be rectified by use of a fine carborundum stone. Do not use emery cloth unless the points are removed first and thoroughly cleaned before reassembly. Renew burned or deeply pitted contacts as follows: **(FIG 3:4)**.

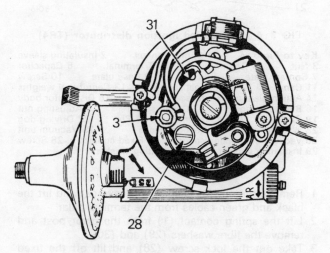

FIG 3:3 Distributor contacts Plus/4

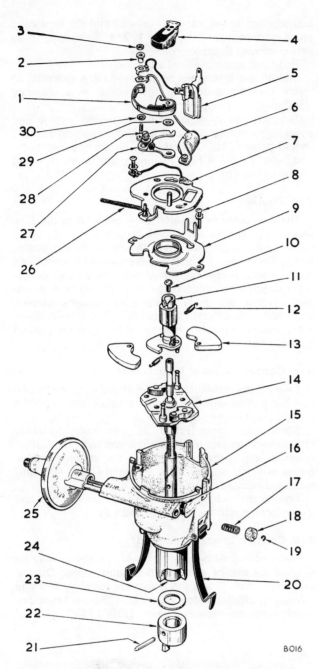

FIG 3 : 4   Dismantled ignition distributor (TR4)

Key to Fig 3 : 4   1 Spring contact   2 Insulating sleeve
3 Nut   4 Rotor arm   5 LT terminal   6 Capacitor
7 Contact plate   8 Screw   9 Base plate   10 Screw
11 Cam   12 Centrifugal spring   13 Centrifugal weights
14 Action plate and shaft assembly   15 Distributor body
16 Ratchet spring   17 Coiled spring   18 Adjusting nut
19 Circlip   20 Cap retainer   21 Pin   22 Driving dog
23 Washer   24 Bearing sleeve   25 Vacuum unit
26 Vacuum connecting spring   27 Fixed contact   28 Screw
29 Insulating washer   30 Insulating washer

1 Remove the nut (3), insulating sleeve (2) and lift the
  black and green cables from the terminal pillar.
2 Lift the spring contact (1) from the pivot post and
  remove the fibre washers (29) and (30).
3 Take out the lock screw (28) and lift off the fixed
  contact (27).

3 : 7 To refit

Reverse the above instructions and adjust the gap
between the contact breaker points.

3 : 8 Distributor capacitor

A short circuit, resulting from the breakdown of the
dielectric between the electrodes of the capacitor, which
is parallel connected across the contact breaker points,
will prevent the interruption of the low tension circuit
and cause ignition failure.

An open circuit in the capacitor is more difficult to
diagnose without the aid of special equipment, but may
be suspect when the points are excessively burnt and
difficult starting is experienced.

Renew the capacitor, or in case of doubt, substitute
the existing one as follows:
1 Remove the distributor cap and rotor arm, unscrew the
  the nut (3) from the spring contact terminal post, and
  lift off the capacitor lead.
2 Take out the capacitor retainer screw and remove the
  capacitor.
3 Secure the new capacitor in place, reconnect the lead
  to the terminal post and refit the nut (3). Refit the rotor
  arm and distributor cap.

FIG 3 : 5   Driving slot aligned with No. 1 pushrod tube
when No. 1 piston is at t d c compression stroke. Note
the offset shown arrowed (Plus/4)

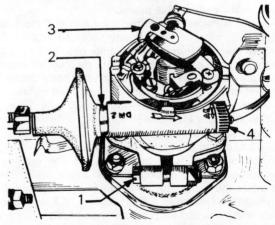

FIG 3 : 6   Distributor (Plus/4)

Key to Fig 3 : 6   1 Clamp bolt   2 Adjusting scale
3 Rotor arm   4 Thumbscrew

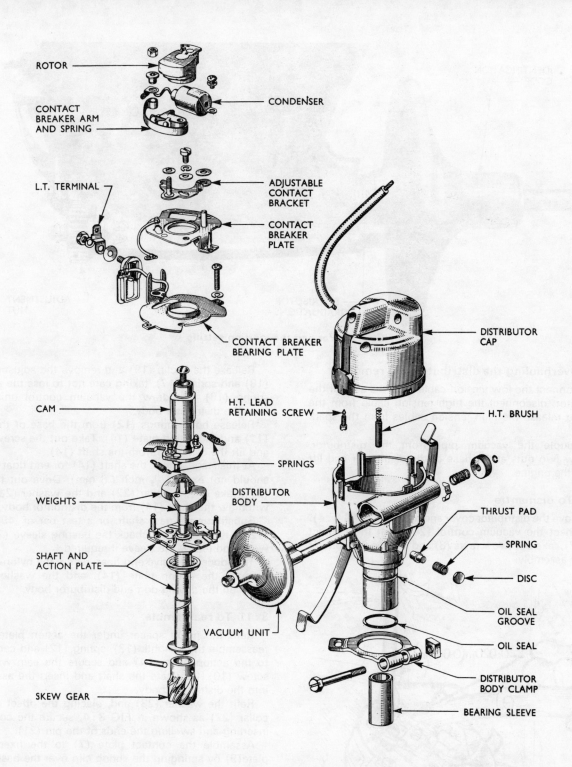

ROTOR

CONTACT
BREAKER ARM
AND SPRING

L.T. TERMINAL

CONDENSER

ADJUSTABLE
CONTACT
BRACKET

CONTACT
BREAKER
PLATE

CONTACT BREAKER
BEARING PLATE

DISTRIBUTOR
CAP

CAM

H.T. LEAD
RETAINING SCREW

H.T. BRUSH

SPRINGS

WEIGHTS

DISTRIBUTOR
BODY

THRUST PAD

SPRING

DISC

SHAFT AND
ACTION PLATE

OIL SEAL
GROOVE

OIL SEAL

VACUUM UNIT

DISTRIBUTOR
BODY CLAMP

SKEW GEAR

BEARING SLEEVE

FIG 3:7   Exploded view of Four/4 Series III distributor

IDENTIFICATION CODE

DISTRIBUTOR GRADUATIONS

ADJUSTMENT NUT

FIG 3:8 Varying the ignition setting

3:9 Overhauling the distributor—to remove

Disconnect the low tension cable from the side of the distributor, disconnect the high tension cable from the coil and release the high tension cables from the spark plugs.

Uncouple the vacuum pipe from the distributor, unscrew two nuts at the base of the distributor and lift it from the engine.

3:10 To dismantle

Remove the distributor cover and rotor arm (FIG 3:4). Disconnect the vacuum control (26) from the contact plate (7), take out two screws (8) and remove the contact breaker assembly.

0·020in (0·64mm)

FIG 3:9 Setting the gap of the contact breaker points. Slacken two screws (black arrows) and use screwdriver in notches

Release the circlip (19) and remove the adjusting nut (18) and spring (17), taking care not to lose the ratchet spring (16). Withdraw the vacuum control unit (25) from the distributor body.

Release both springs (12) from the base of the cam (11) and the action plate (14). Take out the screw (10) and lift the cam (11) from the shaft (14).

At this stage, check the shaft (14) for end float which should not exceed $\frac{1}{32}$ inch (.8 mm). Drive out the pin (21), take off the collar (22) and the washer (23), and withdraw the shaft (14) from the distributor body.

Substituting a new shaft, or a test bar of .490 inch (12.45 mm) diameter check the bearing sleeve (24) for wear, and renew the sleeve if required.

To reduce excessive end float, renew the nylon spacer beneath the action plate (14), and the washer (23) between the driving dog and distributor body.

3:11 To reassemble

Refit the nylon spacer under the action plate (14), reassemble the weights (13), spring (12) and cam (11) to the action plate (14) and secure the cam with the screw (10). Lubricate the shaft and insert the assembly into the distributor body.

Refit the washer (23) and, placing the offset driving collar (22) as shown in FIG 3:4, secure the collar by inserting and swelling the ends of the pin (21).

Assemble the contact plate (7) to the fixed base plate (9) by springing the spring clip over the base plate slot edge, inserting the peg of the contact plate into a slot in the base plate and moving it slightly clockwise. Secure the assembly to the distributor body, using two screws (8).

Insert the vacuum unit (25) into the distributor body and assemble the ratchet spring (16), the coiled spring (17), adjusting nut (18) and the circlip (19). Hook the vacuum connecting spring (26) on to the pin attached to a cranked lug on the contact plate.

Assemble the capacitor and the contact breaker to the contact plate (7) and adjust the contact breaker points as described previously.

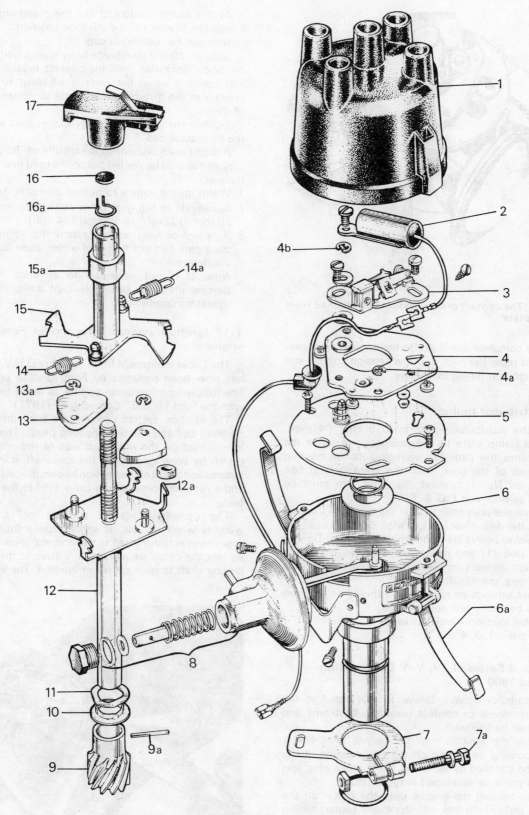

FIG 3:10   Components of the distributor (Ford 1600 GT Capri engine)

Key to Fig 3:10   1 Cap   2 Capacitor   3 Contact plate
4 Upper breaker plate   4a Circlip for vacuum unit post
4b Circlip for pivot post   5 Lower breaker plate   6 Body
6a Spring clip   7 Clamp plate   7a Clamp bolt
8 Vacuum unit   9 Drive gear   9a Roll pin   10 Thrust
washer   11 Wave washer   12 Shaft and action plate
12a Centrifugal advance stop   13 Centrifugal weight
13a Circlip   14 Secondary spring   14a Primary spring
15 Cam spindle   15a Cams   16 Felt pad   16a Circlip
17 Rotor arm

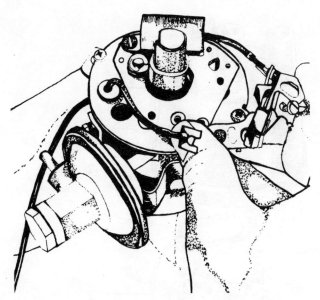

FIG 3:11 The contact breaker assembly detached from the upper plate

Refit the complete distributor to the engine, reconnect the vacuum pipe, the high and low tension cables, and adjust the ignition timing as follows:

3:12 Distributor timing

Adjust the distributor points to .015 inch (.4 mm). Secure the clamp plate to the pedestal and lower the distributor into the pedestal, engaging its driving dog with the slot of the gear. With the crankshaft at tdc and firing on No. 1 cylinder, the rotor arm must be positioned as shown in FIG 3:6.

Set the vernier adjustment (2) in the centre of its scale and adjust the distributor in clockwise direction until the contact breaker points are commencing to open. Tighten the clamp bolt (1) and rotate the screw (4) until one extra division appears on the scale (2). One division is equal to 4 deg. crankshaft angle.

Note: These settings are nominal and should be adjusted to give the best road test performance.

Distributor rotation—anti-clockwise.

Firing order—1, 3, 4, 2.

3:13 Four 4 Series III, IV, V, V Competition Model and 1600

This distributor is very similar to that fitted in the Plus/4 and details of contact breaker adjustment and capacitor can be followed.

To retime the ignition turn the engine until No. 1 piston is coming up to tdc on the compression stroke (this can be checked by removing No. 1 spark plug and feeling the pressure developed in the cylinder).

Continue turning the engine until the notch on the crankshaft pulley is in line with the lower (outer) timing mark on the timing cover.

This will give the initial timing setting of 6 deg. or 10 deg. btdc (static advance), depending on engine.

Check that the fourth line on the ignition timing scale, counting from the vacuum diaphragm housing, is in line with the edge of the distributor body. (FIG 3:8).

At this fourth graduated line the distributor is still at 6 deg. (or 10 deg.) static advance position.

Remove the distributor cap.

Slacken off the distributor body clamp bolt and rotate the body clockwise until the contact breaker points are just opening when the rotor is adjacent to No. 1 HT contact in the distributor cap. Note direction of rotation of arm.

Tighten the distributor body clamp bolt and replace the distributor cap.

A slight readjustment to the distributor may be necessary and should be carried out on the road in the following manner:

1 Warm up the engine to normal operating temperature.

2 Accelerate in top gear on wide throttle opening from 20 mph. (32kph) to 40 mph (64 kph).

3 If heavy pinking occurs, retard the ignition until a trace pink can just be heard under these conditions of acceleration.

Note: It is not necessary to advance the ignition beyond the static setting (except under high altitude operating conditions).

3:14 Ignition system. Late model Ford 1600 GT engines

The Lucas equipment fitted to earlier O.H.V. Four/fours has now been replaced by Ford/Autolite components. The following information applies to those models fitted with the Ford 1600 GT Capri engine (1971).

The ignition system comprises a Ford distributor, an oil-filled coil and Autolite sparking plugs. The distributor is mounted on the righthand side of the engine and is driven by skew gears from the camshaft. It incorporates automatic control of the ignition by centrifugal mechanism, and a vacuum operated unit connected to the inlet manifold.

The centrifugal device consists of spring-loaded weights which fly out as engine speed increases. This movement is transmitted to the contact breaker camshaft so that the cams are advanced relative to the distributor driving shaft to give advanced ignition. The vacuum unit

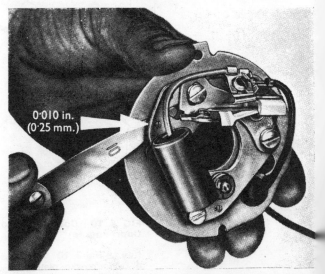

FIG 3:12 Checking clearance between upper and lower plates

is operated by the depression in the inlet manifold, the deflection of the diaphragm in the unit varying with engine load. At small throttle openings with no load on the engine, there is a high degree of vacuum in the manifold and the unit advances the ignition. When the throttle is opened suddenly, or the car is climbing on a large throttle opening, the reduction in manifold vacuum causes the unit to retard the ignition. The two timing controls can be seen in **FIGS 3:10** and **3:13**.

The oil-filled coil is used in conjunction with a starter solenoid and a ballast resistor wire. This ensures that full battery voltage is supplied to the coil when starting, giving better sparking plug performance to facilitate engine firing. The high-tension plug leads are of the suppressor type. The firing order is 1, 2, 4, 3.

3:15 Routine maintenance

At the first 3000 miles and then every 6000 miles, clean and adjust the sparking plugs and the contact breaker points. Also lubricate the distributor and clean the distributor cap, the high-tension leads and the coil.

The sparking plugs:

These are best sand blasted for effective cleaning. Clean up the points with a file so that they are bright, with the centre electrode face flat and square. Adjust the gap by bending the outer electrode. **Never try to bend the centre electrode.** The correct gap is .023 inch on earlier models, .030 inch on later models.

Wipe the insulators clean and dry and renew the gaskets if they are thin and flat, or if oil has been leaking from the plug threads in the head. The correct sparking plugs are Autolite AG.22 and the tightening torque is 24 to 28 lb ft.

The contact breaker:

Before adjusting the points, examine them for defects. These are mainly excessive wear and metal transfer. The latter can be seen as a pip on one point and a corresponding depression in the other. This is normal and does not call for renewal unless the pip is higher than the recommended contact gap. Points in good condition should have a greyish frosted look and be free from pitting. They must meet squarely and be .025 inch apart when checked with a feeler gauge.

Slight pitting can be removed with a fine carborundum stone after the contact breaker has been dismantled as instructed in **Section 3:16**. Clean away all abrasive dust afterwards. This operation needs care to keep the points square and flat. Being relatively cheap, the contact breaker should be renewed if there is any doubt about its condition, as it may adversely affect engine starting and running.

The first step in adjusting the gap between the points is to turn the engine until one of the distributor cams has opened the gap to its fullest extent. Slacken the locking screws arrowed in **FIG 3:9** and provide a feeler gauge .025 inch thick. Insert a screwdriver in the adjusting notches, as shown in the illustration. Turn the screwdriver in the required direction until the gap is correct and then tighten the locking screws. Recheck the gap, and also check the ignition timing, if necessary, as instructed in **Section 3:18**.

FIG 3:13 The centrifugal advance assembly with the slot marked 15L in use as on standard engines. The slot marked 10L is for GT engines as fitted to the Morgan Four/four

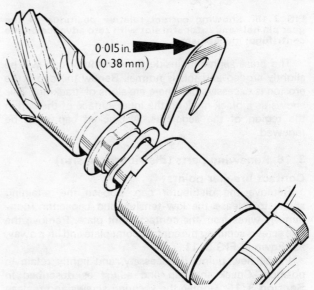

FIG 3:14 Setting the preload of gear and shaft before drilling a new pin hole. Note the specially shaped shim

Lubricating distributor:

This must be done with care, as over-lubricating may lead to oil getting onto the contact breaker points. This will result in burnt points and difficult starting. Clean contaminated points with carbon tetrachloride and a stiff brush.

First lift off the rotor arm 17 (see **FIG 3:10**) and note the pad of felt 16 in the recess in the shaft. Put two drops of engine oil on this pad. Finally, put a slight smear of lithium-base grease on the cams 15a.

Distributor cap, high-tension leads and coil:

Wipe these parts clean and dry, paying particular attention to the inside of the cap. Check the condition of the insulation of the high-tension leads and the security of the end fixings. Make sure that all leads to the coil are secure.

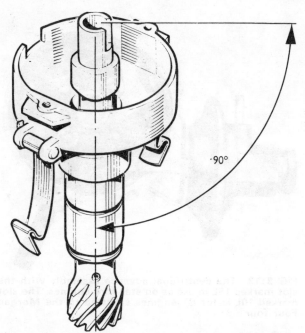

FIG 3:15 Showing correct relative positions of the gear pin hole and rotor arm slot with zero advance on the centrifugal mechanism

The brass segments inside the distributor cap will be slightly eroded and this is normal. Renew the cap if the erosion is excessive or if there are signs of 'tracking'. This shows as a black mark on the inner surface of the cap in the region of the segments. A cracked cap must be renewed.

3:16 Renewing parts (distributor in situ)

Contact breaker points:

Remove the distributor cap. Loosen the retaining screw to release the low-tension and capacitor (condenser) wires from the contact point plate. Remove the two screws securing the contact point plate and lift it away, as shown in FIG 3:11.

Install new points if necessary, and lightly retain in position. Check the gap and adjust as described in Section 3:15. Tighten the securing screws and replace the two wires.

Capacitor (condenser):

Remove the cap, release the capacitor lead from the contact point plate and remove the screw securing the capacitor 2, to the upper breaker plate. Replace in the reverse order.

Breaker plate assembly:

Having removed the contact breaker plate, prise off the circlip 4a from the pivot post of the vacuum unit 8. Remove the two screws securing the lower breakor plate 5 and lift off the assembly. Replace in the reverse order.

To separate the two breaker plates, remove circlip 4b from the pivot post. Remove the flat and wave washers. Turn the upper plate 4 as necessary to disengage the holding-down screw from the keyhole in the lower plate 5. Look out for the short earthing spring between the plates. The low-tension wire is held by a rubber grommet in the lower plate.

When reassembling, make sure there is enough wire passing through the rubber grommet to reach the contact breaker terminal. Fit the earthing spring over the pivot post, followed by the upper plate. .Engage the holding down spindle in the keyhole slot. Retain with the wave and flat washers and the large circlip.

Refer to FIG 3:12 and check the clearance between the nylon pad nearest the holding down pin and the lower plate. It should be .010 inch, and not more. To reduce the clearance, screw the nut further onto the holding down screw.

Governor weights and springs:

With the breaker plates removed, prise off clips 13a and lift off the weights 13. Note the location of the differing springs 14 and 14a and then remove them. When reassembling, make sure the primary spring with the larger coils is fitted to the correct post. Refit the weights with their flat edge adjacent to the cam spindle (see FIG 3:13).

Vacuum unit:

When the breaker plates are lifted off, the vaccum unit link is released as shown in FIG 3:13. The unit is removed by unscrewing the two screws securing the bracket to the distributor body. If the unit is dismantled, note the order for refitting the parts as shown in FIG 3:10. A defective diaphragm cannot be repaired, so renew the whole unit.

3:17 Final overhaul (distributor removed)

Removing:

Disconnect the high-tension leads from the sparking plugs, and the high- and low-tension leads from the coil. Pull the vacuum pipe off the distributor. Unscrew the retaining bolt and lift the distributor away from the engine.

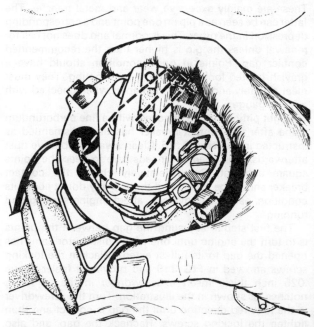

FIG 3:16 When refitting the distributor, the rotor will move from its original position to that shown by dotted lines as the gears mesh

Dismantling:

Having removed all the parts as described in **Section 3 : 16**, remove the cam spindle by extracting felt pad 16 and circlip 16a (see **FIG 3 : 10**). Note which slot is occupied by stop 12a and lift off the spindle 15. Slot 15L is for standard engines and slot 10L for GT engines (see **FIG 3 : 13**).

Remove gear 9 by driving out pin 9a. Note washers 10 and 11. Pull the shaft out of the body and remove the thrust washers below the action plate.

Clean the shaft, cam spindle and bearing surfaces and check without lubricant. Excessive wear calls for renewal, as sideways movement will upset the operation of the cams to give erratic opening of the contact points. A worn drive gear must be renewed as follows:

Fitting a new drive gear:

The new gear will have a pilot drilling for the pin. Fit the thrust washers under the action plate, lubricate the shaft and fit it to the body. Fit the thrust washer, wave washer and a .015 shim, before fitting the gear. A suitable shape of shim is shown in **FIG 3 : 14**. Turn the pilot hole in the gear until it is at 90 deg. to the rotor arm slot at the top end of the cam spindle when the centrifugal advance mechanism is fully retarded. This is the position shown in **FIG 3 : 15**.

Using a suitable clamp, press on the gear until the wave washer is compressed and all slack taken out. **Do not overtighten**. Hold the assembly on a V-block under a pillar drill and use a $\frac{1}{8}$ inch drill. Continue the pilot hole right through the gear and shaft. If the original gear is being fitted to a new shaft, drill a new hole at right angles to the old one. Fit a new roll pin, release the clamp and take out the shim.

Reassembling:

Fit the rest of the parts according to the instructions in **Section 3 : 16**.

Testing:

Elaborate equipment is needed to check the dwell angle to reveal wear in the distributor shaft or bushes. It will also be used to check for wear in the contact breaker assembly, and to check the operation of the centrifugal and vacuum advance mechanisms. Weak springs in the centrifugal assembly will affect engine performance, and adjustment to the spring anchor tabs may be necessary if a new shaft and action plate are fitted. The vacuum unit can be tested and the advance setting adjusted by altering the shims in assembly 8. These tests must be carried out by an accredited agent.

3 : 18 Installing distributor and timing ignition
Installing:

The correct initial advance figure for the C7BH.C distributor used in the 1600 GT engine is 8 deg. when using 97 (4 star) octane petrol.

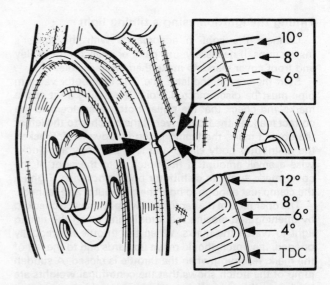

FIG 3 : 17 Ignition timing marks, Ford OHV engine. The upper inset shows the earlier arrangement, the lower the later type

The initial advance is automatically set when the notch in the rim of the crankshaft pulley is in line with the appropriate mark on the front cover as shown in **FIG 3 : 17**. Note that 8 deg. lies between the two raised marks indicating 6 deg. and 10 deg. on earlier models.

Before fitting a distributor, check that it is the correct type (C7BH.C) and also check the octane rating of the fuel to be used in the engine as this will affect the required initial advance.

To install the distributor, turn the crankshaft until the pulley notch is in line with the appropriate timing mark on the front cover when No. 1 piston at the front of the engine is near the top of the compression stroke. On this stroke, both valves will be closed. With the vacuum advance unit pointing to the rear, set the rotor arm so that it points to No. 2 sparking plug. Insert the distributor as shown in **FIG 3 : 16**. As the gears mesh, the rotor arm will turn slightly into the dotted position. If the retaining bolt cannot be fitted because the clamp plate does not line up, slacken the clamp bolt, turn the clamp without moving the distributor and insert the bolt. Tighten the clamps and retaining bolts.

Timing the ignition:

In the absence of a stroboscopic light, set the ignition by keeping the pulley and front cover marks aligned. Slacken the clamp and turn the distributor body as necessary so that the contact breaker points are just opening and the rotor is adjacent to the No. 1 electrode in the cap.

If excessive movement is required before the points are in the correct position, it shows that the gears are meshed incorrectly. Remove the distributor and check that the instructions have been closely followed when refitting it. The firing order is 1, 2, 4, 3 with the rotor moving anti-clockwise.

Do not overtighten the clamp plate bolt 7a in FIG 3 : 10. Just tighten it enough to hold the distributor in position.

Timing the ignition using a timing light:

Connect the light in accordance with the maker's instructions. If necessary, use paint or chalk on the pulley and front cover marks to make them more visible.

Start the engine and let it idle. The distributor vacuum pipe must be disconnected. Point the timing light at the marks and check that the pulley notch is adjacent to the correct mark on the front cover. If the notch is to the left of the correct mark, the timing is too far advanced. Slacken the distributor body clamp and turn the body anticlockwise a small amount. If the notch is to the right of the cover mark, turn the distributor body clockwise. Tighten the clamp just enough to hold the distributor and recheck.

The operation of the centrifugal weights may be checked by opening and closing the throttle and using the timing light to watch the marks. When the throttle is gradually opened, the notch should move upwards and to the left of the mark, returning when the throttle is closed. A sudden jump of the notch shows that the centrifugal weights are binding or the springs are weak. After checking, reconnect the vacuum pipe.

Testing:

This is done with the car on the road. Let the engine reach normal running temperature and move at 20 mile/hr. Open the throttle wide and accelerate in top gear to 40 mile/hr. If there is heavy pinking from the engine, retard the ignition by turning the distributor body anticlockwise a small amount. Test again, and repeat the adjustment until only a trace of pinking can be heard under the same conditions of acceleration.

If the car is normally used at a high altitude, the distributor timing may be advanced by 4 deg. for each 2000 ft above sea level. If altitude varies, set for the lowest altitude at which the car operates.

There is no advantage to be gained by advancing the timing beyond the recommended setting. Neither is it necessary to use a fuel of a higher octane rating than the one specified.

3:19 Ignition testing

In cases of poor starting or complete engine failure on the road, carry out some simple tests to find out whether the ignition system is at fault. Remove one sparking plug lead and arrange the metal end which contacts the plug top so that it is about $\frac{1}{4}$ inch away from a clean metallic part of the engine. Keep it away from any spilt fuel and from the carburetter. Make sure that the fingers are well away from the metal end of the plug lead and turn the engine by means of the starter, with the ignition on. There should be a good snappy spark at regular intervals. A weak or irregular spark shows that something is wrong.

Now remove the distributor cap and the rotor (see **FIG 3:10**). Turn the engine until the contact points have closed and switch on the ignition. Remove the high-tension lead from the coil to the cap (at the distributor cap end). Hold the end about $\frac{1}{4}$ inch from a good earth and open the contact breaker point with a screwdriver, flicking the moving point only. As the points break from the closed position there should be a good spark from the coil HT lead. No spark means a faulty coil or trouble in the low-tension circuit. Check the latter by examining the thin wire from the coil to the terminal plate on the contact breaker. A test of the low-tension wiring is to disconnect the thin wire between the coil and the distributor. Connect a test lamp between the two terminals and turn the engine over slowly. If the lamp lights when the points close, and goes out when they open, the low-tension circuit is in order. If the lamp does not light, the points are dirty or there is a break or loose connection in the low-tension wiring.

A faulty capacitor causes sparking at the contact points and difficult starting. To test for a shorted capacitor, make sure the contact points are open and slide a screwdriver down beside the moving contact until it touches the breaker plate. The screwdriver shank must not contact any other part but the moving contact blade. There should be a spark at the screwdriver tip as it makes and breaks contact with the baseplate. No spark indicates a shorted capacitor or a break in the primary (low-tension) circuit. By removing the securing screw from the capacitor bracket and holding the capacitor clear from all metallic contact (leaving the wire still connected to the contact terminal), the screwdriver test should be repeated. The contact points must still be open. If there is now a spark, when there was none with the capacitor connected, it indicates a short in the capacitor. If there is no spark, there must be a break in the low-tension circuit.

The quickest and easiest test for a suspected capacitor is by substituting with a new one. The correct capacity is .21 to .25 microfarad.

In all these tests it is important to switch on the ignition first.

3:20 Sparking plugs

The routine maintenance of sparking plugs is given in **Section 3:15**. This section also deals with the correct type of plug and the tightening torque.

The following notes are intended as a guide to the condition of the engine and its auxiliaries by careful examination of the sparking plugs after they have been in use for some time.

Examine the firing end of the plugs and observe the type of deposit. Normally it will be a thin powdery coating of a light brown or greyish tan colour. This is the effect of mixed high-speed and low-speed driving with an engine in good tune.

If the deposits are white or slightly yellow, they indicate long periods of constant-speed driving or much low-speed city driving.

Wet black deposits are due to oil entering the combustion chamber past worn pistons and bores, past broken piston rings or down valve stems. Do not confuse this oily deposit with the wetness on plugs due to excessive fuel being introduced into the combustion chamber through over-choking. The cure for oil contamination is an engine overhaul.

Dry, black, fluffy deposits are the result of running with a rich mixture, or incomplete fuel combustion due to defective ignition. Excessive idling may also be a cause.

Overheated sparking plugs will have a white, blistered look about the electrodes, and these may be heavily eroded. The cause may be weak mixture, poor cooling, defective ignition or sustained high speeds with heavy loads.

It is false economy to run an engine with old sparking plugs and a new set should be fitted every 10,000 miles.

3:21 Fault diagnosis

(a) Engine will not fire

1 Battery discharged
2 Contact breaker points dirty, pitted or maladjusted
3 Distributor cap dirty, cracked or 'tracking'
4 Rotor arm not making contact with cap electrode
5 Faulty cable or loose connection in low-tension circuit
6 Distributor rotor arm cracked or 'tracking'
7 Faulty ignition coil
8 Broken contact breaker spring
9 Contact points stuck open
10 Defective ignition switch
11 Plug leads wrongly connected

(b) Engine misfires

1 Check 2, 3, 5 and 7 in (a)
2 Weak contact breaker spring
3 High-tension plug or coil leads wet, cracked or perished
4 Sparking plug(s) loose
5 Sparking plug insulation cracked
6 Sparking plug gap incorrectly set
7 Ignition timing too far advanced
8 Excessive wear of distributor spindles and bushes

(c) Engine lacks power

1 Check 2 and 3 in (a); and check (b)
2 Ignition timing retarded
3 Defective centrifugal or vacuum units in distributor
4 Vacuum unit suction pipe disconnected or leaking
5 Sparking plugs worn out
6 One plug lead detached

NOTES

CHAPTER 4

COOLING SYSTEM

4 : 1 Maintenance
4 : 2 Removal
4 : 3 To dismantle pump
4 : 4 To reassemble pump

4 : 5 The thermostat
4 : 6 Removal
4 : 7 Removal
4 : 8 Fault diagnosis

The cooling system on the original Morgan 4/4 was by thermo-syphon only. No fan or thermostat was incorporated, and the running temperature was approximately 90°C.

With the introduction of the 'Standard Special' engine a fan was introduced. All models since this time have been fitted with a water pump and a bellows thermostat.

4 : 1 Maintenance

Little maintenance is required except for periodic checking of the belt tension and the water level. With regard to the latter, never remove the filler cap when the engine is hot, as the water is under pressure. The fan belt should be adjusted to allow for $\frac{1}{2}$ inch side movement on the belts longest span. Antifreeze is recommended for cold climates, it is advisable to check all hoses and hose clips for signs of perishing and slackness before it is added. It is good practice to flush the system at least once a year, open all draining taps and place a hose in the neck of the radiator and allow fresh water to flow for approx. 15 minutes. When the radiator is badly choked, it is often possible to clear the tubes by removing the filler cap and the bottom hose connection, and forcing water from a hosepipe into the bottom stub, using a suitable adaptor on the hosepipe so as to obtain adequate water pressure. When refilling the system, check that the drain plugs are properly tightened and if a heater is fitted make sure that its water valve is open to prevent an airlock in the heater. Always fill the system slowly as this allows air bubbles to escape and reduces the chance of an air lock.

PLUS/4 WATER PUMP

4 : 2 Removal

Remove radiator (it is possible to remove pump with radiator *in situ*, but the fan blades will have to be removed).

Take out the two short set screws holding the pump body to the cylinder block, and undo the long setscrew passing through the flange of the bearing housing behind the pulley flange and take out dynamo setscrew. To refit, reverse the removal procedure and tension the driving belt.

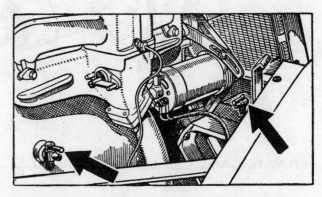

FIG 4 : 1   Draining taps on Plus/4 (1951)

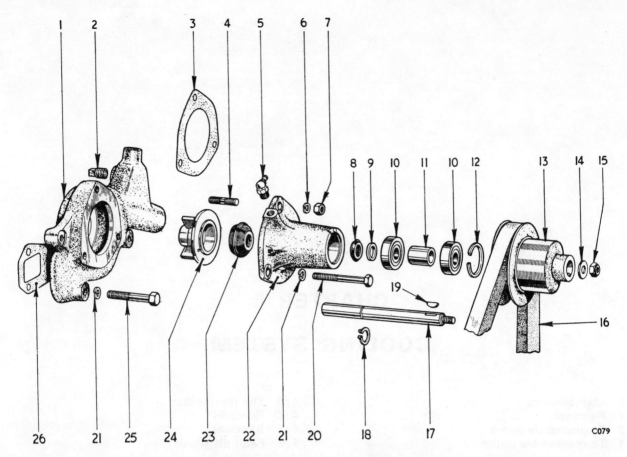

FIG 4:2 Water pump exploded—Plus/4

Key to Fig 4:2   1 Body   2 Heater return pipe blanking plug   3 Gasket   4 Stud   5 Grease nipple   6 Spring washer
7 Nut   8 Spinner   9 Distance washer   10 Ball race   11 Distance tube   12 Circlip   13 Pulley   14 Plain washer
15 Nyloc nut   16 Driving belt   17 Shaft   18 Circlip   19 Woodruff key   20 Bolt   21 Spring washer   22 Bearing housing
23 Seal and bellows assembly   24 Impeller   25 Bolt   26 Gasket

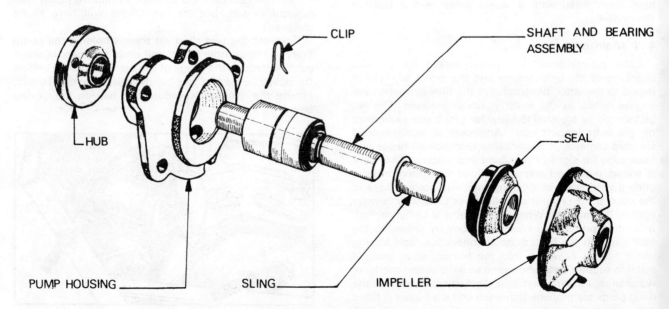

FIG 4:3 Water pump exploded—Four/4 Series II

4 : 3 To dismantle pump

Refer to **FIG 4 : 2**.

1 Remove items (14) and (15) and detach pulley (13).
2 Remove impeller and seal assembly, a press is necessary.
3 Remove circlip (12) and drift out shaft and ball race assembly.
4 Remove the spinner (8), circlip (18), washer (9) and woodruff key (19) from the shaft (17) and press off items (10) and (11).

4 : 4 To reassemble pump

1 Fit items (9), (18) and (8) to the shaft (17). Pack the ball races (10) with grease and press them onto the shaft with their scaled faces outwards and the spacer (11) between them.
2 Using a tubular drift, drive the bearings with the shaft (17) into the housing and secure with circlip, press the seal assembly (23) into the impeller (24).
3 Using a .085 inch (2.159 mm) thick spacer, press the impeller (24) on to the shaft (17). Solder the impeller to the end of the shaft to prevent leakage.
4 Fit the woodruff key (9) and pulley (13) to the shaft (17), securing with a Nyloc nut (15) and plain washer (14).

The water pump shaft and pulley is shortened from the original Standard/Triumph unit by Morgans; all Plus/4 fans are driven from the water pump.

4 : 5 The thermostat

A bellows thermostat is fitted in a housing bolted to the front of the cylinder head and is designed to commence to open at 70°C and is fully open at 92°C.

Four/4 Series II water pump

4 : 6 Removal

1 Drain radiator.
2 Loosen the generator mounting bolts at the generator.
3 Unscrew the bolts securing the fan and water pump pulley to the water pump flange and remove these complete with fan belt.
4 Unscrew the five bolts securing the water pump to the front face of the cylinder block and remove the pump. Replace in the reverse order, using a new gasket, and use a smear of white lead on the bolts.

The thermostat is located in the cylinder head water outlet flange and commences to open at 170°–179°F and is fully open at 190°F.

Four/4 Series III, IV, V, 1600 and Competition Models—water pump
4 : 7 Removal

1 Drain system.
2 Slacken generator and remove fan belt.
3 Remove 4 bolts holding the fan blades and pulley to the hub.
4 Unscrew the three bolts which attach the pump to the block and take off the pump and its gasket. Replace in reverse order using a new gasket.

The pump is of the impeller type with double-row ballbearings. The pumpshaft cannot be removed from the double-row ballbearings; if necessary the shaft and bearing should be replaced as an assembly. During pump

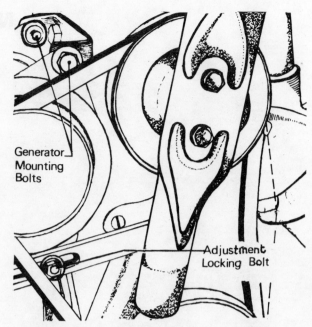

FIG 4 : 4   Fan belt adjustment—Four/4 Series II

overhaul, the impeller should be pressed on to the pump shaft until the clearance between the impeller blades and the rear face of the water pump housing is .030 inch.

The thermostat is located beneath the water outlet of the cylinder head and starts to open at 170°–179°F and is fully open at 199°F.

4 : 8 Fault diagnosis

(a) Internal water leakage

1 Cracked cylinder wall
2 Loose cylinder head nuts
3 Cracked cylinder head
4 Faulty head gasket
5 Cracked tappet chest wall

(b) Poor circulation

1 Radiator core blocked
2 Engine water passages restricted
3 Low water level
4 Loose fan belt
5 Defective thermostat
6 Perished or collapsed radiator hoses

(c) Corrosion

1 Impurities in the water
2 Infrequent draining and flushing

(d) Overheating

1 Check (b)
2 Sludge in crankcase
3 Faulty ignition timing
4 Low oil level in sump
5 Tight engine
6 Choked exhaust system
7 Binding brakes
8 Slipping clutch
9 Incorrect valve timing
10 Retarded ignition
11 Mixture too weak

NOTES

CHAPTER 5

THE CLUTCH

A single dry plate clutch is used on all models. Apart from the 1600 GT engine cars introduced in 1971 all Ford engined cars use hydraulic clutch operation and all other models mechanical operation.

5 : 1 Four/4 Series I

The Borg and Beck clutch calls for no adjustment, nor is such provided. Clutch troubles are infrequent and are usually confined to slip. The most common cause of slip is due to incorrect pedal adjustment; check free movement of pedal and adjust stop to give $\frac{1}{16}$ inch play. A second cause for slip although much less frequent is oil on the driven-plate facings. To remedy this it is necessary to remove the whole unit and replace the clutch plate—a temporary cure is to wash off all traces of oil with spirit.

In the event of trouble being experienced with the clutch not freeing, it is probably due to an excessive amount of travel in the pedal—adjust to $\frac{1}{16}$ inch as previously.

5 : 2 Four/4 Series II, III, IV, V, V Competition Model and 1600

The clutch is released hydraulically on all these models.

5 : 3 Operation

The release mechanism comprises of a hydraulic master cylinder operated by the pedal, the cylinder being flexibly piped to an operating cylinder mounted on the clutch housing, see **FIGS 10 : 5** and **10 : 6** in Chapter 10 for clutch hydraulic layout. The operating cylinder piston operates a pushrod acting on the end of the clutch release arm, which pivots on a fulcrum inside the housing. The release arm carries the release bearing which on actuation presses on the clutch release levers at the pressure unit, to withdraw the pressure plate and thus free the driven plate. The only maintenance normally required is to keep the fluid reservoir topped up to the correct level and to ensure that the adjustment on the

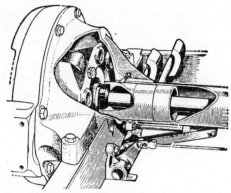

FIG 5:1 Clutch operating mechanism (Four/4 Series I)

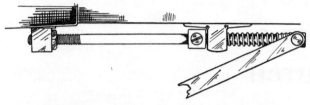

FIG 5:2 Clutch adjuster Four/4 Series I

FIG 5:3 Clutch Slave Cylinder Four/4 Series II

operating cylinder gives the necessary free movement. When the pedal moves through the whole of its return travel, there should be $\frac{1}{16}$ inch clearance between the operating cylinder pushrod and the release arm. This is adjusted by releasing the tension spring on the release arm **(FIG 5:3)** slackening the locknut, and while holding the pushrods at its flats (put there for the purpose) turning the adjusting nut until the clearance is obtained between the nut and the release arm end. The locknut is then tightened, clearance rechecked, and the spring refitted.

The fluid level should be kept within $\frac{1}{2}$ inch of the top of the reservoir.

5:4 Clutch master cylinder—before October 1961

The clutch master cylinder is mounted on the front face of the engine bulkhead **(FIG 5:4)**

The front spigot end of the piston accommodates the valve stem and carries the valve spring retainer. The return spring, under compression, is fitted between the spring retainer and the valve spacer at the forward end of the cylinder.

A reservoir port, drilled at the front of the cylinder, allows fluid from the reservoir to enter the cylinder. The pipe line to the clutch operating cylinder leaves the master cylinder at a port inclined at an angle to the master cylinder body.

With the clutch pedal in the fully released position, fluid is free to flow from the reservoir into the cylinder.

When the pedal is depressed, the piston moves forward advancing the valve spacer and seal. The spacer contacts the end of the cylinder, the wave shim between the flange on the valve stem and the valve spacer pushes the valve seal into contact with the end of the cylinder, so sealing off the reservoir port, preventing the fluid from being pumped back into the reservoir. The fluid is, therefore, pumped through the outlet port to the operating cylinder on the clutch housing, the increase in hydraulic pressure assisting the action of the valve seal.

When the pedal is released the return spring pushes back the piston, reducing pressure in the cylinder, and the release arm retracting spring acting on the operating cylinder piston, via the pushrod, pushes the fluid back into the master cylinder. As the piston reaches the end of its rearwards travel the valve spacer and seal will be pulled away from the reservoir port by the valve stem. The valve uncovers the reservoir port so that fluid may be replenished in the cylinder as necessary.

A rubber dust cap fits over the end of the master cylinder and seals off the pushrod, thus preventing dirt entering the cylinder.

5:5 Removal

1 Disconnect the clutch master cylinder pushrod from the pedal by unscrewing the nut and withdrawing the spring washer and concentric bolt.
2 Detach the fluid line by unscrewing the union nut, using a blanking plug to prevent dirt entering the line.
3 Withdraw the master cylinder after removing the two spring washers and nuts securing the master cylinder to the bulkhead.
4 Empty the contents of the fluid reservoir into a clean container.

5:6 To dismantle

1 Remove the rubber boot. Then withdraw the circlip and remove the pushrod.
2 Withdraw the piston and valve assembly from the cylinder.
3 Remove the piston from the valve assembly. The spring retainer is held in position on the spigot end of the piston by a tab which engages under a shoulder on the front of the piston. Prize up the tab and remove the spring retainer, spring and valve assembly from the piston.
4 To dismantle the valve assembly, compress the spring and move the valve stem to one side in the retainer, so releasing the end of the valve stem from the key slot hole in the retainer. Slide the valve spacer and shim off the valve stem.

5 Remove the rubber valve seal and the piston seal if necessary.

6 Wash the parts in methylated spirit, brake fluid or commercial alcohol. Do not use mineral fluids such as engine oil or paraffin for washing the parts. Carefully inspect the piston rubber seal and renew if there is any sign of damage to the sealing lip. It is not advisable to turn the seal inside out when examining as distortion will be caused. Examine the piston and cylinder bore for scores or damage.

5 : 7 To reassemble

1 Replace the piston seal with the lip away from the larger diameter of the piston.

2 Fit the valve seal to the valve stem with the lip outwards and away from the spring. Slide the shim, the valve spacer, with the legs over the valve seal, and the return spring, in this order, over the valve stem (see **FIG 5 : 4**). Ensure that the convex face of the shim abuts the valve stem flange.

3 Fit the spring retainers in the rear end of the return spring, compress the spring and locate the valve stem in the keyhole slot in the end of the spring retainer.

4 Insert the front of the piston in the spring retainer, and secure it by locating the spring retainer tab under the front shoulder of the piston.

5 Dip the piston and seal in hydraulic fluid. Insert the piston assembly in the cylinder, valve seal end first. Ensure that the piston seal is not damaged as it enters the master cylinder.

6 Install the pushrod in the master cylinder. Locate the washer and fit the retaining circlip.

7 Refit the rubber boot to the clutch master cylinder.

5 : 8 To refit

1 Refit the master cylinder to the engine bulkhead, replace the two securing spring washers and nuts and tighten securely.

2 Reconnect the fluid pipe, tighten the union nut securely, but do not overtighten.

3 Reconnect the clutch master cylinder pushrod to the pedal by passing the concentric bolt through the pushrod and then the pedal. Fit the spring washer and nut.

4 Top-up the master cylinder reservoir with clean approved fluid, and then bleed the system, as described in Chapter 10. If necessary, readjust the clutch. Check the action of the clutch on road test.

5 : 9 The clutch operating cylinder

The clutch operating cylinder or slave cylinder is mounted in the clutch housing flange on the lefthand side and is retained by a circlip.

5 : 10 To remove

1 Disconnect the retracting spring from the operating cylinder.

2 Detach the fluid line by unscrewing the union nut, using a blanking plug to prevent dirt entering the line.

3 Withdraw the pushrod and rubber boot from the operating cylinder.

4 Remove the operating cylinder after extracting the circlip.

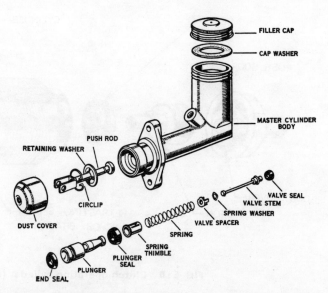

FIG 5 : 4 Brake and clutch master cylinder (exploded) Up to October 1961 (Four/4s only)

5 : 11 To dismantle

1 To remove the piston and seal, lightly tap the cylinder on a block of wood. Withdraw the piston and rubber seal from the cylinder body (FIG 5 : 5).

2 Unscrew the bleed valve on the side of the cylinder body and remove the ball.

3 Pull the rubber piston seal off the spigot at the front of the piston.

4 Wash all parts in hydraulic fluid, methylated spirit or commercial alcohol and examine the rubber piston seal carefully. Renew the seal if there is any sign of damage to the sealing lip. Never use mineral fluids such as engine oil or paraffin for washing hydraulic system parts.

5 - 12 To reassemble

1 Locate the piston seal on the spigot at the front end of the piston with the recess in the seal away from the piston.

2 To fit the piston dip the piston and seal in hydraulic fluid and carefully insert, spigot end first, into the cylinder.

3 Replace the ball and bleed valve but do not tighten.

5 : 13 To refit

1 Slide the cylinder into its location in the clutch housing flange from the front. Retain with the circlip, ensuring that it is correctly located in its groove.

2 Fit the rubber boot to the operating cylinder and insert the pushrod.

3 Reconnect the fluid pipe. Tighten the union nut, but do not overtighten.

4 Adjust the free movement and bleed the system, afterwards ensuring that the rubber cap is replaced on the bleed valve.

5 : 14 Clutch master cylinder—after October 1961

After October 1961 the Four/4 model changed to a $\frac{5}{8}$ inch CV master cylinder with a common non-integral

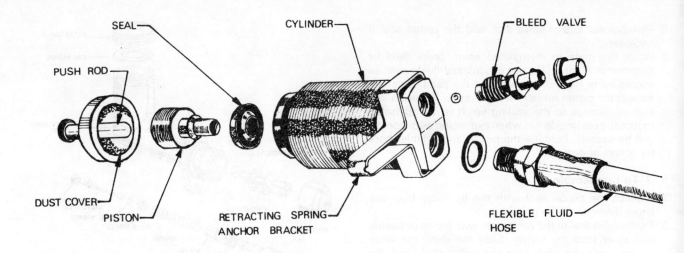

FIG 5:5 Clutch operating cylinder (slave cylinder) exploded Four/4 Series II

Labels: SEAL, PUSH ROD, CYLINDER, BLEED VALVE, DUST COVER, PISTON, RETRACTING SPRING ANCHOR BRACKET, FLEXIBLE FLUID HOSE

tank for both clutch and brake. The dual feed supply tank is placed above the two master cylinders on the bulkhead. The two master cylinders for clutch and brake are similar in operation but the latter is a ¾ inch unit similar to that fitted to the Plus/4. For details of this master cylinder see Chapter 10, **FIGS 10:15** and **10:16**.

The clutch, release bearing and pilot bearing assembly

5:15 To remove

1 Remove the gearbox and clutch housing assembly.

2 Remove the clutch disc and pressure plate assembly after unscrewing the six retaining bolts.

3 Inspect the clutch disc and pressure plate. Check that the linings are secure and free from oil. The disc should also be checked for excessive wear and signs of overheating. If the linings are worn down near to the rivet heads, or, if any of the above conditions are apparent, the disc should be renewed.

Check the condition of the pressure plate surface and the compression springs. Should any sign of scoring, overheating or distortion be present, change the assembly.

5:16 To refit

1 Place the clutch disc in position on the flywheel with the hub away from the flywheel. Align the disc with the pilot bearing using a locator.

2 Refit the pressure plate assembly, locating it on the three dowels. Replace the six securing screws and spring washers, tightening them evenly to a torque of 12 to 15 lb ft. Remove the clutch disc locator.

3 Refit the gearbox and clutch housing assembly.

5:17 The pilot bearing

The clutch pilot bearing located in the centre of the crankshaft flange is a sintered bronze bush. The bearing is impregnated with lubricant in manufacture and does not require attention in service.

5:18 To remove

1 Remove the gearbox and clutch housing assembly.

2 Detach the clutch disc and pressure plate assembly after unscrewing the six retaining bolts.

3 Remove the flywheel.

4 Withdraw the pilot bearing with the aid of a suitable puller.

5:19 To refit

1 Position the bearing in the crankshaft flange with its flat face towards the crankshaft, and tap the bearing gently into position, ensuring that it fits squarely into the bore.

2 Refit the flywheel.

3 Fit the clutch, as described previously.

4 Refit the gearbox and clutch housing.

THE RELEASE BEARING

5:20 To remove

1 Remove the gearbox and clutch housing assembly.

2 Disconnect the retracting spring and remove the rubber gaiter.

3 Withdraw the clutch release bearing and release arm assembly from the clutch housing, after releasing the retaining spring securing the release arm to the fulcrum pin.

4 Slide the release bearing link from the release bearing and arm assembly.
5 Detach the two release bearing locating springs from the clutch release arm.
5 Detach the two release bearing locating springs from the clutch release arm.

5:21 To dismantle

Hold the clutch release bearing assembly, which is a light press fit on the hub, with the bearing downwards and tap the shoulder of the hub sharply on a block of wood.

5:22 To reassemble

Assemble the bearing on the hub with the thrust face of the bearing away from the hub. Press the hub into position, ensuring that it enters the bearing bore squarely.

5:23 To refit

1 Fit the release bearing link between the release arm and release bearing, ensuring that the link is located in the grooves provided in the arm and bearing.
2 Assemble the release bearing locating springs to the release bearing and the release arm. The ends of the springs with the almost complete coils must be fitted to the bearing and the other ends attached to the release arm.
3 Pass the clutch release arm through the clutch housing and locate the release bearing and hub on the main drive shaft bearing retainer, after first inspecting the sleeve for burrs, and smearing it lightly with high melting point grease.
4 Locate the release arm on the fulcrum pin and secure with the retaining spring. The retaining spring ends should be located in the two holes provided in the release arm, then slide the central loop of the retaining spring under the fulcrum pin head.
5 Fit the gaiter over the clutch release arm, ensuring that the arm is correctly located in the clutch housing.
6 Refit the gearbox and clutch housing assembly.

5:24 Plus/4

The clutch is of the single dryplate type which is totally enclosed. An aluminium sleeve, sliding within the electron casting enclosing the shaft to the gearbox, operates the Borg and Beck clutch through a graphite thrust bearing.

5:25 External adjustments and lubrication

The only external adjustments are for thrust block clearance and pedal travel. The clearance adjustment is on the pushrod below the shaft housing, which has a left and righthand threaded rod (FIG 5:6). Turn the rod to give ½ inch free movement at the pedal pad. The link is normally fitted in the upper hole in the relay lever. The pedal stop is a ring, locked by a setscrew on the pedal shaft with a lug making contact with the crossmember.

Grease should be applied every 3,000 miles to the clutch thrust located behind the clutch housing, access to this is through a hole in the top of the gearbox shaft tunnel.

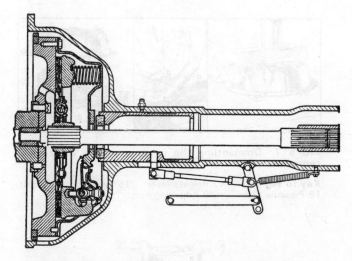

FIG 5:6 Section through clutch showing position of adjusting push rod (Plus/4 1952)

5:26 The graphite thrust block

The graphite block is shrunk into an aluminium alloy sleeve sliding in the clutch shaft housing and connected to the operating pushrod by an eyebolt screwed into the sleeve. The eyebolt on earlier cars was ⅜ inch BSF and was then increased to ½ inch.

To renew the thrust block, heat the sleeve in boiling water and push in the block. The clutch shaft is connected to the gearbox primary shaft by a splined muff coupling. Both shafts should be a tight push fit in the coupling. It is necessary to remove the engine/gearbox to carry out this and all other work on the clutch. Remember that the engine can be removed as a unit with the gearbox, or the gearbox can be removed first, but the unit should never be split at the bellhousing flange until the gearbox has been removed.

5:27 Removal of the clutch from flywheel

1 Slacken the six holding bolts in the outer rim of the cover pressing a turn at a time by diagonal selection until the thrust spring pressure is relieved.
2 Remove the six bolts and lift away the cover assembly and driven plate assembly from the two locating dowels.
3 Inspect the two dowels in the flywheel for looseness and burrs and replace if necessary.

5:28 Replacement of the clutch to flywheel

1 Place the driven plate assembly on the flywheel with the larger portion of the splined hub towards the gearbox and centralize the plate.
2 Fit the cover assembly over the driven plate and locate it on the two dowels in the face of the flywheel.
3 Secure the cover assembly to the flywheel with six bolts and lock washers, tightening them a turn at a time by diagonal selection to the correct tightening torque, 20 lb ft.
4 Remove the driven plate centralizer only when the cover assembly is attached to the flywheel.

It is essential that the driven plate assembly is central at all times during the assembly of the cover to flywheel.

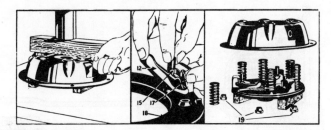

FIG 5 : 7 Dismantling the cover assembly utilizing a ram press

Key to Fig 5 : 7   12 Release lever   15 Eye bolt   17 Strut
18 Pressure plate   19 Adjusting nuts.

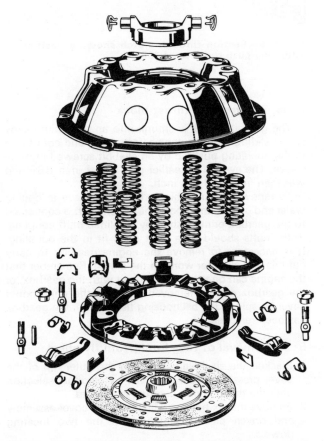

FIG 5 : 8   Exploded view of a typical Borg & Beck clutch

Failure to observe this point may lead to difficulty in attaching the gearbox, for the constant pinion shaft may not have a free passage to the pilot bearing bush in the rear end of the crankshaft.

5 : 24 Dismantling the cover assembly

Note: A hydraulic or fly press and two suitable wooden blocks are needed for this operation. **(FIG 5 : 7).**

Before dismantling the cover assembly suitably mark the following parts so that they can be reassembled in the same relative positions to each other and so preserve the balance of the cover assembly:

(i)   Cover pressing,
(ii) Lugs on the pressure plate,
(iii) Release levers.

1 Lay the assembly on the bed of the press with the pressure plate resting on the two wooden blocks so arranged that the cover pressing is free to move downwards when pressure is applied.
2 Lay another wooden block on top of the cover pressing in such a manner that it will contact the ram of the press and will also move downward between the release levers.
3 Lower the ram of the press sufficiently to bring the cover pressing in contact with the bed of the press. Secure the ram and remove the three adjusting nuts, considerable torque will be necessary as the staking of these nuts has to be overcome.
4 Release the pressure of the press slowly to prevent the thrust springs from flying out.
5 Remove the cover pressing and collect the component parts.

5 : 30 To assemble cover assembly

Before assembly note the markings on the various components and return them to their original positions. Grease the components slightly at their contact faces with Lockheed Expander Lubricant or other suitable lubricant.

1 Fit the pins to the eye bolts and locate these parts within the release levers. Hold the threaded end of the eye bolt and the inner end of the lever as close together as possible and, with the other hand, engage the strut within the slots in a lug on the pressure plate and the other end of the strut push outwards to the periphery of the pressure plate. Offer up the lever assembly, first engaging the eye bolt shank within the hole in the pressure plate, then locate the strut in the groove of the release lever. Fit the remaining levers in a similar manner.
2 Place the pressure plate on the wooden blocks on the base of the press and position the thrust springs on the bosses on the pressure plate.
3 Place the cover pressing, with the anti-rattle springs fitted, over the pressure plate ensuring that the lugs protrude through the cover slots.
4 Arrange a wooden block across the cover and apply pressure to compress the whole assembly. Screw the adjusting nuts on to the eye bolts sufficiently so that pressure can be released.

5 : 31 Inspection of cover assembly

Before reassembling the clutch unit the parts should be cleaned and inspected. Any components which show considerable wear on its working surface should be replaced. The thrust springs and anti-rattle springs should be checked against new ones of the correct strength, and any found to be obviously weak should be replaced. The anti-rattle springs should be assembled to the cover pressing. The working face of the cast iron pressure plate should also be inspected and if the ground face is deeply scored or grooved it should be either reground or replaced by a new plate.

If any parts are changed or a new pressure plate fitted, it is essential it should be statically balanced.

5 : 32 Adjusting the release levers utilizing the driven plate assembly

In service, the original adjustments made by the clutch manufacturer, will require no attention and readjustment is only necessary if the cover assembly has been dismantled.

1 Utilizing the actual flywheel, lay the driven plate in position and clamp the cover plate assembly over it and accurately centralize it.
2 By turning the adjusting nut adjust the height of the lever tips to 1.895 inches from the flywheel face utilizing a suitable depth gauge.
3 Operate the clutch by using a small press several times in order to settle the mechanism.
4 Check the height of the release lever tips and readjust if necessary.
5 Slacken the cover assembly and turn the drive plate 90°. Reclamp the cover assembly to the flywheel and check the height of the release lever tips as a safeguard against any lack of truth in the driven plate.

A more accurate method of setting up is to use Churchill Clutch Fixture No. 99A.

5 : 33 Condition of clutch facings

The possibility of further use of the driving plate assembly is sometimes raised, because the clutch facings have a polished appearance after considerable service. It is perhaps natural to assume that a rough surface will give a higher friction value against slipping, but this is not correct.

Since the introduction of non-metallic faces of the moulded asbestos type, in service, a polished surface is a common experience, but it must not be confused with a glazed surface which is sometimes encountered due to conditions discussed hereafter.

The ideal smooth polished condition will provide a normal contact, but a glazed surface may be due to a film or a condition introduced, which entirely alters the frictional value of the facings. These two conditions might be simply illustrated by the comparison between a polished wood and a varnished surface. In the former the contact is still made with the original material, whereas in the latter instance a film of dried varnish is interposed between the contact surfaces.

The following notes give useful information on this subject.

1 After the clutch has been in use for some time, under perfect conditions, with the clutch facings working on a true and polished or ground surface of correct material, without the presence of oil, and with only that amount of slip which the clutch provides for under normal condition, then the surface of the facings assumes a high polish, through which the grain of the material can be clearly seen. This polished facing is of a mid-brown colour and is then in perfect condition, the co-efficiency of friction and the capacity for transmitting power is up to a very high standard.
Note: The appearance of wound or woven type facings is slightly different but similar in character.

2 Should oil in small quantities gain access to the clutch in such a manner as to come in contact with the clutch facings it will burn off, due to the heat generated by slip which occurs during normal starting conditions. The burning off of the small amount of lubricant, has the effect of gradually darkening the clutch facings, but providing the polish on the facing remains such that the grain of the material can be clearly distinguished, it has very little effect on clutch performance.
3 Should increased quantities of oil or grease attain access to the facings, one or two conditions or a combination of the two, may arise, depending on the nature of the oil, etc.
(a) The oil may burn off and leave on the surface facings a carbon deposit which assumes a high glaze and causes slip. This is very definite, though very thin deposit, and in general it hides the grain of the material.
(b) The oil may partially burn and leave a resinous deposit on the facings, which frequently produce a fierce clutch and may also cause a 'spinning' clutch due to a tendency of the facings to adhere to the flywheel or pressure plate face.
(c) There may be a combination of 1 or 2 conditions, which is likely to produce a judder during clutch re-engagement.
(4) Still greater quantities of oil produce a black soaked appearance of the facings, and the effect may be slip, fierceness or judder in engagement, etc., according to the conditions. If the conditions under (3) or (4) are experienced, the clutch driven plate assembly should be replaced by one fitted with new facings, the cause of the presence of oil removed and the clutch housing assembly and flywheel thoroughly cleaned.

5 : 34 Reconditioning of driven plate assembly

Whilst a much more satisfactory result is obtained by the complete replacement of this assembly, circumstances may force the renewal of the clutch facings. The after-mentioned notes will prove useful.

1 Ensure that the metal components of the assembly are in good condition and pay particular attention to the following:
(a) Uneven spline wear.
(b) Cracked segments.
(c) Springs are not broken.
(d) Test the drive and over run.
2 Drill out the rivets securing the facings to the plates.
3 Rivet the new facings onto the plate assembly. It is suggested that an old flywheel is used as an anvil and the rivets supported by short pieces of $\frac{3}{16}$ inch dia. mild steel rod.
4 Mount the driven plate assembly on a mandrel between the centres of a lathe and check for 'run out' with a dial test indicator set as near to the edge of the assembly as possible.

Where the 'run out' exceeds .015 inch locate the high spot and true the assembly by prizing over in the requisite direction. Care must be taken not to damage the facings.
Note: When offering up the driven plate assembly to the flywheel, the LONGER side of the splined hub must be nearer to the gearbox.

5:35 1971 Ford 1600 GT models

For these cars the clutch has been adapted to mechanical operation through a system of rods due to lack of space for the normal Ford type of arrangement described earlier.

Adjustment:

The amount of free movement on the clutch operating push rod should be .10 inch (2.54 mm). This rod is on the bottom of the clutch linkage lever situated below and to the rear of the petrol pump. Adjustment is made by slackening the yoke and locknut, removing the dowel pin and then screwing the yoke end in or out as required. Do not forget to retighten the locknut and replace the splitpin in the dowel.

In the case of lefthand drive cars it is not necessary to remove the dowel pin, just slacken the locknut behind the front yoke end and turn the rod by hand to adjust, the ends being screwed left and righthand. Do not omit to tighten the locknut.

5:36 Fault diagnosis

(a) Drag or spin

1 Oil or grease on driven plate linings
2 Bent engine backplate
3 Misalignment between the engine and the gearbox first motion shaft
4 Leaking master cylinder, slave cylinder or pipeline
5 Driven plate hub binding on first motion shaft splines
6 Binding of first motion shaft spigot bearing
7 Distorted clutch plate
8 Warped or damaged pressure plate or clutch cover
9 Broken driven plate linings
10 Dirty or foreign matter in clutch
11 Air in the clutch hydraulic system

(b) Fierceness or snatch

1 Check 1, 2, 3 and 4 in (a)
2 Worn clutch linings

(c) Slip

1 Check 1, 2 and 3 in (a)
2 Check 2 in (b)
3 Weak pressure springs
4 Seized piston in clutch slave cylinder

(d) Judder

1 Check 1, 2 and 3 in (a)
2 Pressure plate not parallel with flywheel face
3 Contact area of driven plate linings not evenly distributed
4 Bent first-motion shaft
5 Buckled driven plate
6 Faulty engine or gearbox rubber mountings
7 Worn suspension shackles
8 Weak rear springs
9 Loose propeller shaft bolts
10 Loose rear spring clips

(e) Rattle

1 Check 3 in (c)
2 Broken springs in driven plate
3 Worn release mechanism
4 Excessive backlash in transmission
5 Wear in transmission bearings
6 Release bearing loose on fork

(f) Tick or knock

1 Worn first-motion shaft spigot or bearing
2 Badly worn splines in driven plate hub
3 Release plate out of line
4 Faulty Bendix drive on starter motor
5 Loose flywheel

(g) Driven plate fracture

1 Check 2 and 3 in (a)
2 Drag and distortion due to hanging gearbox in plate hub

CHAPTER 6

GEARBOX

All Morgan four wheeled vehicles except the Four/4 Series II have four speed and reverse gearboxes. In the early Four/4s and all Plus/4s the gearbox is situated amidships whilst the Ford engined cars have it in the more conventional position next to the engine/clutch unit. With the Ford powered vehicles it is necessary to remove the engine/gearbox unit to enable any work to be carried out on the gearbox, the sequence for this is described in Chapter 1 Part C.

6 : 1 Plus/4

A Moss four speed gearbox with synchromesh on all but bottom gear is utilized in the Plus/4. This gearbox is similar to the Jaguar gearbox of the pre-XK period, except for the front and rear covers.

6 : 2 To remove the gearbox

1 Detach gearbox cowl and propeller shaft tunnel.
2 Disconnect speedometer drive, clutch linkage, hand-brake cable and front end of propeller shaft.
3 Remove mounting bolts, but leave Silentbloc mountings in place, and support the engine under back end of sump, raising it just enough for gearbox feet to clear the mountings.

4 Remove setscrews which hold gearbox to clutch shaft housing flange and draw gearbox back with clutch shaft.

Reassemble in reverse order to the above, but check to see that the fibre pad on gearbox face is in good condition and is in place in the layshaft spindle recess when reassembling the gearbox on to the clutch shaft housing. Care must be taken not to disturb clutch driven plate if engine to gearbox shaft is removed.

6 : 3 Dismantling the gearbox

This is a task that should not be undertaken lightly and is best left in the hands of a good mechanic.

1 Take off top cover, together with selector rods and forks.
2 Select top and first gears to lock box and undo driving flange nut. Draw off flange, and extract speedometer drive pinion.
3 Take out rear cover setscrews, being careful not to disturb the layshaft and reverse spindle locking plate.
4 Tap layshaft spindle back, and draw cover off with both spindles *in situ*, allowing layshaft cluster and reverse idler to drop to the bottom of the box.

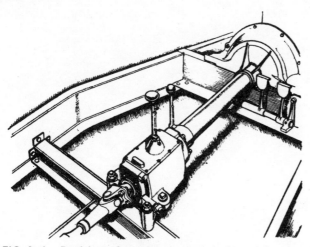

FIG 6 : 1   Position of gearbox in chassis Four/4 Series I

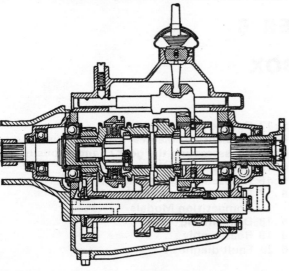

FIG 6 : 2   Section through Moss gearbox as fitted to the Plus/4

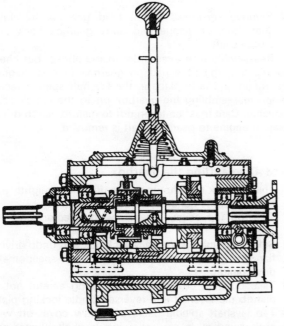

FIG 6 : 3   Section through Meadows gearbox Four/4 Series I

5   Take out front bearing cover setscrews (note copper washers). Turn the primary shaft so that the cutaway on top gear dogs clears layshaft constant mesh gear. Tap mainshaft forward to drive out primary shaft with two ballbearings, and caged roller spigot bearing. Tap mainshaft back until rear ballbearing can be drawn off. The mainshaft assembly can then be lifted out through the top.

6   Remove layshaft cluster with needle roller bearings and thrust washers, and bushed reverse idler.

7   The primary shaft has outrigger ballbearing pressed into the front cover behind lipped oil seal. To dismantle, press shaft out of cover with large ballbearing, retained on shaft with chip shield by spring ring and washer.

8   To dismantle the mainshaft assembly, slide off top and third synchro assembly. Press down plunger in shaft, locking third gear splined thrust washer, and release washer by twisting in line with splines.

9   Slide off third gear together with the 41 needle rollers. Slide off second synchro assembly with sliding first gear, noting interlock plunger and ball which will fall out of extra drilling in hub, and release second gear also with 41 needle rollers and splined washer locked by plunger.

Note: Reverse idler spindle should not be separated from rear cover, as rubber sealing ring recessed in the spindle cannot be replaced without a special thimble.

6 : 4   Reassembling the gearbox

1   Put reverse gear in box. Insert small retaining rings in layshaft cluster needle roller recesses, and insert 29 needle rollers in each end, utilizing thick grease to hold them in position. Insert retaining ring chamfered edge downwards. The other retainer chamfered edge upwards (near bronze washer).

2   Insert outer retaining ring in front end of cluster with large bronze thrust washer. Stick on steel thrust washer (pegged to box).

3   Insert stepped steel washer at rear (pegged to cluster) and small bronze thrust washer. Lower assembly into box and insert thin rod to support same.

4   Assemble second and third gears on mainshaft with 41 needle rollers in each, these being retained by spline washers locked by spring loaded plungers.

5   Slide on Top and third synchro assembly and second synchro assembly with sliding first gear, checking that the interlock ball (towards outside) and plunger are in place in drilling right through hub, and that they are opposite cutaway splines on mainshaft and in first gear. It is important that the half tooth cutaway on third and top operating sleeve are on the right way round, i.e. tapered portion of operating sleeve to face front of box.

6   Grease ends of main case and apply paper gasket.

7   Insert primary shaft assembly, with spigot bearing from front, noting packing ring round outer race of large bearing between box and spring ring. Fit front end aluminium cover and tighten with four $\frac{5}{16}$ inch BSF bolts with plain copper washers.

8   Lift layshaft cluster with rod and insert dummy spindle (.098 inch dia.) with a generous chamfer on end into layshaft so as not to disturb the needle rollers. Fit rear end bearing oil flinger, plain distance piece and speedo drive gear and insert dummy spindle.

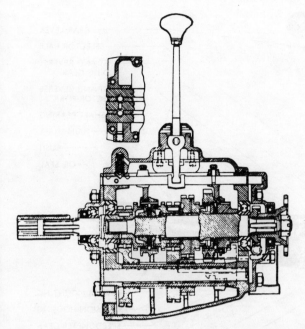

FIG 6:4 Section through early Moss gearbox Four/4 Series I

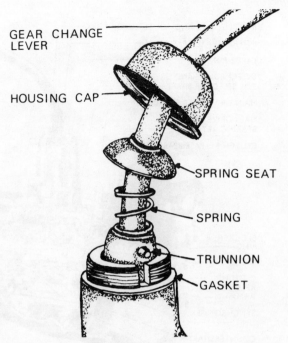

FIG 6:6 Gear change lever Four/4 Series II

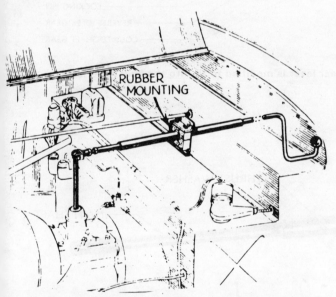

FIG 6:5 Gear linkage Four/4 Series II. Also visible is the windscreen wiper motor and the piping for the 'one shot' lubrication system

9 Offer up rear cover with layshaft spindle and reverse idler (fork groove to front) in place on spindle. Fit rear end cover with large spindle and small spindle (in block).

10 Insert layshaft spindle, pushing out the dummy to the front.

6:5 Four/4 Series I

All Four/4s of the first series were fitted with either a Meadows or a Moss gearbox, (FIGS 6:3 and 6:4), these boxes although made by different manufacturers were very similar in design—the following description of how to dismantle the Moss box will act as a guide to stripping the Meadows gearbox.

6:6 To dismantle the early Moss gearbox

1 Remove the screws from the top of the box and slide the cover backwards to prevent the 3 springs and plungers falling into the gearbox, then remove lid and gear lever together.

2 Remove spider from rear end.

3 Remove front and rear cover.

4 Remove screws from selector rods and take out the rods followed by the selectors.

5 Tap out ball races at front and rear and slide synchromesh hubs forward. The gears can now be removed in one piece.

N.B. A careful note should be made of the position of gears, etc., so that when replacing they are reassembled in the correct order.

6 Slide gears off shaft, first removing first and reverse synchromesh hub, taking care as there are 6 springs and 6 balls located in each of the two hubs.

7 Remove setscrew and steel plate at rear end of box and knock out layshaft. Remove gears through top of box.

8 Remove clip from mainshaft and second gear can then be removed.

6:7 Reassembling

Reassemble in the reverse order to dismantling noting two points.

1 When reassembling the gears, etc., a clip will have to be fabricated which will act as a sleeve to hold springs and balls in position. When all are in position, compress clip and replace synchromesh sleeve.

2 It is very important on the final fitting of the top gear selector rod to fit the steel sleeve in **front** of the selector, otherwise balls and springs will fly out and extensive damage will result.

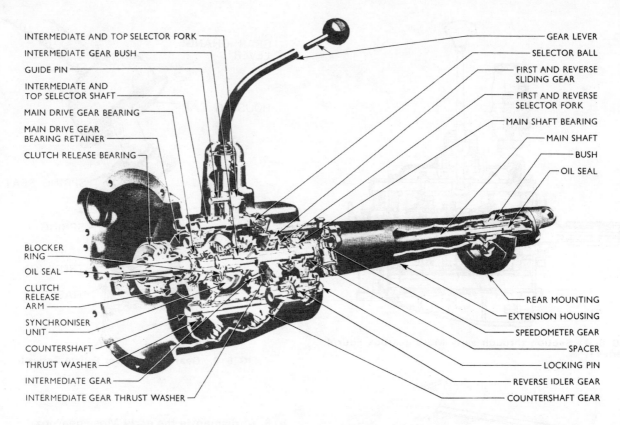

INTERMEDIATE AND TOP SELECTOR FORK
INTERMEDIATE GEAR BUSH
GUIDE PIN
INTERMEDIATE AND TOP SELECTOR SHAFT
MAIN DRIVE GEAR BEARING
MAIN DRIVE GEAR BEARING RETAINER
CLUTCH RELEASE BEARING

GEAR LEVER
SELECTOR BALL
FIRST AND REVERSE SLIDING GEAR
FIRST AND REVERSE SELECTOR FORK
MAIN SHAFT BEARING
MAIN SHAFT
BUSH
OIL SEAL

BLOCKER RING
OIL SEAL
CLUTCH RELEASE ARM
SYNCHRONISER UNIT
COUNTERSHAFT
THRUST WASHER
INTERMEDIATE GEAR
INTERMEDIATE GEAR THRUST WASHER

REAR MOUNTING
EXTENSION HOUSING
SPEEDOMETER GEAR
SPACER
LOCKING PIN
REVERSE IDLER GEAR
COUNTERSHAFT GEAR

FIG 6 : 7   Ford 100E gearbox cutaway view. The gear lever is modified to fit into the Four/4 Series II

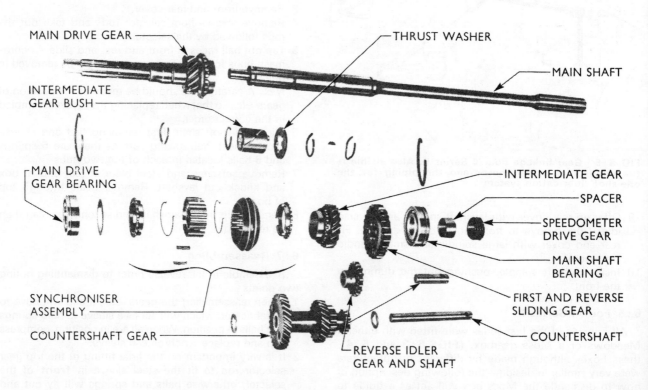

MAIN DRIVE GEAR
INTERMEDIATE GEAR BUSH
MAIN DRIVE GEAR BEARING
SYNCHRONISER ASSEMBLY
COUNTERSHAFT GEAR

THRUST WASHER
MAIN SHAFT
INTERMEDIATE GEAR
SPACER
SPEEDOMETER DRIVE GEAR
MAIN SHAFT BEARING
FIRST AND REVERSE SLIDING GEAR
COUNTERSHAFT
REVERSE IDLER GEAR AND SHAFT

FIG 6 : 8   The Four/4 Series II gearbox exploded

6:8 Four/4 Series II

The gearbox in this model is the identical box (and ratios) as fitted to the Anglia and Prefect (1953–59).

The simplest way to overcome serious gearbox trouble is to fit a replacement box, but this may not always be possible and so a run-down on the procedure is given below.

6:9 Dismantling the gearbox

Remove the clutch release bearing and release arm from the clutch housing. Detach the clutch operating cylinder bracket.

Remove the main drive gear bearing retainer.

Remove four bolts securing the selector housing and detach the housing and gasket.

Before removing the extension housing, the oil seal at the rear of the housing should be extracted.

Unscrew the speedometer driven gear cap from the extension housing and remove the bolts securing the extension housing to the gearbox case. The extension housing may now be slid carefully off the main shaft.

Remove the snap ring securing the speedometer drive gear to the main shaft and detach the gear, key and spacer.

Pull the main shaft carefully to the rear and insert a spacer tool between the rear bearing and the gearbox case. Gently tap the mainshaft through the bearing until the bearing can be separated from the shaft and remove the main shaft assembly through the top of the gearbox case. Pull the main drive gear forward if necessary.

To dismantle the mainshaft, expand the snap ring securing the synchromesh assembly to the front of the shaft and detach the synchromesh assembly, blocking ring and intermediate gear.

To remove the intermediate gear bush from the main-shaft, locate a bush remover over the bush and screw down the two locating pins, so that they enter fully into the holes in the bush. Tighten down the centre bolt of the tool to pull the bush from the mainshaft.

Turn the intermediate gear thrust washer one-twelfth turn in either direction, until it can be pulled along the mainshaft splines.

Remove the first and reverse sliding gear and the snap ring from the mainshaft.

Expand the snap ring on the main drive gear, in front of the bearing and tap the main drive gear into the case, finally removing it through the top of the box. Lift out the bearing and oil baffle.

Drive out the pin locking the countershaft and reverse idler gear shaft, using a thin punch.

To remove the countershaft, use a brass or copper drift to drive the shaft approx. one inch to the rear, then insert a dummy countershaft to push the countershaft out of the box from the front.

Lift the countershaft gear and thrust washers from the gearbox case.

Drive the reverse idler gear shaft out of the box from the front, using a suitable bent driver. Remove the reverse idler gear.

6:10 The synchromesh assembly

Check that suitable mating marks are stamped on the synchromesh sleeve and hub.

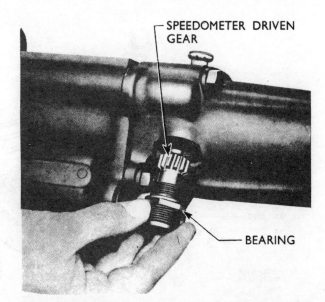

FIG 6:9   Removing the speedometer driven gear Four/4 Series II

To dismantle the synchromesh, carefully pull the sleeve off the hub, when the blocker plates and springs may be detached.

When reassembling, fit a spring in each side of the hub so that both springs are located the same way round, with one end in the same slot in the hub. Position the three blocker plates in the hub slots, so they rest on the springs and carefully replace the sleeve with the mating marks on the sleeve and the hub together.

6:11 Main shaft spigot bush

Hold the main drive gear in a vice and tap a thread in the bush, and with the aid of an extractor withdraw the bush.

Insert a new bush, using a driver and drill the two oil holes through the gear into the bush and then ream the bush.

6:12 Countershaft gear

Hold the countershaft gear in a vice and drive out the old bushes. A stepped driver may be used when refitting the shaft gear bushes, after which they must be reamed in line using a reamer.

6:13 Dismantling the gear change housing

Punch out the guide pin and unscrew the plugs at each side of the housing. Extract the selector balls and springs.

Turn the top and second gear selector fork until the rivet is vertically in line with the turret and drive out the rivet.

With the first and reverse gear selector shaft in the neutral position withdraw the selector shaft forward, holding the fork stationary.

Drive out the rivet from the first and reverse gear selector fork and extract the shaft from the front of the housing.

Tap the housing to allow the interlock plunger to fall out of its location between the two shafts.

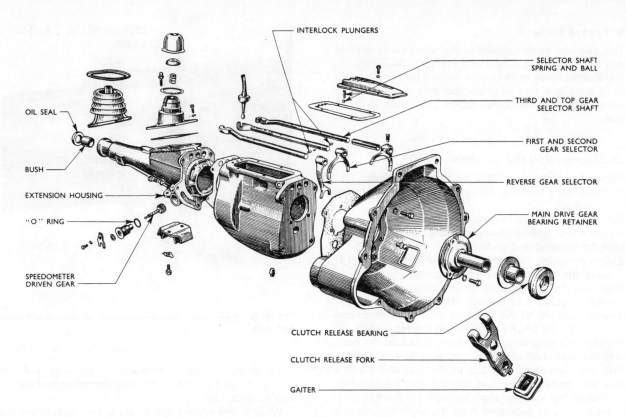

OIL SEAL

BUSH

EXTENSION HOUSING

"O" RING

SPEEDOMETER
DRIVEN GEAR

INTERLOCK PLUNGERS

SELECTOR SHAFT
SPRING AND BALL

THIRD AND TOP GEAR
SELECTOR SHAFT

FIRST AND SECOND
GEAR SELECTOR

REVERSE GEAR SELECTOR

MAIN DRIVE GEAR
BEARING RETAINER

CLUTCH RELEASE BEARING

CLUTCH RELEASE FORK

GAITER

FIG 6:10   Four/4 Series III gearbox—exploded (external)

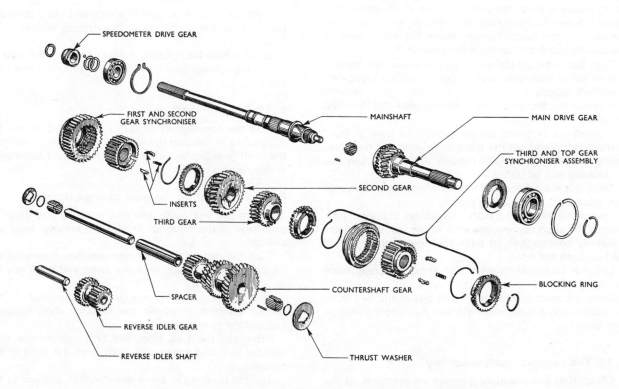

SPEEDOMETER DRIVE GEAR

FIRST AND SECOND
GEAR SYNCHRONISER

INSERTS

THIRD GEAR

SPACER

REVERSE IDLER GEAR

REVERSE IDLER SHAFT

MAINSHAFT

SECOND GEAR

COUNTERSHAFT GEAR

THRUST WASHER

MAIN DRIVE GEAR

THIRD AND TOP GEAR
SYNCHRONISER ASSEMBLY

BLOCKING RING

FIG 6:11   Four/4 Series III gearbox—exploded (internal)

6:14 Reassembling the gear change housing

Install the first and reverse gear selector shaft, rivet-hole end first, in the location farthest from the guide pin. Push the shaft through the front and centre support, and fit the first and reverse selector fork so that the slotted end will line up with the top and intermediate shaft, when inserted.

Turn the shaft to bring the three adjacent notches to the outside, and the gear lever slot towards the guide pin.

Insert the rivet and pin over the end.

Insert the interlock plunger and refit the top and second gear shaft from the front, the end having three notches being inserted first.

After the shaft has passed through the front support, fit the selector fork. The guide pin slot in the fork must be on the same side as the first and reverse selector shaft, which must be in the neutral position, before the second gear shaft can pass the interlock plunger. Push the shaft into position, turn it so that the three notches are to the outside and rivet the fork to the shaft.

Insert the guide pin so that it passes through the slot in the top and second gear selector fork, and replace the selector ball, spring and plug in each side of the housing.

Check that the oil trough is fitted with the opening to the top, and horizontal and that it is flush with the gearbox case at the rear.

6:15 Reassembling the gearbox

Fit the reverse idler gear with the long shoulder to the front, and replace the shaft so that the locking pin hole in the shaft is in line with the hole through the end of the gearbox case. Tap the shaft into position.

Place a thrust washer on each end of the countershaft gear. Lower the countershaft gear to the bottom of the box.

Pass the dummy countershaft or a suitable tool, through the gear and thrust washers from the front of the box, and fit the countershaft from the rear, turning it until the locking pinhole in the shaft lines up with the hole in the casing.

Refit the locking pin.

Enter the main drive gear through the top of the box, so that the gear shaft protrudes through the front bearing aperture.

Locate an oil baffle on the main drive gear so that it overlaps the gear teeth and replace the bearing with the snap ring on the outer diameter to the front. Push the main drive gear forward and tap the bearing on to the shaft, and replace the snap ring securing the bearing.

6:16 Reassembling the main shaft

Fit a new snap ring in the rear groove on the splined portion of the shaft, and replace the first and reverse sliding gear with the selector fork groove to the rear.

Replace the intermediate gear thrust washer in the second groove on the shaft, turning it one-twelfth of a turn, to bring the internal splines in line with the splines on the shaft.

Now drive the intermediate gear bush into position against the thrust washer, using a hollow driver. Note that the key on the bush must engage between two splines of the thrust washer.

Replace the intermediate gear with the coned face to the front and locate a blocker ring on the coned face.

Replace the synchromesh assembly, with the long shoulder of the hub to the front and fit a new snap ring to secure it in place.

Refit the main shaft assembly through the top of the box so that the rear end of the main shaft passes through the rear bearing aperture. Place the other blocker ring on the coned face of the main drive gear and align the main shaft spigot in its bush in the main drive gear.

Fit the gearbox rear bearing over the shaft with the snap ring on the outer diameter to the rear and tap the bearing forward with a spacer tool until the bearing abuts the snap ring on the shaft.

Refit the speedometer driving gear spacer, key and gear and secure with a new snap ring.

Examine the oil seal in the main drive gear bearing retainer and renew if necessary. Drive the new seal into position, with the sealing lip away from the retainer. Replace the retainer over the main drive gear with the drain hole to the bottom and secure with three screws.

If the extension housing bush is worn, it should be replaced. Drive the new bush into position with the split in the bush towards the top of the extension housing and flush with its flange at the rear.

Fit a new oil seal in the rear end of the extension housing.

Replace the extension housing and gasket on the gearbox rear face, securing them with five bolts. Ensure that the gasket holes line up with the holes in the extension housing.

Check that the selector shaft cover plugs are fitted in the clutch housing and then replace the selector housing and gasket, ensuring that the selector forks are aligned with the grooves in the synchromesh sleeve and sliding gear. Secure the housing with four bolts.

Fit the clutch release bearing and release arm, engaging the clips on the release arm around the fulcrum pin head and the fork ends in the spring clips on the bearing hub.

6:17 Four/4 Series III, IV, V, 1600 and Competition Models

The gearbox is of the constant mesh type with four forward gears and one reverse; second, third and top gear are synchronized. The constant mesh gears are of the helical type. An exploded view of the gearbox is shown (FIGS 6:10 and 6:11).

6:18 Dismantling and reassembly

After the gearbox is removed from the car it can be dismantled as follows:

Remove the clutch release bearing, the clutch fork and the clutch housing.

Remove the gear lever housing and gearbox top cover, being careful not to lose the shifter shaft lock springs.

Remove the shifter shaft lock springs and balls; place all gears in the neutral position.

Unscrew the square-headed shifter fork bolts after removing the locking wire.

Pull the reverse shifter fork shaft from the gearbox housing; now hold the spacer sleeve which is fitted on the third/top gear shifter fork shaft with one hand and pull the shifter fork shaft out of the gearbox housing with the other. Remove the spacer sleeve.

Pull back the first/second gear shifter fork shaft until the floating pin can be removed from the front end of it;

then remove the shifter fork shaft from the gearbox housing.

Lift the shifter forks from the locating grooves of the respective gears.

The two interlock plungers which are located in the forward face of the gearbox can now be removed after removing the plug on the righthand side of the gearbox housing.

Remove the bolts and lock washers from the gearbox extension housing and pull the housing approximately $\frac{1}{4}$ inch away from the gearbox housing.

Rotate the extension housing a quarter turn to the left until the recess above the lower lefthand securing bolt hole is located above the countershaft.

Loosen the countershaft from the bore in the front face of the gearbox housing by carefully tapping it with a brass drift; push the countershaft out of the gearbox with the aid of a dummy shaft. The dummy shaft remains in the countershaft gear cluster. Carefully withdraw the extension housing and main shaft assembly from the gearbox.

Locate a nut, a flat washer and the special sleeve (Tool No. P.7043), or a suitable bush on a $\frac{5}{16}$ x 24 UNF 2 inch bolt; screw the bolt into the reverse idler gear shaft and withdraw the shaft by tightening the nut.

Remove the reverse idler gear pinion.

Remove the front bearing cover from the gearbox housing; remove the large circlip from the front bearing and push the bearing and main drive gear pinion into the gearbox, following which it can be taken out of the gearbox through the top. Lift the countershaft gear cluster out of the gearbox housing and remove the dummy shaft, the forty bearing needles (twenty at each end), together with the spacer bush and the four washers. If necessary, the main shaft assembly can be dismantled as follows: Remove the speedometer driving gear from the extension housing; compress the circlip which retains the main shaft bearing in the extension housing and remove the mainshaft assembly from the extension housing.

Remove the speedometer drive worm wheel.

On early models, the worm wheel is retained on the shaft by means of a circlip; on later models it is secured by means of a nut and tab washer.

Remove the locating ball from the main shaft and remove the spacer bush (on later models) or the circlip (on early models).

Expand and remove the main shaft bearing retaining circlip. Press the main shaft bearing off the mainshaft and remove the first gear and second gear synchronizer assembly, the second gear synchronizer ring and the second gear pinion.

Note: The main shaft, the first/second gear synchronizer hub and the sleeve are matched and provided with etched markings. Synchronizer parts are only serviced as a unit, consisting of the first/second gear synchronizer sleeve, the hub, the rear spring for the synchronizer keys and the retaining plate which is permanently secured to the synchronizer hub. The retaining plate should never be removed from the hub, nor should the sleeve and hub be interchanged between assemblies.

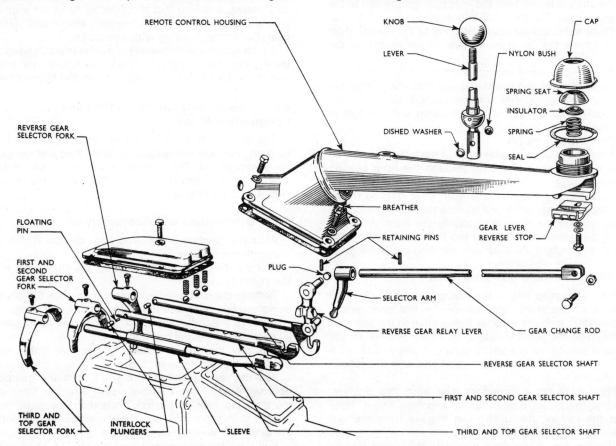

FIG 6:12 Four/4 1600 remote gear change mechanism

Remove the third/top gear synchronizer sleeve from the hub; remove the synchronizer keys and the front spring. Remove the circlip from the groove in the mainshaft.

With the aid of the special tool set, No. P.4090–3, press the third/top gear synchronizer hub, the synchronizer ring and the third gear pinion off the mainshaft.

The mainshaft, the synchronizer hub and the sleeve are matched and provided with etched markings.

If necessary, remove the circlip from the main drive gear and press the bearing off the main drive gear (an oil slinger is installed between the ballbearing and the gear).

If necessary, the oil seal and bearing bush may be removed from the extension housing and new parts installed, taking care that the split in the bearing bush is facing upwards and the lip on the oil seal inwards.

6 : 19 Reassembly

Assemble the first/second gear synchronizer unit.

If a new unit is to be installed, slide the synchronizer sleeve off the hub. Locate the synchronizer keys in the hub so that the flat extensions on the keys are within the retaining plate and that the hooked end of the already installed synchronizer spring is inside one key. Leave the other end of the spring free.

Note in which synchronizer key the spring tag is located and also the direction of rotation of the spring; slide the second gear synchronizer sleeve, with the shifter fork collar, towards the rear, on to the hub, making sure that the mating marks on hub and sleeve coincide.

Install the front synchronizer spring so that the tag end of the spring is in the same synchronizer key in which the tag of the rear spring is located; the front spring should be running in the opposite direction.

Slide the second gear pinion on to the main shaft with the teeth towards the thrust collar on the shaft. Install the synchronizer ring on the tapered face of the second gear. Install the first/second gear synchronizer assembly on the mainshaft, making sure that the marked splines on hub and shaft coincide.

Note: The hub should be pressed on the shaft until the rear face of the hub is level with the bearing shoulder on the mainshaft.

Position the large mainshaft bearing circlip over the mainshaft and locate the bearing on the shaft, so that the radius on the outer bearing race is toward the rear of the shaft. Support the assembly with the aid of a suitable tool and press the shaft in the bearing. On former models, install the small bearing-retaining circlip in its groove in the shaft.

Slide the third gear pinion on to the shaft with the gear teeth toward the thrust collar on the shaft and locate the synchronizer ring on the taper face of the gear.

Install one synchronizer spring in the rear of the third/top gear synchronizer hub and locate the hub on the mainshaft with the long boss towards the front of the shaft.

Support the assembly with the aid of a suitable tool, turn the shaft until the mating marks on hub and shaft coincide and press the synchronizer hub on to the shaft.

Install the circlip in the mainshaft groove. Install the synchronizer keys and front spring, making sure that the tag ends of front and rear springs are in the same

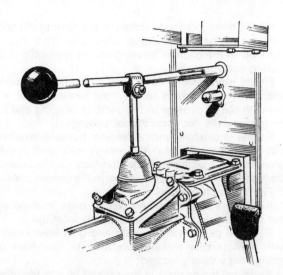

FIG 6:13 Standard gear lever layout for Four/4 Series III, IV and V

synchronizer key and that the springs are running in opposite directions.

Leave the outer end of each spring free. Refit the sleeve to the hub, making sure that the markings coincide.

Fit the front speedometer worm wheel retainer circlip in its groove in the shaft (on early models); install the spacer bushing (on later models).

Fit the locating ball in the mainshaft and fit the speedometer worm wheel with the shoulder towards the rear. Fit the circlip (on early models) or the tab washer and the nut (on later models). Tighten the nut to 20–25 lb ft. and bend over the tab washer.

Install the mainshaft assembly in the extension housing, taking care not to damage the oil seal and bearing bush.

Make sure that the mainshaft bearing is properly seated in the extension housing and fit the retaining circlip so that its two ends are in the recess in the extension housing.

Refit the speedometer drive gear and bearing with a new 'O' seal ring.

Locate the spacer, with a washer at each end, in the countershaft gear cluster and insert the dummy countershaft. Coat the bearing needles with grease and fit twenty bearing needles round the dummy countershaft at each end of the gear.

Fix the retaining washers over each end of the dummy countershaft.

Stick the two thrust washers (large washer to the front) in the gearbox housing with grease, making sure that the tongue on each washer is located in the recess in the gearbox housing.

Carefully place the cluster gear assembly in the gearbox housing, taking care not to dislodge the thrust washers.

Install the reverse idler gear with the large diameter towards the rear.

Fit the dished oil slinger plate on the main drive gear with the concave side towards the gear; fit the bearing on the main drive gear with the groove in the outer bearing race away from the gear and press the bearing on the gear. Fit the small diameter circlip in its groove in the main drive gearshaft.

Fit the thirteen bearing rollers in the bore of the main drive gear; install the main drive gear and bearing assembly in the gearbox housing and fit the circlip in the bearing outer race.

Fit the front bearing cover with a new gasket, making sure that the oil groove in the front bearing cover is in line with the oil passage in the gearbox housing and that the gasket does not cover this oil passage.

Fit the mainshaft and extension housing assembly with a new gasket; install the reverse idler shaft and the countershaft, making sure that the flats on the countershaft and the reverse idler shaft are in the correct position.

Fit the clutch housing.

Refit the shifter forks and related parts, making sure that the interlock plungers are properly located.

Refit the gearbox cover plate and gear lever housing with new gaskets, making sure that the lock balls and springs are properly located.

Re-install the gearbox in the car and fill it to the proper level with the correct grade of lubricant.

6:20 Fault diagnosis

(a) Jumping out of gear

1 Broken spring behind locating ball for selector rod
2 Excessively worn locating indentation in selector rod
3 Fork to selector rod securing screw or rivet loose

(b) Noisy gearbox

1 Insufficient oil
2 Excessive end play in laygear
3 Worn or damaged bearings
4 Worn or damaged gear teeth

(c) Difficulty in engaging gear

1 Incorrect clutch pedal adjustment
2 Worn synchromesh cones

(d) Oil leaks

1 Damaged joint washers
2 Worn or damaged oil seals
3 Front, rear or side covers loose or faces damaged

CHAPTER 7

PROPELLER SHAFT, REAR AXLE AND SUSPENSION

7 : 1   Rear suspension
7 : 2   Propeller shaft
7 : 3   Rear axle Moss type Four/4 Series I
7 : 4   Rear axle removal Four/4 Series I
7 : 5   Rear axle early Plus/4 and Four/4 Series II

7 : 6   Later models Plus/4 and Four/4s
7 : 7   Andrex rear shock absorbers (dampers)
7 : 8   Girling shock absorbers
7 : 9   Armstrong shock absorbers
7 :10   Fault diagnosis

7 : 1 Rear suspension

The suspension at the rear is by half elliptic springs mounted on the inside of the side members and passing underneath the axle.

Silentbloc bushes now anchor the springs at front and rear, and on no account should they be oiled or greased. Until recent years the rear ends worked in cast iron trunnion blocks which formed part of the tubular cross-member. To remove the springs, jack up the rear of the car and drive out the anchorage bolt. Jack up the axle and remove U-bolts, it will then be possible to slide the spring forward out of rear trunnion. The trunnions should be oiled or greased every 250 miles. Grease nipples are provided, but the spare wheels must be removed to get at same.

7 : 2 Propeller shaft

The front and rear universal joints on the propeller shaft are of Hardy-Spicer manufacture and the needle bearings require no attention other than regular lubrication. Usually long and severe service is required before any appreciable wear is noticed. The trunnions and needle bearings are the only parts subject to wear, and when replacement is finally necessary they may be removed

and replaced by hand without the need for special tools. The needle bearings are locked in position with lock rings on recessed grooves in the yokes, requiring only a pair of pliers for removal. If for any reason there is necessity to remove the bearing assembly, be sure to hold the trunnion in an upright position, so that the assembly to be removed is at the bottom. This is necessary in order to prevent the needles from falling out. In the event of their doing so, the assembly should be washed in petrol and then by smearing them with light oil, to hold the needles in position, the bearings can be readily reassembled. Do not use grease when reassembling as this is liable to clog the oil passages, use a light oil. The joints have four independent oil reservoirs which carry the oil to the needle bearing assemblies. On some models each universal coupling is fitted with a grease nipple and a third nipple is provided for the spline shaft.

7 : 3 Rear axle Moss type Four/4 Series I

Most of the adjustments that may be necessary from time to time on the Moss rear axle can be made without removing the complete axle from the chassis.

Differential adjustments are made after removing the differential and pinion housing from the axle case. Hubs, hub-bearing cups, and axle shafts are first removed.

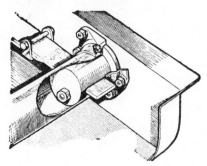

FIG 7:1 The rear trunnion (1936)

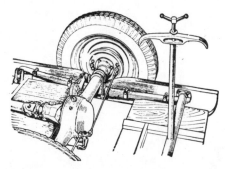

FIG 7:2 Rear suspension showing the underslung frame

FIG 7:3 Rear suspension showing Silentbloc bushes at rear

Bevel pinion adjustments call for removal of propeller-shaft flange, oil retainer, thrust cover, and extraction of bevel pinion with races in position. The method of adjustment is by pressing off the ball race and inserting shims if the pinion is to be adjusted 'in' or removing shims to adjust 'out'. The crownwheel is adjusted by inserting a square bar in the slots on the differential bearing locknut, after slackening off differential cup bolts and turning back the locking tabs.

When setting crownwheel and pinion, endeavour to obtain a marking about $\frac{3}{8}$ inch along the inner portion of the tooth. If possible, run the gears at about 1,000 rpm with some surface blue on the teeth. Apply load by holding a stout stick against the crownwheel.

When rewiring the differential cup bolts, make sure that the wire passes over the locking tabs to keep them in position.

Hub bearings can be adjusted by insertion or removal of shims between cups and brake anchor plates after taking off hubs and drums. Adjust until there is the smallest amount of play possible, allowing the shafts to turn freely. Use a new joint washer when refitting differential assembly.

7:4 Rear axle removal Four/4 Series I

To remove axle from car disconnect propeller shaft and brake connections. Remove wheels and 'U' bolts. Take out setscrews attaching brake backplate to axle casing, which screw into wheel bearing housing. Hub, brake drum, bearing and halfshaft can then be drawn out. Move axle sideways so that dismantled end passes spring. Axle can then be tipped so that other end passes between spring and body. On four-seater propeller shaft tunnel and end board must be dismantled to clear nose-piece.

Taper roller wheel bearings are adjusted by shims between bearing housing and brake backplate. Shafts butt at inner ends on later type axle (BA8A) (FIG 7:6). Earlier type (BA8) has thrust block round differential bevel spindle. Allow minimum play.

Bevel pinion shaft runs on roller inner and ball outer bearings, separated by distance-piece on shaft and pulled up tight by nut securing propeller shaft coupling. On type BA8 ballbearing outer race located by cap flange-bolted to final drive housing.

No adjustment for bearings. Bevel mesh adjusted by shims between ballbearing inner race and distance-piece.

On type BA8A ballbearing is housed in screwed sleeve with locking ring for mesh adjustment.

Crownwheel riveted to differential housing which is one piece on BA8, split on BA8A. Assembly runs in ballbearings, adjustable for mesh by ring nuts. Backlash .003 inch.

7:5 Rear axle early Plus/4 and Four/4 Series II

The Salisbury hypoid bevel drive with semi floating shafts are employed on these models, the Plus/4 having the 3HA (FIG 7:7) and the Four/4 Series II the 6HA type. Both types are similar in design and construction but the overall size of the latter is reduced. Final drive housing integral with axle tubes, rear cover detachable.

To remove axle from car, put wooden blocks between springs and lower flange of frame behind axle, to give clearance for removal of U-bolt nuts. Remove wheels and draw off hubs. Disconnect brake fluid pipe and T-piece from unions on axle, handbrake cable from compensator, and pipes and links from brake backplates. Backplate assemblies can then be removed (four bolts each side, heads outside) with oil seal housings and shims, which should be kept with each backplate. Disconnect rear end of propeller shaft, and take nuts off spring U-bolts. Shock absorbers, linked to inner U-bolts, need not be disconnected separately. Lift axle sideways until one end is clear of chassis frame, then lower and draw other end through.

Hubs keyed on tapered halfshafts (interchangeable). Taper roller bearings in axle tube ends, retained by backplates with shims behind to adjust end float

FIG 7:4 Chassis layout, showing propeller shaft, Andrex Shock absorbers and rear axle Jan. 1936 Four/4

(.001–.005 inch). Inner ends of halfshafts butt on floating thrust block round planet bevel spindle.

To remove halfshaft draw off hub, detach brake backplate assembly with lipped oil seal in housing, and shims. Draw out shaft and bearing carefully through inner oil seal (lip inwards).

If both shafts are withdrawn, when refitting see that shims on both sides are of about equal thickness, so that thrust block remains central. Shims .003, .005, .010 and .030 inch thick available.

Bevel pinion shaft carried in taper roller bearings. Outer races pressed into final drive housing from front and rear. Distance-piece between inner races. Shims (.003, .005, .010, .030 inch thick) between distance piece and inner race of front bearing for bearing adjustment. Shims (.003, .005, .010 inch) between outer race of rear bearing and housing for mesh adjustment.

Pinion setting marked on face of pinion may be zero, plus or minus. This indicates amount in 'thous' above or below nominal distance (2.25 inch on 3HA 2 inch on 6HA) of face from centre line of crownwheel. Use mesh adjusting shims to obtain setting marked, and assemble pinion in bearings with original bearing shims, but without oil thrower or oil seal. Tighten driving flange nut and test for preload (8–12 lb in.).

Crownwheel spigoted and bolted to flange of one-piece differential cage. Side bevel gears run directly in cage with thrust washers behind. Planet bevel pinions have spherical thrust washers, and run on spindle retained by pin peened to lock. Axle shaft thrust block round spindle.

Differential assembly carried on taper roller bearings in split housings with shims (.003, .005, .010, .030 inch thick) between inner races and cage for bearing and mesh adjustment. Install differential assembly without shims and with bevel pinion removed, and mount dial gauge on axle casing with button against back face of crownwheel. Move differential assembly to one side of housing with lever, and set gauge to zero. Lever assembly over to other side and note gauge reading (A). This figure indicates play in bearings, and thickness of shims needed to take up play. Add .008 inch to total to give preload. This total must be divided to obtain correct crownwheel mesh as follows:

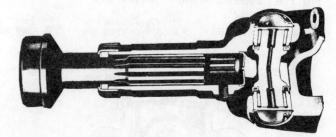

FIG 7:5 Slip spline shaft.

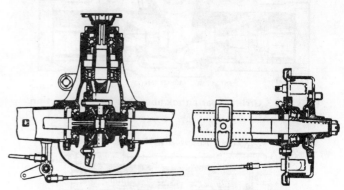

FIG 7:6 Section through BA8A rear axle

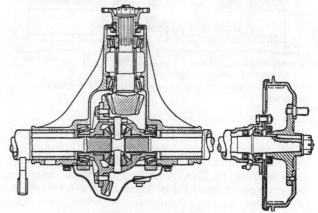

FIG 7:7 Section through 3HA rear axle

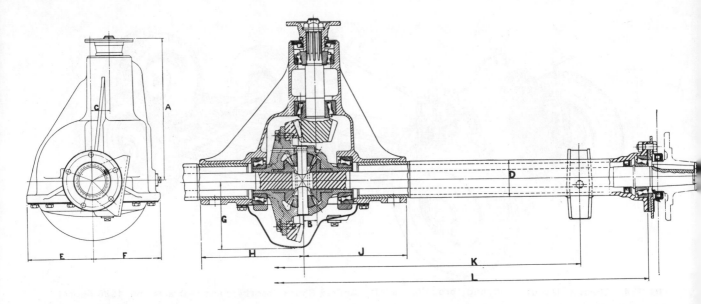

FIG 7 : 8   Sections through 7 HA rear axle

Key to Fig 7 : 8   A—$9\frac{1}{4}$ inch (235 mm)   B—$\frac{3}{4}$ inch (19 mm)   C—1 inch (25 mm)   D—$2\frac{1}{4}$ inch (76 mm)
E—$4\frac{9}{16}$ inch (116 mm)   F—$4\frac{9}{16}$ inch (116 mm)   G—$3\frac{13}{16}$ inch (97 mm)   H—$6\frac{1}{8}$ inch (156 mm)   J—$6\frac{1}{8}$ inch (156 mm)

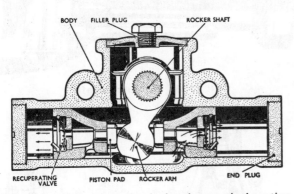

FIG 7 : 9   Girling rear shock absorber vertical section

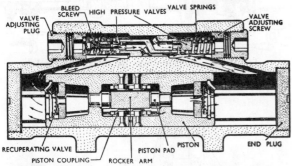

FIG 7 : 10   Girling rear shock absorber, horizontal section

After installing bevel pinion, reassemble differential, again without shims. Lever away from pinion, set indicator to zero, and lever assembly towards pinion. Note reading (B). This, minus backlash figure etched on crownwheel, is thickness of shims to go behind crownwheel side bearing. Remainder of shims from total (A + .008 inch) go behind offside bearing.

When assembling differential with shimmed bearings, use spreader (Salisbury tool No. SE.104) to open out housing or, if this is not available, cock outer races slightly and tap lightly into place with lead hammer.

When assembly is complete, check for backlash (.004 inch minimum). Change shims from one side to other of differential bearings if necessary.

7 : 6   Later models Plus/4 and Four/4s

The Salisbury 3HA and 6HA rear axles were replaced in January 1961 by the 7HA model (**FIG 7 : 8**), which is used in all cars and is similar in design and construction to the earlier types. The zero cone setting distance for this axle is 2.219 inches compared with the 3HA 2.25 inches and the 6HA 2 inches. It is essential to quote engine and chassis numbers when ordering parts for this axle as the driving gear, pinion assemblies, and differential case assemblies have been slightly modified. These 'Phase 2' axles were fitted on both Plus/4 and Four/4 models from approx. February 1964.

7 : 7   Andrex rear shock absorbers (dampers)

On early models Andre Multiplex Shock absorbers were fitted, these were the usual friction type so popular before the war. The best guide to whether they are doing their job is to note the riding qualities of the car when travelling fairly fast over a rough road. If the springing action seems too free and the rear of the car tends to carry on bouncing after hitting a bump, increase the resistance by tightening the centre adjusting nut (clockwise or to the right) by one graduation at a time. On the other hand, if the springing action seems retarded and feels stiff reverse the above procedure.

It is a common fault to increase the resistance more than is necessary and care should be taken on this point.

For racing enthusiasts a considerable increase in pressure may be required.

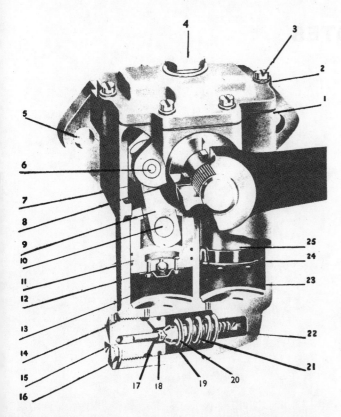

FIG 7:11   Cut-away view of an Armstrong lever type shock absorber

Key to Fig 7:11   1 Gasket   2 Shakeproof washer   3 Lid screw   4 Filler plug   5 Holes for mounting shock absorber to chassis   6 Crank pin   7 Crank plate   8 Gland packing   9 Connecting rod   10 Piston pin   11 Compression or bump piston   12 Recuperating valve   13 Compression or bump cylinder   14 'O' ring seal   15 Valve screw   16 Valve screw washer   17 Rebound valve   18 'O' ring seal   19 Compression valve   20 Compression washer   21 Compression spring   22 Rebound spring   23 Rebound cylinder   24 Rebound piston seal   25 Rebound piston

7:8 Girling shock absorbers

Girling hydraulic dampers **(FIGS 7:9** and **7:10)** took the place of the friction type in the early fifties (1951–52 SA.237/12 lefthand. SA.237/13 righthand. 1952–55 SA.237/16 lefthand. SA.237/16 righthand). Inspect the units and check the rubber bearing bushes for wear or signs of perishing. Provision is made for topping up which can be done with the dampers in position.

The procedure is as follows:

1 Thoroughly clean the unit before removing the filler plug.
2 A shield should be placed over the unit before the plug is removed in order to protect it, and should not be removed until the plug is replaced.
3 Check that the filler can is absolutely clean internally and externally. Use only Girling Piston Type Damper Oil (Thin). It is impossible to over fill.

It is possible to adjust the valves in the Girling unit as they are spring loaded. After being set at the factory to the Morgan Co. specifications it is not recommended that any adjustment be attempted, but it is possible, if desired, providing extreme cleanliness is observed.

7:9 Armstrong shock absorbers

On all post-war Four/4s and on later Plus/4s, Armstrong lever type units are used.

This shock absorber **(FIG 7:11)** is of the hydraulic double acting type and works on the principle of pumping oil backwards and forwards between two cylinders through suitable valves set to give the required degree of restriction in each direction. This design has advantages in that firstly all working parts are submerged in oil, and secondly it is only necessary to recuperate the very small amount of oil which is forced past the pistons by pressure built up as the shock absorber operates.

The servicing procedure is similar to the Girling type but the oil—Armstrong Super (thin) fluid—should be kept at $\frac{3}{8}$ inch from the bottom of the filler plug orifice. There is now no exchange service for these units. Armstrong Selectaride shock absorbers can be fitted if desired.

7:10 Fault diagnosis

(a) Noisy axle

1 Insufficient or incorrect lubricant
2 Worn bearings
3 Worn gears

(b) Excessive backlash

1 Worn gears, bearings or bearing housings
2 Worn axle shaft splines
3 Worn universal joints
4 Loose or broken wheel studs. Worn wire wheel hubs

(c) Oil leakage

1 Defective seals in hub
2 Defective pinion shaft seal
3 Defective seals on universal joint spiders

(d) Vibration

1 Propeller shaft out of balance
2 Worn universal joint bearings

(e) Rattles

1 Rubber bushes in damper links worn through
2 Dampers loose
3 Spring 'U' bolts loose
4 Loose spring clips
5 Worn bushes in spring eye
6 Broken spring leaves

(f) 'Settling'

1 Weak or broken spring leaves
2 Badly worn bushes
3 Loose spring anchorages

NOTES

CHAPTER 8

THE FRONT SUSPENSION

The original Morgan Four/4 utilized a similar (but strengthened) front axle and suspension unit to that used in the Morgan 3/wheeler for so many years. Each front wheel is controlled by helical springs arranged in a near vertical tubular member. Two main tubes lay one above the other and were connected by vertical and diagonal tubes to give great rigidity. Each front wheel was damped by a Newton-Bennett shock absorber. Detail improvements were incorporated up to 1939, such as, the 'vertical' spindle was inclined backwards and was increased from $\frac{3}{4}$ to 1 inch in diameter. The sliding member became a steel forging with phosphor bronze bushes at top and bottom and a space was left between the bushes which acted as a reservoir for lubricant which was filled via a grease gun nipple. **(FIG 8 : 1).**

The first post-war vehicles that appeared, were similar except for different spring characteristics, particularly with regard to the rebound spring, also shock absorbers were not always fitted. A steering damper was now placed between the sliding axle and the top spring and connected to the chassis side which reduced wheel wobble.

The Plus/4 in 1950 employed the same system, but the main coil springs were increased by 3 inches to give greater wheel movement and a softer ride, and shock absorbers were fitted to all cars. **(FIG 8 : 2).**

Also the 'one shot' lubrication system was incorporated for the first time.

With the sliding-axle type of front suspension it is vital that adequate lubricant reaches the sliding member, up to this time grease nipples only were employed. With the 'one shot' system the upper ends of the suspension spindles are connected by steel piping to a metered two-way union adjacent to the dash, this union being connected via a pedal-operated valve to the pipe leading to the engine oil gauge line. Thus momentary pressure on the pedal opens the valve and allows oil under full engine pressure to flow into the pipes and thence to the suspension units. In practice, one 'shot' every 100 miles or so is sufficient to provide all the lubrication that is required by both suspension and steering movements. This lubrication and suspension system has continued to be used, with slight modifications, to all Morgan models to date.

8 : 1 The 'one shot' front suspension lubricator

About every 100 miles the foot plunger should be depressed and this actuates a mushroom valve, which admits oil under pressure to the front suspension. If too much oil reaches this area, it is indicative of two things— either the driver is keeping his foot on the plunger too long or that the valve is leaking. If the latter is suspected, disconnect all four unions, and detach the valve from the dash panel. Insert a screwdriver in the front hole to hold the slotted valve whilst the cap is unscrewed from the valve stem, this will release the conical valve and spring (a stronger spring is now available for early models). **(FIG 8 : 4).**

The valve should be ground very lightly with fine paste and finished off with metal polish. Reassemble, securing the cap by light riveting.

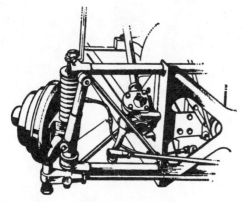

FIG 8:1 Front suspension and steering gear layout Four/4 Series I

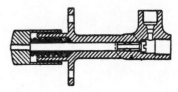

FIG 8:4 Section through front suspension lubrication valve

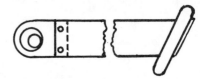

FIG 8:5 Showing steering damper positioned with hole eccentric to king pin

FIG 8:2 Front suspension Plus/4 1950

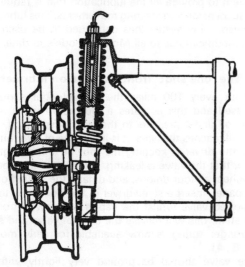

FIG 8:3 Section through Plus/4 (1952) front suspension

8:2 Front suspension—dismantling (Plus/4)

It is possible to remove the complete front suspension assembly from the chassis once the radiator has been detached, but this should only be done in cases of damage, all other operations can be carried out with this assembly *in situ*. To dismantle the front suspension, jack up the front of the car to a height of at least 15 inches and remove the road wheels. It is advisable to place blocks under the front of the car as a precaution. Disconnect the lower end of the shock absorber and the track rod end, together with the brake fluid pipe (chassis end) and the oil pipe union at the top of the king pin. Loosen the large setscrew (auto lubrication bolt) at the top end of the kingpin, supporting the stub axle, which will drop when the setscrew is taken away, and the king-pin, with rebound spring, will fall out, releasing the main spring and inner cover. The stub axle thrust is taken by the phosphor bronze plate between the stub axle and the lower end of the spring, this is bolted to a spring steel blade the other end of which is secured to the chassis frame. On the early models the steel blade was drilled for the kingpin, and the phosphor bronze washer was riveted to the underside. With this type it was necessary to dismantle the whole suspension if the steel blade needed replacing. On later models the steel plate can be detached without further dismantling.

The procedure for reassembling is as follows—place the steering damper, spring and dust cover on stub axle, and the rebound spring on to the kingpin. Thread the kingpin up into the stub axle and press upwards with the jack until the top end registers in the top lug, and bolts can be inserted in lower plate, and the large setscrew in the upper end of the kingpin. It will be found advantageous to grease the thrust pad on the end of the steering damper before assembly.

Before the chassis clamp bolts are tightened check position of the hole in steering damper—this should be eccentric to kingpin (FIG 8:5) under full deflection.

The hubs run on ballbearings with a distance-piece between the inner races and a packing ring covering the radius of stub axle behind the inner bearing. The outer race of the inner bearing is kept in the hub by a screwed ring which has a lipped oil seal. Later models have roller bearings with no distance-piece.

Ball joints on the transverse drag link are of the screwed end plug type and are spring-loaded (on recent models a Thompson track rod is fitted). The track rod has loose rubber bushed knuckle joints with shouldered bolts, these should be fully tightened. The other socket is screwed on and held there by a locknut.

On certain cars which have covered considerable mileage, faults are sometimes noticed in respect of front wheel vibration. This can be overcome by making certain that the flat spring sheet blade mounted from the stub axle to the chassis side member is secured without any radial movement at the chassis end. This blade should slide inwards and outwards only. Any sideways or radial movement should be reduced to a minimum by adjusting the shims. These shims are locked in place by the two bolts which secure the flat steel clamps to the chassis. It may also be necessary to renew the damper blades if worn edges are apparent.

8 : 3 Fitting new front suspension cross frame

New front suspension cross frames are now supplied undrilled. To ascertain the correct position of holes on the new, cut a template in cardboard of the original, marking the position of the holes carefully and place it on the new frame and mark out the position of the holes and then drill, etc.

8 : 4 Fitting a new rebound spring

1 Remove road wheel and auto lubrication pipe.
2 Remove track rod from steering arm.
3 Slacken auto lubrication bolt at top of assembly.
4 Remove shock absorber from hanger pin.
5 Remove 2 bolts from flange on bottom lug.
6 Place jack underneath kingpin and raise.
7 Remove auto lubrication bolt release jack and kingpin will then fall away.
Replace in the reverse order to the above.

8 : 5 Front shock absorbers

Newton hydraulic dampers of the 11,000 series with a 2¾ inch (70 mm) stroke were fitted on the early Four/4s. These require very little attention and if they are giving a satisfactory ride and there is no apparent leak, the best advice is to leave well alone. The early series of the 11,000 unit are of the sealed construction type and cannot be dismantled. This type which is recognized by the end of the cylinder being rolled over on to the gland has been replaced by the later type.

To replenish with fluid if necessary the unit should be taken from the vehicle and dismantled as follows:

Holding the eye end at the bottom of the unit in a vice, remove the top mounting rubbers and lift off the dust cover. This will expose the gland nut, which is unscrewed, but not withdrawn from the piston rod. Withdraw the complete inner assembly, take off the foot valve assembly from the end of the inner cylinder, give a sharp pull on the piston rod, holding the cylinder in the other hand. (Inspect the piston rod, and if scratched replace it or return shock absorber for a Service Exchange unit). This will withdraw the piston and gland from the cylinder. (The foot valve and spring may have remained in the outer cylinder when the inner assembly was withdrawn, but these may be retrieved when fluid is

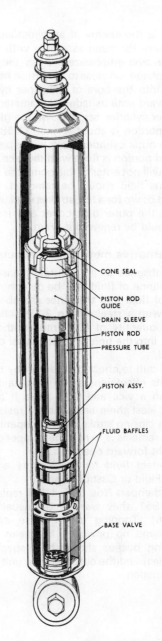

FIG 8 : 6   Girling direct action telescopic shock absorber

CONE SEAL
PISTON ROD GUIDE
DRAIN SLEEVE
PISTON ROD
PRESSURE TUBE
PISTON ASSY.
FLUID BAFFLES
BASE VALVE

drained from the outer cylinder). Do not withdraw the gland assembly from the piston rod unless it is intended to replace the inner and outer synthetic rubber seals. If there are no signs of leaking at the gland, indicated by fluid in the body of the unit, the seals need not be renewed, although this is recommended if spares are available. If dismantled, reassemble in the opposite order and feed back over the piston rod using a taper thimble to prevent damage to the seals when passing over the threaded end of the piston rod. Thoroughly wash all parts in clean paraffin before reassembly and proceed as follows:

Fit the foot valve assembly into the end of the inner cylinder, replace the foot valve and spring. To prevent the valve and spring from falling out, keep the assembled parts upright and feed up the bore of the outer cylinder until properly seated; turn the assembled cylinders upright and stand in a vice, pour in 1.7 fluid ounces of fluid. Dirt is the enemy of all hydraulic equipment and the necessity for clean assembly with the correct fluid cannot be over-emphasized. Push the gland assembly along the piston rod close to the piston head and assemble the head into the bore of the inner cylinder; push the gland forward until its reduced diameter fits into the end of the inner cylinder, screw down the gland nut until the threaded portion is about $\frac{1}{16}$ inch (1.58 mm) below the end of the outer cylinder. Push in the piston rod until the shouldered portion is flush with the face of the gland nut. If the rod will not enter to this point, the unit is over-filled and surplus fluid should be removed. Work the piston rod up and down for a few strokes until uniform resistance is felt. Fit the outer dust cover and mounting rubbers, which should be renewed if worn.

8 : 6 Alternative method of measurement

In the absence of an accurate measuring vessel, the correct volume of fluid may be determined by pouring a quantity of fluid into the outer chamber and measuring the level with a steel rule to 2.33 inches. Pour out the measured quantity of fluid into another container and pour back into the unit when the inner cylinder has been assembled.

It is difficult to check the damper by hand but a rough guide to its effectiveness can be obtained by placing it **upright** in a vice and then press it home (maximum stroke) at least three times—more resistance should be felt on the closing stroke than the opening stroke.

All that remains is to refit the damper on the car, which is a straight forward operation.

The correct fluid for these units is Newton Shock Absorber Fluid or Castrol Shockol.

Girling dampers Nos. DAS 4/131 replaced the Newton units in 1951, they were of the usual telescopic type. **(FIG 8 : 6)**. Topping up of these dampers is never necessary and no provision has been made to do so. The bearing bushes should be inspected occasionally (6,000 miles) and the outside of the unit kept clean to aid head dissipation.

The Girling equipment was replaced by Armstrong shock absorbers and again no provision is made for topping up; the same maintenance instructions apply.

Important: All models with wire wheels have splined hubs and therefore if a disc wheeled model is to be fitted with wire wheels, the whole assembly must be changed.

8 : 7 Fault diagnosis

(a) Wheel wobble

1 Worn hub bearings
2 Broken or weak front springs
3 Uneven tyre wear
4 Worn suspension linkage
5 Loose wheel fixings

(b) 'Bottoming' of suspension

1 Check 2 in (a)
2 Dampers not working

(c) Heavy steering

1 Neglected swivel pin lubrication
2 Wrong suspension geometry

(d) Excessive tyre wear

1 Check 4 in (a), 2 in (b) and 2 in (c)

(e) Rattles

1 Check 2 in (a)
2 Lubrication neglected, rubber bushes worn
3 Damper mountings loose
4 Radius arm mountings loose or worn

(f) Excessive 'rolling'

1 Check 2 in (a) and 2 in (b)

CHAPTER 9

THE STEERING

The very first Four/4 models were fitted with a simple reduction gear mounted halfway down the steering column similar to the three-wheeler, but after only a few months this was changed to the familiar Burman worm and nut box, which continued up to the mid fifties. From this time cam gear steering has been fitted to both Plus/4 and Four/4 models.

9 : 1 The Burman steering gear

This is non-adjustable for wear, though end-play of the column may be taken up by adjustment of the two large locknuts under the steering wheel. Special flat spanners will be needed for this, as normal spanners will be found to be too thick. These locknuts tighten a ball-race at the top of the column, and the tightening must not be overdone or the steering will be rendered unduly stiff.

Apart from this small adjustment, all wear in the box must be taken up by fitting new parts, although several 'dodges' give temporary improvement. A diagram of the steering is shown (FIG 9 : 1) and it will be seen that the bottom of the inner column A has a square thread which screws into a bronze nut B. A rocker arm C, which is pivoted at P, engages, with its pegged end, a sleeved hole in the bronze nut. It will be seen, then, that when the steering wheel is turned the bronze nut moves up or down the column, taking with it the pegged end of the rocker arm. The movement of the rocker arm turns the rocker shaft and actuates the drop-arm which is attached to the splined end of the shaft.

The points of wear are obviously—between the thread of the column and the thread of the nut; between the peg and the sleeved hole in the nut; in the bearings supporting the shaft; between the splines on the shaft and the drop-arm.

9 : 2 Testing for wear

To test for wear in the box, first ensure that there is no movement between the drop-arm and the splined shaft by tightening the clamp nut, then get someone to hold the drop-arm and gently rock the steering wheel back and forth. The person holding the drop-arm can tell when he feels that it is being actuated. There will undoubtedly be some play, unless all the parts are new, but more than 1 inch measured along the circumference of the steering wheel, should be deemed excessive. Now check to see where the play is in the box. The box is easily worked upon, but access is greatly assisted by jacking up the offside, removing the front wheel and pushing the thin tension bar out of the way. This bar comes directly in front of the steering box end cover and may be removed by undoing the locknut at the bottom of it and then unscrewing from the top. It need not be taken right out, but merely pushed up into a position where it will not be obstructive.

Remove the end cover, which is secured by three $\frac{1}{4}$ inch B.S.F. bolts, and ask your assistant to rock the steering wheel slowly. With the end cover removed (FIG 9 : 2), the end of the column and the nut will be seen, and it should be possible to detect whether there is any perceptible back-lash on the thread, i.e. see if the nut begins to move immediately the column turns. If so the play is not in the nut but, if any play exists, attention must be given to it. Do not, however, merely fit immediately a new column and nut, but test for play in the rest of the box first.

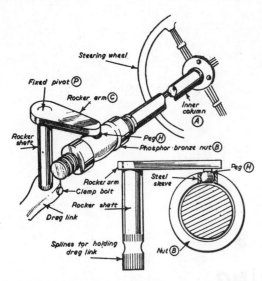

FIG 9:1   Diagram of Burman Steering Gear

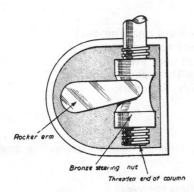

FIG 9:2   Top of steering with cover removed

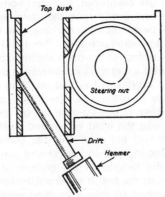

FIG 9:3   Method of drifting out the top bush

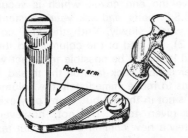

FIG 9:4   Spreading the peg

Hold the drop arm firmly with both hands and try to push and pull it. If movement is possible, then wear exists either upon the rocker shaft or on the bronze rocker shaft bushes or on both. Finally test for wear between the peg and the bronze nut. This is done by removing the cover from the top of the box (four $\frac{1}{4}$ inch B.S.F. Bolts). Ask your assistant again to move the steering wheel and place your fingers on the rocker arm, with finger tips touching the nut. It is then easy to feel whether there is a slight time-lag between movement of the nut and movement of the rocker arm. If so then play exists between the peg and the sleeved hole in the nut.

The only permanent method of rectifying these faults is by fitting new parts. If play exists between the nut and the column, a new .005 inch undersize nut should be fitted. (There are two types of steering nut—5 and 6 start—it is recommended to send a pattern when ordering). If, however, play is really excessive, then a new column and nut will be required. The old column is easily removable in the following manner. Undo the large nut in the centre of the steering wheel. On post-war cars the wheel may then be removed with the aid of a puller. On pre-war cars it is easier to unscrew the four $\frac{1}{4}$ inch nuts on the wheel boss, and split the wheel, when only the small rear part of the boss will have to be pulled off. The two large locknuts and cone are then unscrewed. Take off the drop arm and tap up the rocker shaft, when the column and nut may be withdrawn through the end of the box. Take care not to allow any of the loose ball-bearings at the top of the column to run down inside, or they may cause endless trouble.

The bronze bushes which form the bearing for the rocker shaft may be drifted out by using a long bolt **(FIG 9:3).** A fairly heavy hammer should be used, since movement is restricted. The new bushes may be driven in, using a piece of wood between the bush and the hammer or mallet. Notice that the top bush is bevelled off to leave room for the steering nut to turn. Both bushes have a slight lead on them, so no difficulty should be encountered in inserting them. Since they are made to size, no reaming is necessary, and the rocker shaft may be pushed down immediately.

9:3 Assembly

Great care should be taken to ensure absolute cleanliness when assembling. It is advisable to use an assembly compound between the column and the nut. Assemble the column first and adjust the two locknuts until no end play exists and yet there is no stiffness. Assemble the steering wheel. Screw on the steering nut (if it is an undersize nut a slight lead may have to be filed on the column) and assemble the rocker shaft. Make sure that the peg really is over the sleeved hole in the nut before any pressure is exerted, otherwise the nut may be damaged. Paper gaskets and jointing compound should be used when replacing the covers on the steering box in order to make it oiltight. Grease should on no account be used since it will not reach the rocker shaft bearings and they will wear excessively.

If it is necessary to take up wear between the peg and the sleeved hole in the steering nut, but it is not thought economical to fit new parts, an improvement can sometimes be effected by spreading the peg with a hammer **(FIG 9:4),** although this is certainly not workshop practice. This will prove successful and has been known to last for about 3,000 miles.

9 : 4 The drag link

The drag link has screwed ends which are designed so that wear may be taken up. The split pin should be removed and a screwdriver should be inserted into the end of the rod and the inner screw removed (FIG 9 : 5). Clean and grease it and the ball, reassemble, tightening right home, and replacing the splitpin. This should be done to both ends of the drag link.

9 : 5 The track rod

To test for wear in the track rod ends, ask an assistant to rock the steering wheel just enough to actuate the track rod and wheels. Any wear will immediately be apparent. New parts are the only remedy, but these are not expensive. Two new bolts and conical bearings will be all that are required.

Since no provision is made on these cars to grease the track rod ends without dismantling, they are usually neglected and wear sets in. A popular modification consists of drilling and reamering out the steering arms on the brake back plates, and making up special bolts which are tight fits into them (FIG 9 : 6). The bolts are drilled as in the diagram and have angled grease nipples on their heads. The spring washer, nut and splitpin, are assembled as shown. The greasing of track rod ends is thus much simplified, and wear between the bolts and the steering arms is no longer possible.

9 : 6 Swivel pins, bushes and hub bearings

Wear on these is easily checked by pulling and pushing the top of each front wheel. If much movement is perceptible attention should be given.

To refit swivel pin bushes jack up the front of the car as high as possible. Remove the front wheels and shock absorbers. The hub should then be removed by unscrewing the greasing nut, taking out the splitpin and nut then exposed, when the hub may be withdrawn with the aid of a puller. Strip off the brake shoes and the brake cable. Unscrew the nut at the top of the swivel pin, and, if the car is post-war, unscrew the two bolts which retain the rebound spring at the bottom tube. The swivel pin can then be removed downwards, when the springs, dustcover (if fitted), brake back plate and large bronze washer will come away.

Unless there is a fair amount of wear on the swivel pins it will only be necessary to renew the bushes.

The old bushes may be drifted out and the new ones inserted and driven in, using a wooden block to avoid damaging the bronze. The swivel pins and stub axle assembly bushes should be reamered to fit the swivel pins.

Reassemble in the reverse order to dismantling, and again absolute cleanliness must be insisted upon, and an assembly compound is advised. Check the ball races before refitting, and if any roughness is apparent after cleaning them, or if they may be rocked, however slightly, they should be renewed. Replace the hubs and the track rod and splitpin the hubs. Pack with grease and adjust brakes.

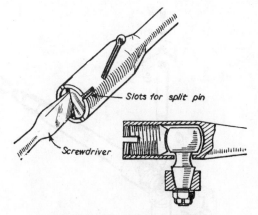

FIG 9 : 5   Details of drag link

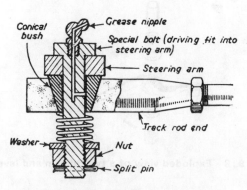

FIG 9 : 6   The modified track rod end

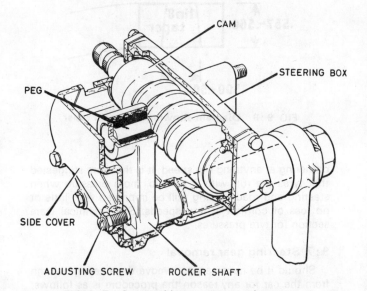

FIG 9 : 7   Cam and lever type steering gear

The tracking should be set. Toe-in should be $\frac{1}{8}$ inch and on no account should the wheels be allowed to toe-out. If the steering is erratic over rough ground, the trouble is probably in the shock absorbers. See Chapter 8 regarding front shock absorbers.

It must not be forgotten that tyre pressures play a large part in steering and road holding, and it pays to check them frequently. With the recommended tyre pressures, tyres tend to squeal and this is very noticeable when

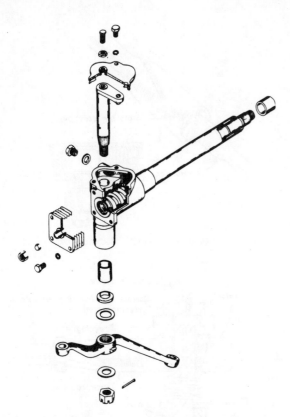

FIG 9 : 8   Exploded view of a typical cam and lever box

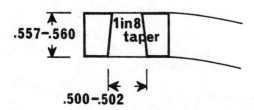

FIG 9 : 9   Diagram showing drop arm taper

cornering at anything like speed. It is therefore suggested that tyres are run with 2 to 4 lb. more pressure when steering and road holding will be improved with little or no loss of comfort at low speeds. See Technical Data section for tyre pressures.

9 : 7 Steering gear removal

Should it be necessary to remove the steering column from the car for any reason the procedure is as follows:
1 Remove steering wheel from car (taper and Woodruff key on Burman Box and serrated taper Cam Gearbox), slacken the column tube support bracket and pull out rubber grommet to facia panel.
2 Remove the front suspension diagonal stay rod in front of steering box, disconnect drag link from the arm, and take out the two large setscrews holding the box to the chassis frame, taking care to note the position of the tapered light alloy packing pieces on either side of the frame side member (Burman Box only).

3 Withdraw steering column out to front.
Note: When refitting stay rod, screw the lower end right in and lock with nut, then tighten upper nuts evenly so that rod is neither in compression nor tension.

9 : 8 Track rod adjustment

1 Slacken bolt in clip on track rod.
2 Loosen locknuts at end of track rod.
3 Twist track rod tube with hand to either right or left to reduce or widen the track, this should be $\frac{1}{8}$ inch toe-in on the rim.

9 : 9 Cam gear steering

Since the mid-fifties cam and lever type steering gear has been fitted to both Plus/4 and Four/4 models. The main feature of this type of steering gear is that it relies on a rotating cylindrical cam engaging with a stud mounted on a lever which is an integral part of the output shaft **(FIG 9 : 7)**.

The cam itself is not actually a worm, but is generated on a special machine the cutter of which travels in the same arc as the peg in the rocker shaft. This ensures accurate peg engagement at all positions. At the centre of the cam, corresponding to the straight ahead position of the road wheels, there is a 'high spot', details of which are explained below.

To test the steering gear, disconnect the drag link from the ball pin of the drop arm so that the steering wheel may be freely rotated from lock to lock. At the central position it should be possible to feel some resistance as the peg passes over the high spot referred to above. If this cannot be discerned and it is possible to spin the wheel from lock to lock without feeling the cam centre, then the thrust screw on the top cover should be turned clockwise a small amount at a time until a torque of approximately 12 lb. inch at the rim of the steering wheel is required to move over the centre. The thrust screw is secured in place by a locking nut. It should be noted that when connected up with the steering linkage on the chassis, this high spot cannot be noticed when the vehicle is driven on the road and therefore does not cause any feeling of discomfort to the driver. If it does, the adjustment is excessive and will harm the mechanism.

It should be observed that in properly adjusted condition, there will be no backlash or lost motion of the drop arm at the central position. But at any other position it will be found that the drop arm can have a certain amount of shake, which reaches a maximum at each lock. This comes about due to clearance of the peg in the cam track at all positions other than the straight ahead.

During manufacture the shims in the end cover are adjusted to allow a maximum of only .002 inch end float of the cam in the box. In time it may be necessary to remove a shim to prevent this amount being exceeded due to normal wear in service. Shims are usually provided in three sizes: .0024, .005, .010 inch.

If one or more shims are removed, the end cover should then be replaced and tightened up, care being taken to ensure that the ball cages are running true and have not been allowed to become askew and forced home in this way. (Should this occur, the cages will break up and the ballbearings will drop out into the box and cause considerable damage). It should then be possible to rotate the column by hand to guard against pre-loading if too many shims have been removed. To facilitate shim adjustment, it is advisable to carry this out ·with the steering gear held vertically upside down in a suitable fixture after draining off the lubricating oil. When clamped horizontally in a vice, the ball cages may slip out of position before the end cover has been resecured.

When it is necessary to remove the drop arm from the taper splined end of the rocker shaft, a proper extracting tool must be employed. Hammering is likely to damage the gear and often leads to no further progress in any event due to the firm hold of the arm on the taper.

After the vehicle has been initially run-in and oil changes are made to engine and gearbox, etc., the high spot on the cam may have been lost due to 'bedding down' of the new parts. Therefore it is recommended that at this stage the appropriate thrust screw adjustment should be made (in the manner already described) to ensure that the centre is correct. It should then remain in adjustment for some time.

9 : 10 The Thompson track rod

On models since late 1953 a Thompson·track rod has been utilised—this can be fitted to any model, but in all cases a new drop arm will be necessary. Also the steering arms must be altered to take the taper of the taper pin as per **FIG 9 : 9.**

9 : 11 Fault diagnosis

(a) Wheel wobble

1 Unbalanced wheels and tyres
2 Slack steering connections
3 Incorrect steering geometry
4 Excessive play in steering gear
5 Broken or weak front springs
6 Worn hub bearings

(b) Wander

1 Check 2, 3 and 4 in (a)
2 Front suspension and rear axle mounting points out of line
3 Uneven tyre pressures
4 Uneven tyre wear
5 Weak dampers or springs

(c) Heavy steering

1 Check 3 in (a)
2 Very low tyre pressures
3 Neglected lubrication
4 Wheels out of track
5 Steering gear maladjusted
6 Steering columns bent or misaligned
7 Steering column bearing pre-loaded excessively

(d) Lost motion

1 End play in steering column
2 Loose steering wheel
3 Worn steering box
4 Worn ball joints
5 Worn suspension system

NOTES

130

CHAPTER 10

THE BRAKING SYSTEM

Morgan 4 wheeler models have always been fitted with Girling brakes. As the car has developed more power over the years, so the braking system has been improved to cope with the increased speed. Up to 1950 non-servo cable and rod operated brakes were fitted, but from this time on they have been hydraulically operated.

At the front type HLS/S (two leading shoe) units were fitted from 1950 until they were superseded by disc brakes. The rear brakes from 1950 to 1956 were type HW and these were then replaced by HL3 units.

10:1 Mechanical brake adjustment

Adjustment for lining wear is taken up by the brake shoe adjuster, which protrudes from the backplate and has four machined flats on it. Turn in a clockwise direction until resistance is felt and then slacken off one full notch or two clicks. The car need not be jacked up for this operation.

10:2 Mechanical brake relining

1 Jack up car and remove wheels.
2 Remove drums—rear by means of undoing the two countersunk screws, and the front by taking off the complete hub. A suitable puller would be needed for this.
3 Prize one shoe out of the groove in the plunger at the expander end with a screwdriver. Both shoes and springs can now be removed, leaving expander and adjuster units in position on the backplates.

4 Clean down the backplates, check expander and adjuster units for free working. Slack back adjuster (anticlockwise) to full off position. Adjuster cone spindle should screw quite easily into the housing.
5 Replace old springs with new if possible and fit to new shoes. Check that the springs are between the shoe webs and backplate and fit the shoe ends to the adjuster grooves. Shoes have half round slots at one end; fit these slots to the adjuster plungers; then insert the other end of the shoe in expander plunger. Place screwdriver under web of the remaining shoe and ease into plunger groove.

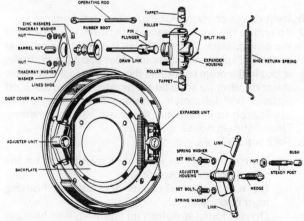

FIG 10:1 Exploded view of Girling non-Servo brake

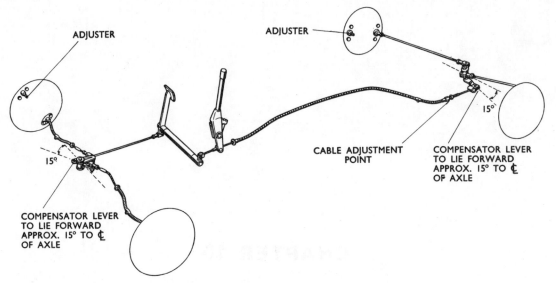

FIG 10:2 Brake layout Four/4 1945 to 1950

In the figure:
- ADJUSTER
- ADJUSTER
- CABLE ADJUSTMENT POINT
- COMPENSATOR LEVER TO LIE FORWARD APPROX. 15° TO ₵ OF AXLE
- 15°
- 15°
- COMPENSATOR LEVER TO LIE FORWARD APPROX. 15° TO ₵ OF AXLE

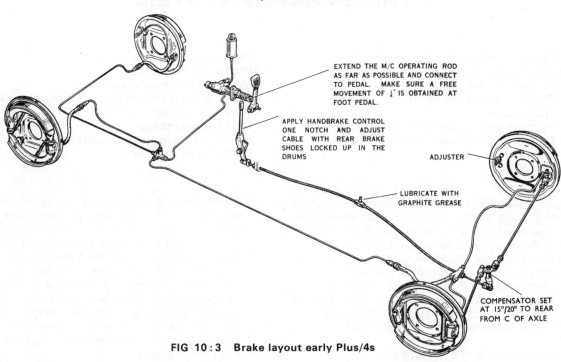

FIG 10:3 Brake layout early Plus/4s

In the figure:
- EXTEND THE M/C OPERATING ROD AS FAR AS POSSIBLE AND CONNECT TO PEDAL. MAKE SURE A FREE MOVEMENT OF ⅛" IS OBTAINED AT FOOT PEDAL.
- APPLY HANDBRAKE CONTROL ONE NOTCH AND ADJUST CABLE WITH REAR BRAKE SHOES LOCKED UP IN THE DRUMS
- ADJUSTER
- LUBRICATE WITH GRAPHITE GREASE
- COMPENSATOR SET AT 15°/20° TO REAR FROM C OF AXLE

6 Refit drums checking for cleanliness beforehand.
7 To ensure the correct clearance between the shoes and the drums, slack off the set pins that hold the adjuster to the backplate one complete turn and lock up brake shoes in the drum by turning the adjuster in a clockwise direction. Bolt up adjuster set pins tightly and slack off adjuster one full notch. Give the brake pedal a firm application to ensure that the shoes have centralized. Drums should not be quite free.
8 Refit road wheels.

Note: **Do not** tighten up the brass expander nut on the outside of the backplate.

Do not remove expander and adjuster housing from backplate.

Do not forget to tighten up firmly adjuster housing set pins.

10:3 Hydraulic brake adjustment

The HLS/S (two leading shoe) brake **(FIG 10:4)** fitted to front wheels is adjusted by a pair of knurled snail cams. Jack up the car (it is recommended to remove the wheels, although this is not essential), and place a spanner on one of the two adjuster nuts and turn in a clockwise direction until the shoe contacts the drum, spin the wheel to ascertain this, then slacken off until the drum is just free, then repeat the process with the second adjuster nut. These nuts are situated fore and aft of each backplate.

Both HW type and HL3 type rear brakes **(FIGS 10:8 and 10:9)** have a single adjuster and this is placed in a forward position on the backplate. To adjust the brakes jack up the car and turn adjuster in a clockwise direction until the shoe contacts the drum, then slacken off one or two notches until the drum is free. There is a

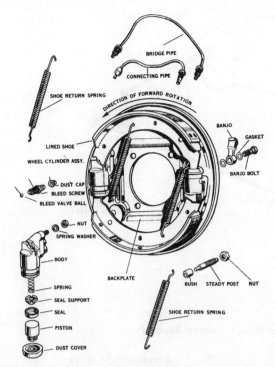

FIG 10 : 4 Exploded view of Girling HLS/S brake

constant drag on the rear wheels due to the action of the differential and axle oil, this should not be confused with brake drag.

10 : 4 Relining hydraulic brakes

The procedure for fitting new brake shoes to hydraulically operated brakes is similar to fitting them to mechanical brakes, but the following precautions should be taken:

1 After removing the original shoes place a rubber band round the pistons to keep them in position.

2 Avoid the use of paraffin, etc., when cleaning down the backplates.

3 When lubricating the moving parts with Girling cleaning fluid, be sure that none comes into contact with any hydraulic component or brake lining.

10 : 5 Disc brakes

In 1959 disc brakes became an optional extra on the Plus/4 **(FIG 10 : 10)** and more recently have become standard fittings on all models. The discs are 11 inches in diameter and the caliper is of the two piece pattern with $\frac{7}{16}$ inch quick detachable pads.

The disc, which is attached to and rotates with the hub, is straddled by the caliper held by two studs on the stub axle flange. On each side the caliper cylinder contains a rubber sealing ring positioned in a groove in the body and a piston protected by a dust cover. Inserted between the piston and the disc is the segmental lining pad bonded to a steel plate which is held in the body by a retainer plate secured by a set bolt and a shakeproof washer.

Upon application of the brake pedal the hydraulic pressure generated in the system causes the co-axially aligned pistons to apply equal and opposite pressure by the friction pads on the rotating disc in direct proportion to the foot effort applied to the pedal.

When the pressure is released and the compression on the disc relieved, the segmental pads and the pistons remain in a relaxed position and ready for the next application. In this manner adjustment for lining wear is automatic and no manual adjustment is required. Pads should be renewed when they are worn to within $\frac{1}{8}$ inch or 3 mm of the pad backing plate.

If the pads are allowed to become thinner than this, there is a danger of transmitting heat to the fluid and causing vaporization during a period of heavy braking.

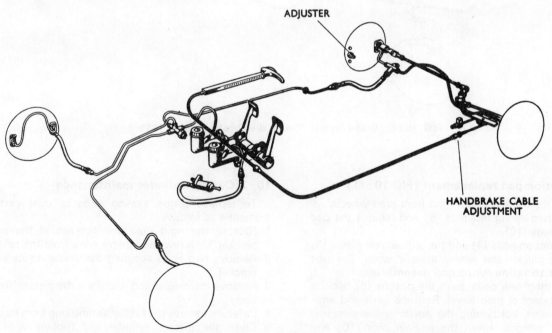

FIG 10 : 5 Hydraulic brake and clutch layout Four/4 Series II

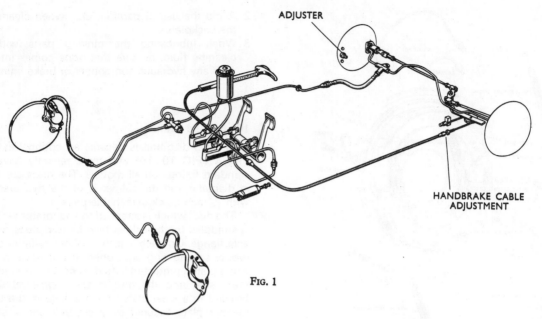

ADJUSTER

HANDBRAKE CABLE
ADJUSTMENT

FIG. 1

FIG 10:6 Hydraulic brake and clutch layout Four/4 Series IV

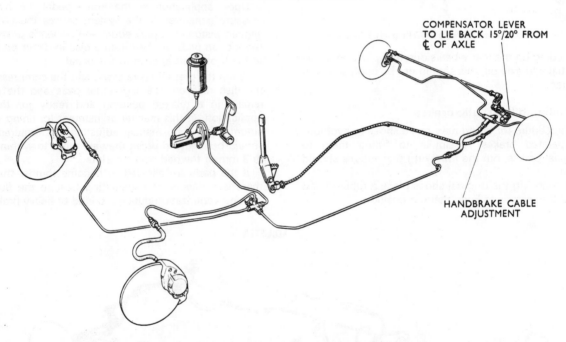

COMPENSATOR LEVER
TO LIE BACK 15°/20° FROM
℄ OF AXLE

HANDBRAKE CABLE
ADJUSTMENT

FIG 10:7 Brake layout Plus/4, disc brake version 1959

10:6 Friction pad replacement (FIG 10:11)

1 Jack up the car and remove the front road wheels.
2 Release two spring retainers (9) and remove the pad retainer pins (10).
3 Lift the friction pads (4) and the anti-squeal plates (5) from the caliper and renew them if worn. **Do not attempt to reline worn pad assemblies.**
4 Before fitting new pads, push the pistons (6) back to the full extent of their travel. Refit the pads and anti-squeal plates, positioning the arrow in the direction of wheel rotation. Insert the retainer pins (10) and secure them with the spring retainer clips (9).

10:7 Caliper cylinder maintenance

To replace piston sealing rings or dust excluders, dismantle as follows:
1 Release the rigid pipe and locknut at the support bracket. Unscrew the flexible hose from the caliper.
2 Remove two bolts securing the caliper to its support bracket.
3 Remove the caliper and withdraw the pistons from the body.
4 Carefully remove the rubber sealing ring from its recess.
5 Clean the piston, cylinder and rubbers with clean brake fluid **only.**

6 Examine all components for serviceability and renew where necessary.

10 : 8 Reassembly

Lubricate the surfaces of the bore and piston with clean brake fluid.

1 Fit a new piston seal into the recess in the cylinder.
2 Locate the projecting lip of the rubber dust excluder in its recess in the cylinder.
3 Insert the piston, closed end leading, into the cylinder, taking care not to damage the polished surface. Push piston fully home and engage the outer lip of the dust excluder with the recess in the piston. Replace the friction pads.
4 Assemble the caliper over the disc, and refit shims between caliper and mounting bracket.
5 Refit the flexible brake hose and bleed the system.

10 : 9 Discs

Maximum permissible run-out on the friction faces of the disc is .002 inch (.0508 mm).

The discs may be machined to a thickness of .440 inch (11.18 mm) to rectify excessive run-out or scored faces. Minimum permissible finish of the disc machining:

15–30 micro inches measured circumferentially.
50 micro inches measured radially.

10 : 10 The handbrake

Adjustment of the rear brake shoes automatically re-adjusts the handbrake mechanism. The handbrake cable can be adjusted for stretch, but must be slack when the brakes are off. The adjustment on early models is on the handbrake lever, but was moved to near the rear axle (**FIG 10 : 13**) on later models. If after adjusting the rear brakes, there is still excessive free play on the handbrake lever, lock up the shoes in the drum, apply the handbrake one notch and remove any slack in the cable by means of the adjuster on the rear end of the cable, ensuring that the handbrake compensator lever is set back approximately 15/20 deg. from the centre line of the rear axle.

10 : 11 The hydraulic system

The Plus/4 has always had hydraulic brakes operated by a master cylinder with a non-integral tank. Four/4 models have only had this system since October 1961: before that time the master cylinder and tank were in one unit, details of this type of layout are to be found in Chapter 5 dealing with the clutch.

10 : 12 Master cylinder—non-integral tank type

The following information holds good for the clutch master cylinder on Four/4 models after October 1961, it is however a $\frac{5}{8}$ inch unit as opposed to a $\frac{3}{4}$ inch unit for the brake.

The operating principal is as follows for all master cylinders fitted to Morgan cars.

When pressure is applied to foot pedal the pushrod contacts the plunger and pushes it up the bore of the cylinder. During the first $\frac{1}{32}$ inch of movement the spring washer fitted under the valve head is allowed to resume its natural 'bowed' shape and closes the port to the supply tank (**FIG 10 : 15**). As the plunger continues to move up the bore, fluid is forced through the pipelines to the wheel cylinders.

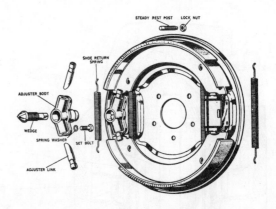

FIG 10 : 8 Exploded view of the Girling type HW rear brake

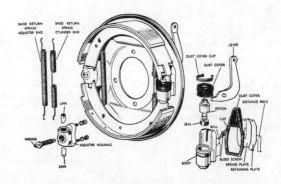

FIG 10 : 9 Exploded view of the Girling type HL3 brake

FIG 10 : 10 Disc-brake on Plus/4 1959

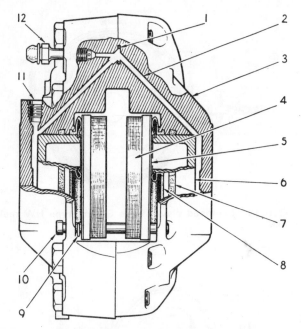

FIG 10:11   Details of caliper assembly

Key to Fig 10:11   1 Rubber 'O' ring   2 Fluid transfer channels   3 Caliper body   4 Brake pad   5 Anti-squeal plate   6 Piston   7 Piston sealing ring   8 Dust cover   9 Retaining clip   10 Retaining pin   11 Flexible hose connection   12 Bleed nipple

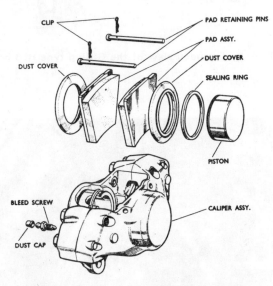

FIG 10:12   Exploded view of disc brake

On the return stroke the plunger moves back with the return of the fluid and the final movement of the plunger compresses the spring washer, lifting the valve seal off its seat and opening the supply tank port **(FIG 10:16)**. The fluid can now move unrestricted between system and tank.

10:13 Servicing

After every 40,000 miles or a period of three years, whichever occurs first, all master cylinders should be replaced by new guaranteed units. However, the cylinders may be serviced at this period when new seals from the

appropriate Girling Service Kit should be fitted, but only if the cylinder plunger bore is in perfect condition.

10:14 Dismantling

Drain the system of fluid by attaching a rubber tube to a wheel cylinder bleed screw, unscrew half a turn and pumping out the fluid by operating the foot pedal. Discard the fluid.

Disconnect the pipe, or pipes, from the cylinder. Unscrew the securing bolts, disconnect the pushrod and remove the cylinder from its mounting. Drain out any surplus fluid by removing the filler cap.

Pull back the rubber dust cover and remove the circlip with a pair of long-nosed pliers. If a diaphragm type of dust cover is fitted, the metal retaining band should be carefully removed without damage. The plunger assembly can now be removed either by shaking the cylinder or by compressed air pressure.

If the seals are loose on the plunger and appear oversize, suspect contamination. Compare the old seals with the new, but do not let them touch. If the old seals are appreciably larger, contamination is indicated and the system should be thoroughly flushed out with Girling Cleaning Fluid and all seals and hoses changed without delay.

Lift the leaf of the spring retainer and remove the spring assembly from the plunger. Compress the spring to free the valve stem from the keyhole of the spring retainer, thus releasing the tension of the spring. Remove the spring, valve spacer and spring washer from the valve stem and the valve seal from the valve head.

Remove the seal from the plunger.

Remove the cap washer from the filler cap.

10:15 Bleeding the hydraulic system

The process of removing air from the pipe line and cylinders is known as 'bleeding' and is necessary whenever any part of the system has been disconnected, or the level of fluid in the supply tank has been allowed to fall so low that air has been drawn into the master cylinder.

When seals are worn it is possible for air to enter the wheel cylinders, without any sign of leaking fluid, and cause a 'spongy' pedal, which is the usual indication of air bubbles in the system.

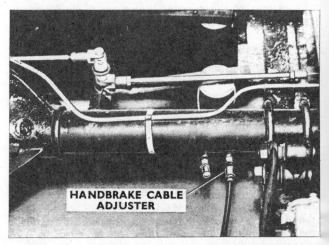

FIG 10:13   Handbrake adjustment Four/4 Series II

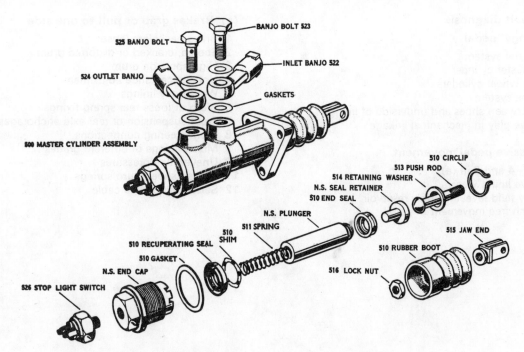

FIG 10:14 Exploded view of early Plus/4 master cylinder

Labels on figure:
525 BANJO BOLT
BANJO BOLT 523
524 OUTLET BANJO
INLET BANJO 522
GASKETS
800 MASTER CYLINDER ASSEMBLY
510 CIRCLIP
513 PUSH ROD
514 RETAINING WASHER
N.S. SEAL RETAINER
510 END SEAL
N.S. PLUNGER
511 SPRING
515 JAW END
510 RECUPERATING SEAL
510 SHIM
510 GASKET
510 RUBBER BOOT
516 LOCK NUT
N.S. END CAP
526 STOP LIGHT SWITCH

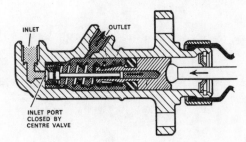

FIG 10:15

(Labels: INLET, OUTLET, INLET PORT CLOSED BY CENTRE VALVE)

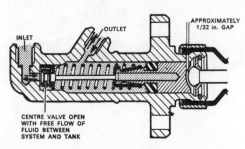

FIG 10:16

(Labels: INLET, OUTLET, APPROXIMATELY 1/32 in. GAP, CENTRE VALVE OPEN WITH FREE FLOW OF FLUID BETWEEN SYSTEM AND TANK)

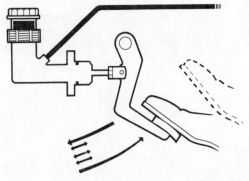

FIG 10:17 Pedal action when bleeding braking system

It is vital that scrupulous cleanliness is maintained throughout the entire bleeding operation. Never use a rag of linty texture and ensure that dirt and grit is not allowed to enter the system—especially at the supply tank.

To prepare the brakes for bleeding the adjusters on front drum brakes should be slackened off (anticlockwise) until against their stops. This will reduce space in the wheel cylinders and economise in time and fluid.

Top up the supply tank direct from a can of unused Castrol-Girling Brake and Clutch Fluid of the recommended grade. Never under any circumstances use fluid which has been bled from a system to top up the supply tank as it may be aerated, have too much moisture content and possibly be contaminated.

Ensure that the supply tank is kept topped up with fluid as it is essential that at no time during the bleeding operation should the fluid reservoir level be allowed to fall to a point where air may be admitted into the hydraulic system via the supply tank.

Bleeding should commence at the rear near side wheel if the vehicle has drum brakes all round; but, if the vehicle has disc front and drum rear brakes the front disc brakes should be bled first, commencing with the front near side wheel.

Unscrew the bleedscrew enough to allow the fluid to be pumped out (half a turn is normally sufficient) and close the bleedscrew immediately after the last downward stroke of the pedal when air bubbles no longer appear. Repeat this procedure at each wheel in turn.

The operation of the brake pedal is most important. The pedal should be pushed down through the full stroke, followed by three short rapid strokes and then the pedal should be allowed to return quickly to its stop by removing the foot from the brake pedal (FIG 10:17) this action should be repeated until the air is dispelled at each bleed screw.

10:16 Fault diagnosis

(a) 'Spongy' pedal

1 Leak in the system
2 Worn master cylinder
3 Leaking wheel cylinders
4 Air in the system
5 Gaps between shoes and underside of linings
6 Excessive play in mechanical linkage

(b) Excessive pedal movement

1 Check 1, 4 and 6 in (a)
2 Excessive lining wear
3 Very low fluid level in supply reservoir
4 Too much free movement of pedal

(c) Brakes grab or pull to one side

1 Brake backplate loose
2 Scored, cracked or distorted drum
3 High spots on drum
4 Unbalanced shoe adjustment
5 Wet or oily linings
6 Worn or loose rear spring fixings
7 Front suspension or rear axle anchorages loose
8 Worn steering connections
9 Mixed linings of different grades
10 Uneven tyre pressures
11 Broken shoe return springs
12 Seized handbrake cable

CHAPTER 11

THE ELECTRICAL SYSTEM

All Morgan 4 wheeler models have been fitted with a 12 volt Lucas electrical system using one 12 volt battery or two 6 volt batteries in series. Wiring diagrams are given in the Technical Data Section to enable those with some electrical experience to trace and correct wiring faults.

Serious mechanical and electrical defects in the generator and starter motor, etc., are best cured by fitting new units on an exchange basis, but instructions for those adjustments which can be made by a reasonably competent engineer have been included in this chapter. To carry out such adjustments to the electrical control gear demands the use of precise measuring instruments. Unreliable instruments will make accurate adjustment impossible.

11 : 1 Earth connection

On early Four/4s the negative battery terminal was connected to earth, but this was reversed before 1939 giving a positive earth system. This continued up to September 1965 for the Plus/4 when again Negative earth was adopted. The Four/4 series reverted to Negative earth with the Four/4 1600 model.

11 : 2 The battery

The battery(ies) used are the lead acid type using dilute sulphuric acid as an electrolyte. The life of a battery is a hard one and it will be considerably shortened by the lack of regular maintenance. An obvious sign of trouble is corrosion of the terminals and surrounding parts. This causes both electrical resistance and electrical leakage. Clean off the corrosion by washing with dilute ammonia then dry the parts and smear the terminal posts with petroleum jelly. Use anti-sulphuric paint on adjacent metal parts such as the battery bolts, the strap, etc. The top of the battery must always be dry and clean. Dampness encourages the spread of corrosion and provides a path for electrical leakage.

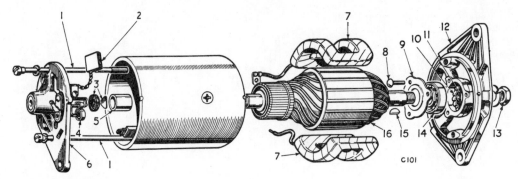

FIG 11:1   Dismantled generator

Key to Fig 11:1   1 Bolts   2 Brush   3 Felt ring and aluminium seal   4 Brush spring   5 Bearing bush   6 Commutator end bracket   7 Field coils   8 Rivet   9 Bearing   retainer plate   10 Corrugated washer   11 Felt washer   12 Driving end bracket   13 Pulley retainer nut   14 Bearing   15 Woodruff key   16 Armature

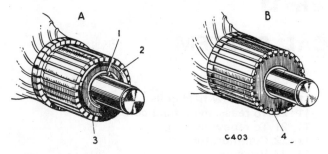

FIG 11:2   Commutator details

Key to Fig 11:2   A—Fabricated commutator   B—Moulded commutator   1 Metal roll-over   2 Insulating cone   3 Slot depth .032 inch (.81 mm) max.   4 Slot depth .02 to .035 inch (.508 to .89 mm)

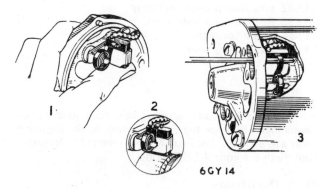

FIG 11:3   Fitting commutator end bracket to 'windowless' yoke generator

Key to Fig 11:3   1 Method of trapping brush in raised position with spring   2 Normal working position   3 Method of releasing brush on to commutator

11:3 The electrolyte

The level must be maintained just above the tops of the separators. Never add acid but top-up with distilled water. The condition of the battery can be checked by measuring the Specific Gravity of the electrolyte in each cell with a hydrometer. The indications are as follows:

For climates below 27°C or 80°F

Cell fully charged   Specific Gravity 1.270 to 1.290
Cell half-discharged   1.190 to 1.210
Cell fully discharged   1.110 to 1.130

These figures are for an electrolyte temperature of 16°C or 60°F. Add .002 to, or subtract .002 from the hydrometer readings for each 3°C or 5°F rise or fall from that temperature.

All six cells should read approximately the same. If one cell differs radically from the rest it may be due to an internal fault or possibly there has been spilling or leakage of the electrolyte. If it has been spilled, add more with the same Specific Gravity. This can be made by adding sulphuric acid to distilled water. It is highly dangerous to add water to acid.

If the battery is in a low state of charge, take the car for a long daylight run or put it on a charger at 4 amps until it gasses freely, taking out the vent plugs and refraining from using a naked light when it is gassing.

If the battery is unused for long periods, give a freshening-up charge every month. Never leave it in a discharged condition.

11:4 Generator—to dismantle

Remove the generator from the engine, extract the driving pulley and take out the woodruff key (15). Remove two bolts and withdraw the commutator end bracket (6) from the yoke **(FIG 11:1)**. Note the fibre thrust washer adjacent to the commutator.

Withdraw the armature (16) and drive end bracket (12) complete with bearing. Support the bearing retaining plate (9) and press the shaft from the drive end bracket.

11:5 Field coils

Renew as follows:

1 Drill out the rivet securing the field terminal assembly to the yoke and unsolder the field coil connections.
2 Remove the insulation piece which prevents the junction of field coils from contacting the yoke.
3 Mark the yoke and pole shoes so that they can be refitted to their original positions.
4 Unscrew the pole shoe retaining screws, remove the pole shoes and lift off the coils.

5 Fit the new field coils over the pole shoes and re-position them inside the yoke.

6 Locate the pole shoes and field coils by lightly tightening the retaining screws; fully tighten them by using a wheel operated screwdriver. Lock the screws by caulking.

7 Replace the insulation piece between the field coil connections and the yoke.

8 Re-solder the field coil connections to the field coil terminal tags and rivet the assembly to the yoke.

11 : 6 Commutator

Burned commutator segments may be caused by an open-circuit in the armature windings. If armature testing facilities are not available, test the armature by substitution.

The commutator should be smooth and free from pits or burned spots. Slight burning may be rectified by careful polishing with a strip of fine glass paper while rotating the armature. To remedy a badly worn commutator, mount the armature, with or without the drive end bracket, in a lathe. Rotate the armature at high speed and take a light cut with a very sharp tool, removing as little metal as is necessary to clean up the commutator. Polish the commutator with very fine glasspaper and undercut the insulators between segments to a depth of $\frac{1}{32}$ inch (0.8 mm), using a hacksaw blade ground to the thickness of the insulator (FIG 11 : 2).

11 : 7 Brushes

Check that the brushes move freely in their holders, by holding back the tension springs and pulling gently on the flexible connectors. If a brush is inclined to stick, remove it from its holder and clean its sides with a petrol-moistened cloth.

Replace the brushes in their original position or renew those which are less than $\frac{11}{32}$ inch (8.7 mm) in length (FIG 11 : 3).

Test the brush spring tension using a spring scale. Fit new springs if the tension is below 15 ozs.

11 : 8 Bearings

Replace the bearing bush in a commutator end bracket as follows:

Remove the old bearing bush from the end bracket by screwing a $\frac{5}{8}$ inch tap squarely into the bush for a few turns and pulling out the bush with the tap.

Insert the felt ring and aluminium disc (3) in the bearing housing and using a shouldered mandrel press the new bearing bush into the end bracket until the bearing is flush with the inner face of the bracket (FIG 11 : 4).

Replace the ballbearing at the driving end as follows:

1 Drill out the rivets (8) and remove the plate (9) (FIG 11 : 1).

2 Press the bearing (14) from the end bracket (12) and remove the corrugated washer (10), felt washer (11) and oil-retaining washer.

3 Clean and pack the replacement bearing with high melting point grease, such as Energrease RBB.3 or equivalent.

4 Place the oil retaining washer, felt washer and corrugated washer in the bearing housing and press in the bearing housing and press in the bearing.

5 Fit and rivet the retaining plate to the end bracket.

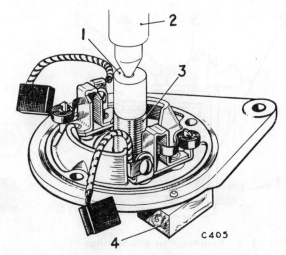

FIG 11 : 4 Fitting a new bearing to the commutator end bracket

Key to Fig 11 : 4   1 Mandrel   2 Press   3 Bush
4 Wood blocks

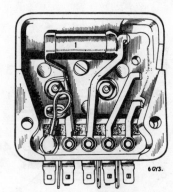

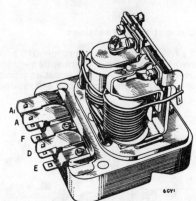

FIG 11 : 5 The voltage regulator and cut-out

11 : 9 Reassembly

1 Supporting the inner journal of the bearing to prevent damage, press the armature through the bearing assembled in the drive end bracket.

2 Assemble the armature and end bracket to the yoke.

3 Hold the brushes up by positioning each brush spring at the side of its brush.

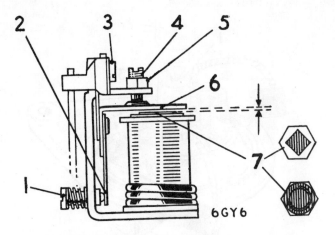

FIG 11 : 6 Regulator air gap settings

Key to Fig 11 : 6 1 Voltage adjusting screw   2 Armature
tension spring   3 Armature securing screws   4 Fixed
contact adjustment screw   5 Locknut   6 Armature
7 Core face and shim

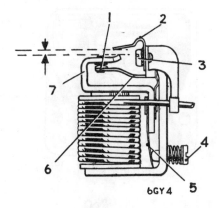

FIG 11 : 7 Cut-out air gap settings

Key to Fig 11 : 7   Follow through .010 to .020 inch
(.254 to .508 mm)   2 Stop arm   3 Armature securing screws
4 Cut-out adjusting screw   5 Armature tension spring
6 Fixed contact blade   7 Armature tongue and moving contact

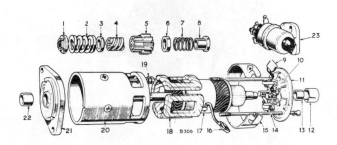

FIG 11 : 8 Dismantled starter motor

Key to Fig 11 : 8   1 Starter drive nut   2 Starter drive spring
3 Thrust washer   4 Screwed sleeve   5 Pinion   6 Thrust
washer   7 Spring   8 Collar   9 Brush   10 Brush spring
11 Commutator end bracket   12 Cover   13 Bush   14 Bolt
15 Brush cover   16 Brush   17 Field coil connection
18 Field coil   19 Terminal   20 Yoke   21 Drive end cover
22 Brush   23 Starter solenoid

4 Fit the commutator end bracket on the armature shaft
until the brush boxes are partly over the commutator.
Press each brush down on the commutator and move
its spring to the operating position.

5 Fit the commutator end bracket to the yoke and refit
the bolts (1).

11 : 10 Control box

The control box shown in **FIG 11 : 5** contains two
units—a voltage regulator and a cut-out. Although
combined structurally, the regulator and cut-out are
electrically separate.

The regulator is set to maintain the generator terminal
voltage between close limits at all speeds above the
regulating point, the field strength being controlled by
the automatic insertion and withdrawal of a resistor in
the generator field circuit.

11 : 11 Cleaning contacts

1 Regulator Contacts—use fine carborundum stone or
silicon carbide paper.

2 Cut-out Relay Contacts—use a strip of fine glasspaper
—never carborundum stone or emery cloth.

11 : 12 Voltage Regulator—electrical setting

It is important that only a good quality MOVING COIL
VOLTMETER (0 to 20 volts) is used when checking the
regulator.

Remove the cover and insert a thin piece of cardboard
between the armature and the core face of the cut-out
to prevent the contacts from closing.

Start the engine and slowly increase its speed until
the generator reaches 3,000 rpm, when the open circuit
voltage reading should be between the appropriate
limits given below according to the ambient temperature.
Open circuit settings:

Ambient Temperatures	Open Circuit Voltages
10°C (50°F)	16.1–16.7
20°C (68°F)	16.0–16.6
30°C (86°F)	15.9–16.5
40°C (104°F)	15.8–16.4

If the voltage, at which the reading becomes steady,
occurs outside these limits, adjust the regulator by
turning the adjusting screw clockwise to raise the
voltage or counter clockwise to lower.

Adjustment of regulator open-circuit voltage should
be completed within 30 seconds otherwise heating of
the shunt windings will cause false settings to be made.

Remove the cardboard.

11 : 13 Voltage regulator—mechanical setting

A copper separator, in the form of a disc or square, is
welded to the core face of the voltage regulator, and
affects the gap setting between the core-face and the
underside of the armature as follows:

Where a round separator is used, the air gap should be
.015 inch (.38 mm).

Where a square separator is used, the air gap should be
.021 inch (.53 mm).

To adjust the air gap.: **(FIG 11 : 6)**.

Slacken the fixed contact locking nut and unscrew
the contact screw until it is well clear of the armature
moving contact.

Slacken the voltage adjustment spring-loaded screw until it is well clear of the armature tension spring.

Slacken the two armature assembly securing screws.

Insert a gauge of sufficient width to cover the core face, and of the appropriate thickness, between the armature and copper separator.

Press the armature squarely down against the gauge and retighten the two armature assembly securing screws. Without removing the gauge, screw in the fixed contact adjustment screw until it just touches the armature contact. Retighten the locking nut.

Recheck the electrical setting of the regulator.

11:14 Cut-out—electrical setting

If the regulator is correctly set but the battery is still not being charged, the cut-out may be out of adjustment. To check the voltage at which the cut-out operates, remove the control box cover and connect the voltmeter between the terminals D and E. (FIG 11:5). Start the engine and slowly increase its speed until the cut-out contacts are seen to close, noting the voltage at which this occurs. This should be 12.7–13.3 volts (FIG 11:7).

If operation of the cut-out takes place outside these limits, it will be necessary to adjust. To do this, turn the adjusting screw in a clockwise direction to raise the voltage setting or in a counter clockwise direction to reduce the setting. Turn the screw only a fraction of a turn at a time and test after each adjustment by increasing the engine speed and noting the voltmeter readings at the instant of contact closure. Electrical settings of the cut-out, like the regulator, must be made as quickly as possible, because of temperature rise effects. Tighten the locknut after making the adjustment. If the cut-out does not operate, there may be an open circuit in the wiring of the cut-out and regulator unit, in which case the unit should be removed for examination or replacement.

11:15 Cut-out relay

Slacken the adjustment screw until it is well clear of the armature tension spring.

Slacken the two armature securing screws.

Press the armature squarely down against the core face (copper sprayed in some units, fit with a square of copper in others) and retighten the armature securing screws. No gauge is necessary.

With the armature still pressed against the core face, adjust the gap between the armature stop arm and the armature tongue to .032 inch (.81 mm) by bending the stop arm.

Adjust the fixed contact blade so that it is deflected .015 inch (.38 mm) by the armature moving contact when the armature is pressed against the core face.

Recheck the electrical setting of the cut-out.

11:16 To remove starter motor

1 Disconnect the cables from the battery and the starter motor.
2 Remove two (or three) bolts, nuts and spring washers securing the starter motor to the cylinder block and clutch housing flanges.

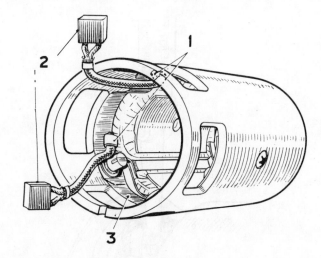

FIG 11:9   Brush connections

Key to Fig 11:9   1 Field coil connections   2 Brushes   3 Yoke

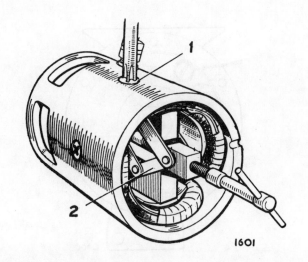

FIG 11:10   Using a pole shoe expander to refit the field coils and retainer screws

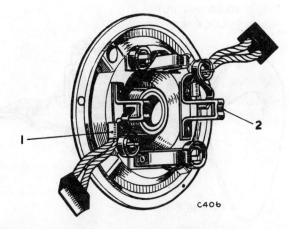

FIG 11:11   Commutator end bracket

Key to Fig 11:11   1 Brush connections   2 Brush boxes

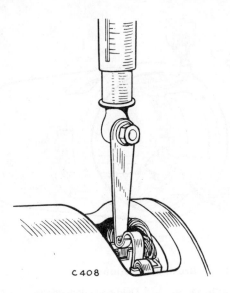

FIG 11:12 Using a spring scale to test the brush spring tension

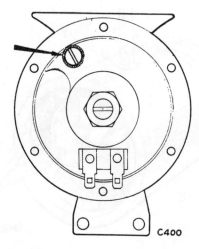

FIG 11:13 Horn adjusting screw (indicated by arrow) on Model 9H Horns.

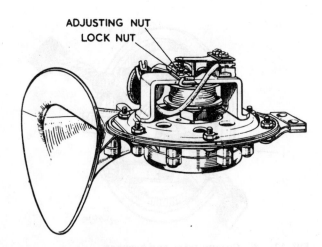

ADJUSTING NUT
LOCK NUT

FIG 11:14 Model WT.614 windtone horn with cover removed as fitted to early Plus/4 cars

3 Withdraw the starter motor from the clutch housing and manoeuvre it out.

11:17 To refit starter motor

Reverse the removal procedure, ensuring that the shoulder on the starter motor bolting face registers correctly with the cylinder block flange face.

Reconnect the cables to the battery and starter motor terminals.

11:18 Dismantling starter motor

Loosen the brush cover screw and slide the cover (15) from the unit. Lift the brush springs (10) and withdraw the brushes (9) from their holders **(FIG 11:8)**.

Unscrew the terminal nuts (19), the two bolts (14) and remove the end bracket (11). Withdraw the drive end bracket (21) and armature from the yoke (20).

Extract the split pin, unscrew the nut (1), removing items 2–8 and slide the drive end bracket (21) from the shaft.

Reassembly—reverse the dismantling procedure.

11:19 To renew field coils

Unscrew the four-pole-shoe retaining screws, using a wheel operated screwdriver and pole expander tool for obstinate cases.

Mark the yoke and pole-shoes so that they can be refitted to their original positions.

Take out the pole-shoes, lift off the coils and unsolder the field coil tappings from the terminal post.

Fit new field coils by reversing the procedure, and replace the insulating pieces used to prevent the inter coil connectors from contacting the yoke.

11:20 To reassemble field coils.

Assemble the components 1 to 8 in order shown on **FIG 11:8** and secure the retaining nut (1) with a splitpin.

11:21 To renew bearings

Using a shouldered mandrel of the same diameter as the shaft, drive out the old bush and press the new bearing bush into the end bracket.

The bronze bushes are porous and must not be opened out after fitting, otherwise the porosity of the bush may be impaired.

11:22 Commutator

A commutator in good condition is clean, smooth and free from pits or burned spots. If cleaning with a petrol-moistened cloth is ineffective, carefully polish the commutator with very fine glasspaper while the armature is rotating. Do not use emery cloth.

To rectify a badly worn commutator, mount the armature in a lathe, rotate at high speed and take a light cut with a sharp tool, removing the minimum of metal to obtain a clean finish. Finally, polish with very fine glasspaper.

Note: Do not undercut the mica insulators between segments.

11:23 Brushes

Check that the brushes move freely on their holders by

holding back the brush springs and pulling gently on the flexible connectors. If a brush is inclined to stick, remove it from its holder and release its sides with a smooth file.

Replace the brushes in their original positions or renew excessively worn brushes as follows:

Cut off the original brush flex $\frac{1}{8}$ inch (3 mm) approximately from the aluminium and tin the brazed joint. Open out the loop, taking care not to allow solder to run towards the brush.

Place the original joint within the loop, squeeze up and solder. The brushes are preformed so that bedding to the commutator is unnecessary.

11 : 24 Starter drive

When the starter motor is removed from the engine, check the pinion for cleanliness and freedom of action. If necessary wash the drive assembly in paraffin to remove dirt and grease, which is the usual cause of a sticking pinion. Do not lubricate the components.

11 : 25 To dismantle

Extract the split pin (FIG 11 : 8), unscrew the retaining nut (1), and slide the components 2-8 from the starter armature shaft.

11 : 26 Wind tone horns, model 9H

Lucas miniature wind tone horns, model 9H operate on the principle of a resonating air column vibrated by a diaphragm, actuated electro-magnetically by a self-interrupting circuit. The horns are intended to be sounded in matched pairs, each pair consisting of a high note and a low note horn—the notes differing by a definite musical interval.

11 : 27 Maintenance

If a horn fails to sound or its performance is unsatisfactory, check the following and rectify as necessary:
1 Battery condition.
2 Loose or broken connection in the horn circuit.
3 Loose fixing bolts.

If the above points are in order, adjust the horn as follows:

11 : 28 Adjustment

Adjustment does not alter the pitch of the note but merely takes up the wear of moving parts.

Disconnect one horn whilst adjusting the other, and take care to avoid earthing disconnected live wires. Connect a first grade moving-coil 0–10A ammeter in series with the horn and adjust the small serrated adjustment screw on the side of the horn at which the cables terminate.

Turn the adjusting screw (FIG 11 : 13) clockwise to increase the current, or anticlockwise to decrease it, until the best performance is obtained with the least current.

If adjustment is being made without an ammeter, turn the adjusting screws anticlockwise until the horn just fails to sound; then turn it back one quarter of a turn. *Warning:* Do not disturb the central slotted stem and locking nut.

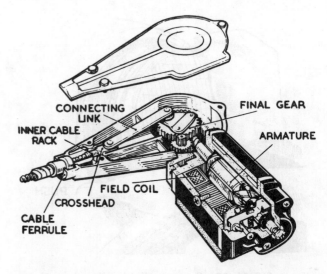
FIG 11 : 15 Wiper motor cutaway with gearbox cover removed (CRT 15)

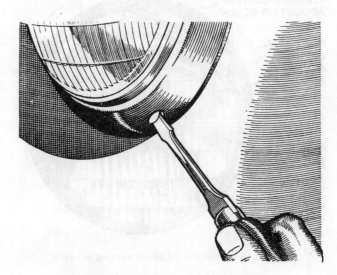
FIG 11 : 16 Removing lamp ring

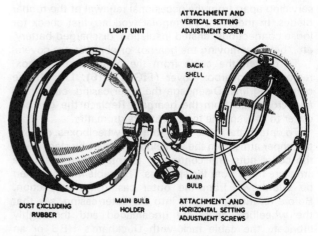
FIG 11 : 17 Diagramatic view of bulb position

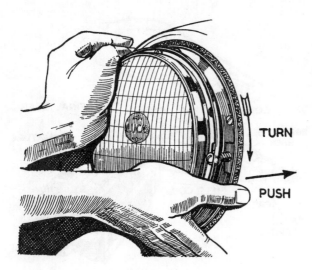

FIG 11:18 Replacing light unit

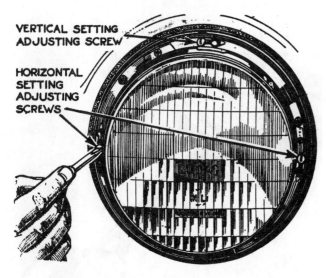

VERTICAL SETTING ADJUSTING SCREW

HORIZONTAL SETTING ADJUSTING SCREWS

FIG 11:19 Position of beam setting screws

11:29 Windscreen wiper CRT15

Normally the windscreen wiper will not require any servicing apart from the occasional renewal of the rubber blades. In the event of irregular working, first check for loose connections, chafed insulation, discharged battery, etc., before removing the gearbox or commutator covers.

To detach the cable from the motor and gearbox, remove the gearbox cover (FIG 11:15). Lift off the connecting link. Disengage the outer casing, cable rack and crosshead from the gearbox. Replace the gearbox cover to prevent the ingress of foreign matter.

To detach the cable rack from the wheelboxes, remove the wiper arms from the wheelbox spindles by slackening the collet nuts and continuing to rotate them until the arms are freed from the spindles. The cable rack can then be withdrawn from the outer casing for inspection. Before refitting the cable into the outer casing, see that the wheelbox gears are undamaged and thoroughly lubricate the cable rack with Duckham's HBB or an equivalent grease.

Inspection of commutator; disconnect the wiper at its terminals and withdraw the three screws securing the cover at the commutator end. Lift off the cover and clean the commutator, using a petrol-moistened cloth, taking care to remove any carbon dust from between the commutator segments.

Inspection of brush gear; check that the brushes bear freely on the commutator. If they are loose or do not make contact, a replacement tension spring is necessary. The brush levers must be free on their pivots. If they are stiff, they should be freed by working them backwards and forwards. Brushes which are considerably worn must be replaced.

If the motor operates but does not transmit motion to spindles, remove the gearbox cover. A push-pull motion should be transmitted to the inner cable of the flexible rack. If the crosshead moves sluggishly between the guides, lightly smear a small amount of medium grade engine oil in the groove formed in the die-cast housing.

When overhauling, the gearbox must be lubricated by packing it with a grease of the zinc oxide base type.

11:30 To remove headlamp bulb

1 Remove the screw securing the front rim to the headlamp unit (FIG 11:16).
2 Remove the dust excluding cover to expose the three-spring-loaded adjustment screws (FIG 11:19).
3 Press the light unit inwards against the tension of the adjusting spring and turn it in an anticlockwise direction until the heads of the screws can be disengaged through the slotted holes in the light unit rim. *Note:* Do not disturb the screws as this will alter the lamp setting.

11:31 To replace headlamp bulb

1 Install the replacement bulb in the holder, taking care to locate it correctly (FIG 11:17).
2 Engage the projections on the inside of the adaptor with the slots in the holder, press on and secure by twisting in a clockwise direction.
3 Position the light unit so that the heads of the adjustment screws protrude through the slotted holes in the flange, press the unit in and turn in a clockwise direction (FIG 11:18).
4 Replace the dust-excluding cover and refit the front rim.

11:32 Headlamp beam setting

The lamps should be set so that the main driving beams are straight ahead and parallel to one another, and parallel to the road surface. If adjustment to the setting is required, first remove the front rim and rubber as previously described. Set each lamp to the correct position in the vertical plane by means of the vertical adjustment screw at the top of the reflector unit (FIG 11:19). Turn the screw in a clockwise direction to raise the beam and in an antickockwise direction to lower it. Horizontal adjustment can be altered by turning the adjustment screws on each side of the light unit.

The setting of the lamps can best be carried out by placing the car in front of a blank wall at the greatest possible distance, taking care that the surface on which the car is standing is level and not sloping relative to the wall.

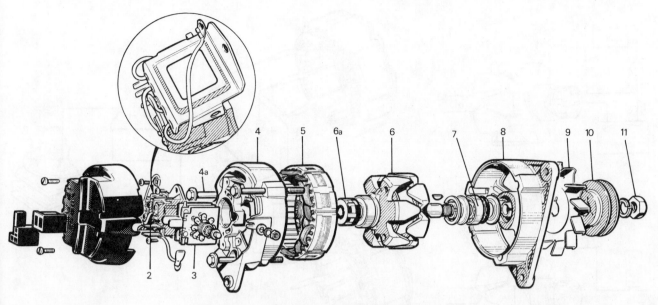

FIG 11:20   Components of type 15ACR alternator

Key to Fig 11:20   1 Plastic cover   2 Brushgear   3 Rectifier   4 Slip ring end bracket   4a Long bolt   5 Stator
6 Rotor   6a Slip ring moulding   7 Bearing   8 Drive end bracket   9 Fan   10 Pulley   11 Pulley nut

It will be found an advantage to cover one lamp while setting the other.

11:33   Replacing a light unit

In the event of damage to either the front lens or reflector, a replacement light unit must be fitted as follows:

1 Remove the light unit as already described.
2 Withdraw the three screws from the unit rim and remove the seating rim and unit rim from the light unit.
3 Position the replacement light unit between the unit rim and setting rim, taking care to see that the die-cast projection at the edge of the light unit fits into the slot in the seating rim, and also check that the seating rim is correctly positioned. Finally secure in position by means of the three fixing screws.
Note: In certain instances a sealed beam unit is fitted in place of the Lucas light unit.

11:34   The alternator

The C40L generator has been replaced on later Four/four engines with a Lucas 15 ACR alternator of 28 amp output, incorporating a built in regulator. This three phase alternator is much lighter than the DC generator it replaces and has a much higher output at lower engine revolution.

The well ventilated rotor is carried at each end on ball bearings which are lubricated for life. Two aluminium die-cast mounting brackets house the stator and rotor to form the main structure of the machine.

If you suspect the alternator, before carrying out any dismantling make sure that all connections are firm, clean and free from corrosion.

Overhauling the alternator:
Removal:

1 Disconnect the battery and unplug the leads at the rear of the alternator.

2 Slacken the three securing bolts and tilt the alternator towards the engine to remove the fan belt.
3 Remove the securing bolts and lift off the alternator. Refit in the reverse order, ensuring that the fan belt has $\frac{1}{2}$ inch (13 mm) free movement at a point midway between the alternator and fan pulleys.

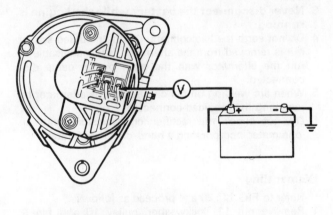

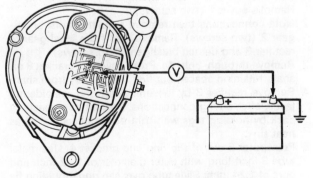

FIG 11:21   Alternator voltage drop tests

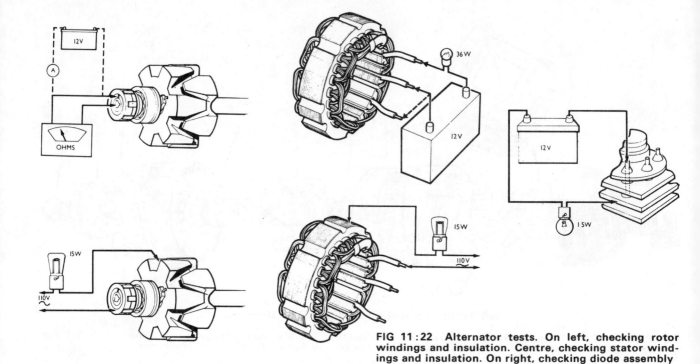

FIG 11:22 Alternator tests. On left, checking rotor windings and insulation. Centre, checking stator windings and insulation. On right, checking diode assembly

Precautions:

It is essential to be aware of the following important points when dealing with an alternator:
1 Alternator is used with negative earth only.
2 Refit battery by first connecting the negative battery terminal to the earthing strap and then fitting the positive lead.
3 **Never disconnect the battery while the engine is running.**
4 Do not earth the live connector in the moulded socket if it is removed from the alternator. It is inadvisable to run the alternator with the main output cable disconnected.
5 When arc welding on the car, isolate the alternator by removing the moulded connectors.
6 Do not check the rectifier or transistors with an ohmmeter incorporating a hand-driven generator.

Dismantling:

Refer to **FIG 11:20** and proceed as follows:
1 Remove nut 11, lockwasher, pulley 10 and fan 9. Remove cover 1 (two screws).
2 Note connections then remove regulator from brushgear 2 (two screws). Remove lead from brushgear to rectifier 3 and detach brushgear (two screws).
3 Remove through-bolts 4a. Press drive end bracket 8 off shaft, retaining spacer, but first remove key from shaft.
4 Remove rectifier 3 by loosening nut and unsoldering leads, after noting connections. Prevent heat reaching pack by holding tags with thin-nosed pliers, to act as heat sink.
5 Press rotor 6 out of slip ring end bracket 4. Use metal tube 3 inch long with outer diameter of 1.32 inch and bore of 1.24 inch. Slide tube over slip ring moulding 6a and use it to drive the outer race of the bearing from its housing.

6 If necessary, unsolder field connections from slip ring moulding and withdraw moulding. Pull off bearing if renewal is required.
7 Carefully prise stator 5 out of bracket 4. Remove circlip from bracket 8 to remove bearing 7. Note order of grease seal assembly.

Testing and adjusting charging circuit:

When the charging circuit appears to be faulty, first check that the fan belt is not slipping. Ensure that the battery is in good condition as outlined in **Sections 11:2** and **11:3**. Carry out further tests as follows:

Voltage drop test:

1 Refer to **FIG 11:21**. Connect a low-range voltmeter to positive terminal of battery and positive terminal on alternator (top view). Voltmeter must be high-grade moving coil instrument with a scale suitable for readings of .25 volt.
2 Switch on headlamps (main beam) and start engine. Run at about 3000 rev/min. If meter reads in excess of .5 volt, there is a high resistance in the positive side of the charging circuit.
3 Repeat test with negative connections (lower view). If meter reading exceeds .25 volt there is a high resistance in the negative side of the charging circuit.
4 Check for high resistance due to loose, dirty or corroded connectors. These must be clean and tight.

Rotor tests:

1 Refer to both lefthand views in **FIG 11:22**. Connect ohmmeter between slip rings of rotor (top view). Resistance should be 4.3 ohms. Alternatively, use a 12-volt battery and ammeter in series. Reading should be approximately 2.8 amp.

2 Test insulation with 110-volt AC supply and 15 watt lamp (lower view). Connect between one of slip rings and a rotor pole. Coil is earthed to rotor if lamp lights. Fit new rotor.

Stator tests:

1 Refer to central views in **FIG 11 : 22**. Test continuity of windings as in top view. Connect any two of the three stator cables across a 12-volt battery and test lamp taking not less than 36 watts. Repeat, replacing one of the two cables with the third. Failure of lamp to light means a break in part of the stator winding. Renew the stator.

2 Test insulation with 110-volt AC supply and 15 watt test lamp. Connect between one of stator cables and laminations (lower view). Lamp will light if coils are earthed. Renew stator.

Diode tests:

1 Refer to single view on right in **FIG 11 : 22**. If alternator output test indicates a fault in one or more of the diodes, remove the rectifier from the alternator (see under 'Dismantling').

2 Connect each of the nine diode pins in turn, in series with a 1.5 watt test bulb and one side of a 12-volt battery. Connect the other battery terminal to the particular heat sink into which the diode is soldered.

3 Now reverse the connections to the diode pin and the heat sink. The bulb should light in one test only.

4 If the bulb lights in both tests, or not in either, fit a new rectifier.

Reassembling:

This is mainly a matter of reversing the dismantling instructions. Having fitted the brushgear, check the brush springs by placing new brushes in their holders. Press down until the brushes are flush with the holder, using a spring compression scale. The scale should read 7 to 10 oz. The Ford tool No. for the scale is CP.9501.

When soldering the leads onto the rectifier, use thin-nosed pliers as a heat sink to prevent soldering heat from reaching the rectifier.

Fit the drive end bearing after packing with suitable grease. The slip ring end bearing is fitted to the rotor shaft with its shielded side facing the rotor. Then re-engage the slip ring moulding with the slot on the rotor shaft and resolder the field connections.

Fit the stator into the slip ring end bracket, ensuring that the slots in the stator line up with the through holes for the bolts.

11 : 35 Fault diagnosis

(a) Battery discharged

1 Terminals loose or dirty
2 Lighting circuit shorted
3 Generator not charging
4 Regulator or cut-out units not working properly
5 Battery internally defective

(b) Insufficient charging current

1 Loose or corroded battery terminals
2 Generator driving belt slipping

(c) Battery will not hold a charge

1 Low electrolyte level
2 Battery plates sulphated
3 Electrolyte leakage from cracked casing or top sealing compound
4 Plate separators ineffective

(d) Battery overcharged

1 Voltage regulator needs adjusting

(e) Generator output low or nil

1 Belt broken or slipping
2 Regulator unit out of adjustment
3 Worn bearings, loose pole pieces
4 Commutator worn, burned or shorted
5 Armature shaft bent or worn
6 Insulation proud between commutator segments
7 Brushes sticking, springs weak or broken
8 Field coil wires shorted, broken or burned

(f) Starter motor lacks power or will not operate

1 Battery discharged, loose cable connections
2 Starter pinion jammed in mesh with flywheel gear
3 Starter switch faulty
4 Brushes worn or sticking, leads detached or shorting
5 Commutator dirty or worn
6 Starter shaft bent
7 Engine abnormally stiff

(g) Starter motor runs but does not turn engine

1 Pinion sticking on screwed sleeve
2 Broken teeth on pinion or flywheel gears

(h) Noisy starter pinion when engine is running

1 Restraining spring weak or broken

(j) Starter motor inoperative

1 Check 1 and 4 in (f)
2 Armature or field coils faulty

(k) Starter motor rough or noisy

1 Mounting bolts loose
2 Damaged pinion or flywheel gear teeth
3 Main pinion spring broken

(l) Lamps inoperative or erratic

1 Battery low, bulbs burned out
2 Faulty earthing of lamps or battery
3 Lighting switch faulty, loose or broken wiring connections

(m) Wiper motor sluggish, taking high current

1 Faulty armature
2 Bearings out of alignment
3 Commutator dirty or short-circuited
4 Commutator brushes worn or sticking
5 Wheelbox spindle binding, cable rack tight in housing

(n) Wiper motor operates but does not drive arms

1 Wheelbox gear and spindle worn
2 Cable rack faulty
3 Gearbox components worn

(o) Fuel gauge does not register

1 No battery supply to gauge
2 Gauge casing not earthed
3 Cable between gauge and tank unit earthed

(p) Fuel gauge registers 'FULL'

1 Cable between gauge and tank unit broken or disconnected

CHAPTER 12

BODYWORK

The first Morgan four wheeler was introduced in 1936 with a two seater body. The following year a four seater version was made available and in 1938 a coupe was added to the range. Two of these three styles have remained in one form or another to date. Late in 1953 the two seater body style changed, the radiator was replaced by a sloping cowl at the front and the headlamps became in-built. The coupe and four seater model adopted these changes soon afterwards. The Four/4 was re-introduced in October 1955 with a body similar to the Plus/4 but with a scuttle lower by $2\frac{1}{2}$ inches and other small variations. In September 1957 the Plus/4s frontal appearance was altered slightly by the extension of the cowl downwards by 3 inches and by curtailing the depth of the grille by a like amount, also the two and four seater body sides were 'pushed-out' which gave 4 inches more width internally and increased the screen width by 2 inches. The most radical change in Morgan bodywork took place in 1963 when the Plus/4/Plus was introduced. This was a Plus/4 chassis with a fibre-glass two seater body, and about 60 were produced.

In October 1968 the Plus/4 four seater was replaced by the Four/4 four seater. The car is similar in most respects to the two seater version but has the rear part of the body reshaped to accommodate the extra seats.

As the drophead coupé body was never offered on the Four/4, this style ceased to be available when the Plus/4 was discontinued in January 1969.

12:1 Body removal

The body of the Four/4 Series I was removed by first taking away the pedal board and disconnecting the wiring. Removing the seven body bolts each side and undoing the clip under the dash to the steering column, the body was then free to be lifted clear. To remove the body from the chassis of the early Plus/4, disconnect batteries (two-seater and coupé, behind seat) or remove battery (four-seater, on scuttle). Remove front wings (stay bolts, bolts to bonnet valances, below running boards and to rear wings). Separate body trim from floorboards (tacks) and propeller shaft tunnel from heelboard (which is part of body). Take out woodscrews along lower edge of heelboard. Detach trim panel behind seats. Disconnect all pipes, wires and controls, and remove spare wheels. Draw off steering wheel and remove column. Disconnect petrol pipe from pump, and tie up to stop syphoning if tank is full. Take out seven bolts each side holding scuttle to valances and cross-member, and eight coachbolts each side holding body to top flanges of frame.

Instrument and switch wiring can be reached from underneath, but for complete access facia panel must be detached. Instrument panel, screwed to back of facia panel, need not be separated. Draw off steering wheel disconnect speedo drive and oil gauge pipe, and take out four screws holding panel to body (on coupé, panel is

FIG 12:1   Post-war Four/4 Series I Four seater

FIG 12:2   Plus/4 Coupé. Pre-Sept. 1957. Note narrow cowl

FIG 12:3   Plus/4 Two seater (1959)

held by bracket below each end with two screws). Draw panel over steering column, taking care not to strain water temperature gauge pipe.

12 : 2 Hood

When erecting the hood, always fix the eyelets in the back curtain over the turn-buttons first and then fix snaps across the top of the windscreen. If secured at the front first some strain will be necessary to pull the eyelets over the eyes, which in time will pull away from the fabric.

However, it is recommended that if the hood is tight when dismantling it is advisable to release it at the rear which avoids straining at the eyelets.

It is not intended that the tonneau cover over the rear compartment should remain in position when the hood is up as the turn-buttons do not allow for the double thickness, and unnecessary strain is placed on the hood fabric and turn-buttons alike.

When standing and rain is imminent it may be noted that the loose hood top makes a useful tonneau cover if fitted in the usual way without erecting the hood frame.

12 : 3 Side curtains

It should be remembered that Vybak is easily scratched and soiled, spoiling vision at the sides. When not in use, therefore, do not throw the side curtains carelessly into the rear compartment or they may move about and become damaged.

NOTES

APPENDIX

LUBRICATION DIAGRAMS

        Four/4 Series I
        Four/4 Series II
        Four/4 Series IV and V
        Plus/4

WIRING DIAGRAMS

        Four/4 Series I (1936)
        Four/4 Series I (1939)
        Four/4 Series I Coupé (1939)
        Four/4 Series I (1946-47)
        Plus/4 (1950-51)
        Plus/4 and Four/4 Series I (1956)
        Plus/4 and Four/4 Series II (1960)
        Plus/4 and Four/4 Series IV (1961-62)
        Plus/4 (1965 onwards)

TECHNICAL DATA

        Engine   Ignition system
        Carburetter details   Gearbox and rear axle
        Electrical   Cooling system
        Front suspension and steering   Dimensions

HINTS ON MAINTENANCE AND OVERHAUL

GLOSSARY OF TERMS

METRIC CONVERSION TABLE

NOTES

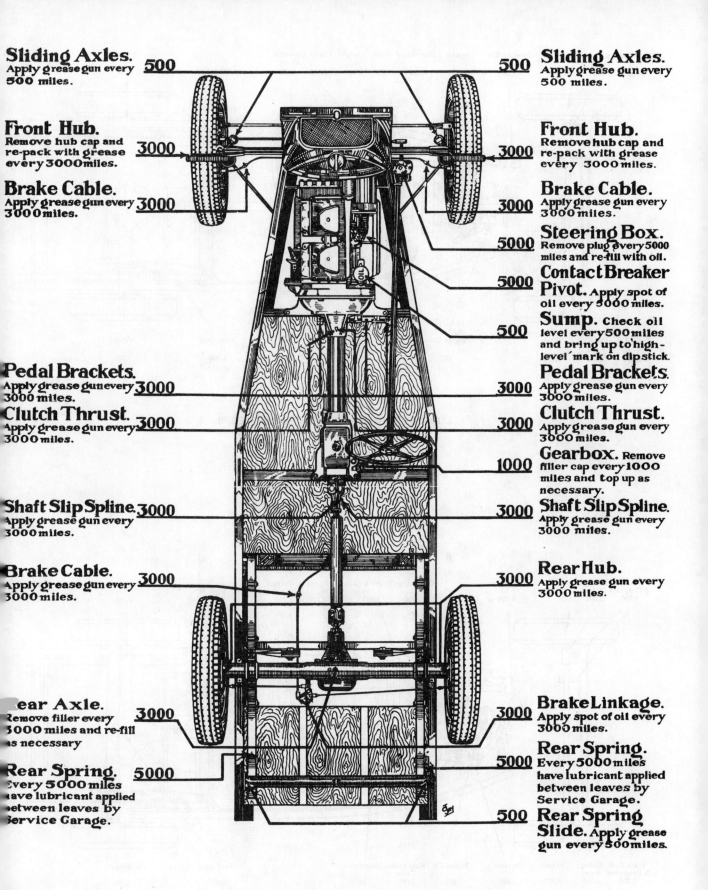

Sliding Axles.
Apply grease gun every 500 miles. — 500

Front Hub. Remove hub cap and re-pack with grease every 3000 miles. — 3000

Brake Cable. Apply grease gun every 3000 miles. — 3000

Pedal Brackets. Apply grease gun every 3000 miles. — 3000

Clutch Thrust. Apply grease gun every 3000 miles. — 3000

Shaft Slip Spline. Apply grease gun every 3000 miles. — 3000

Brake Cable. Apply grease gun every 3000 miles. — 3000

Rear Axle. Remove filler every 3000 miles and re-fill as necessary — 3000

Rear Spring. Every 5000 miles have lubricant applied between leaves by Service Garage. — 5000

500 — **Sliding Axles.** Apply grease gun every 500 miles.

3000 — **Front Hub.** Remove hub cap and re-pack with grease every 3000 miles.

3000 — **Brake Cable.** Apply grease gun every 3000 miles.

5000 — **Steering Box.** Remove plug every 5000 miles and re-fill with oil.

5000 — **Contact Breaker Pivot.** Apply spot of oil every 5000 miles.

500 — **Sump.** Check oil level every 500 miles and bring up to 'high-level' mark on dipstick.

3000 — **Pedal Brackets.** Apply grease gun every 3000 miles.

3000 — **Clutch Thrust.** Apply grease gun every 3000 miles.

1000 — **Gearbox.** Remove filler cap every 1000 miles and top up as necessary.

3000 — **Shaft Slip Spline.** Apply grease gun every 3000 miles.

3000 — **Rear Hub.** Apply grease gun every 3000 miles.

3000 — **Brake Linkage.** Apply spot of oil every 3000 miles.

5000 — **Rear Spring.** Every 5000 miles have lubricant applied between leaves by Service Garage.

500 — **Rear Spring Slide.** Apply grease gun every 500 miles.

**LUBRICATION CHART FOUR/4 SERIES I
LUBRICATE AT MILEAGE SHOWN**

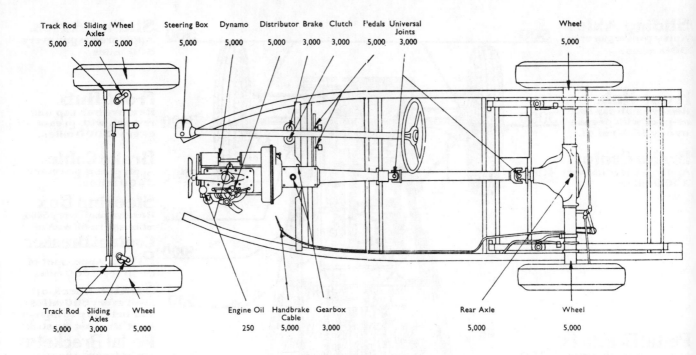

LUBRICATION CHART FOUR/4 SERIES II
LUBRICATE AT MILEAGE SHOWN

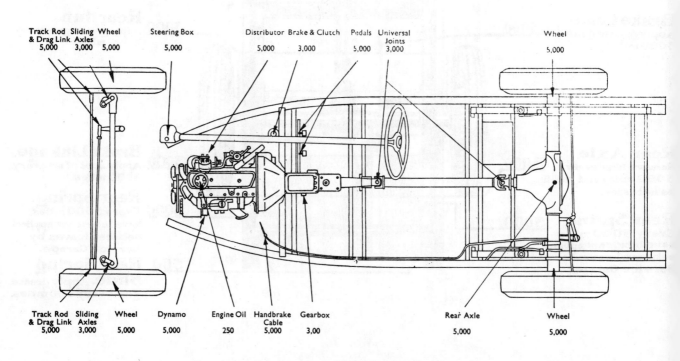

LUBRICATION CHART FOUR/4 SERIES IV and V
LUBRICATE AT MILEAGE SHOWN

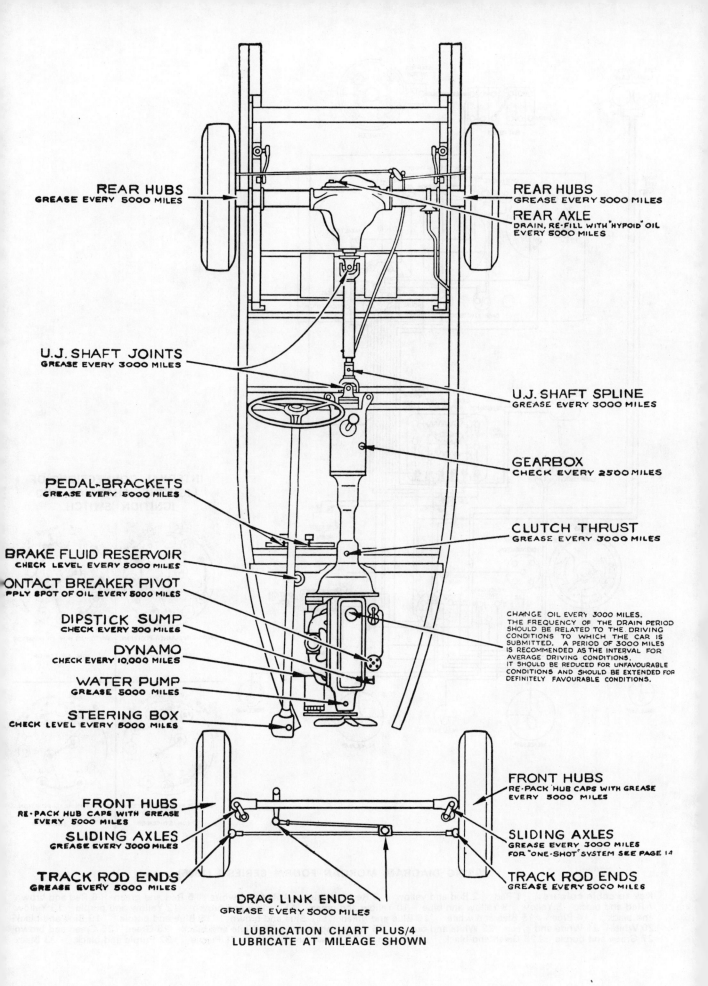

REAR HUBS
GREASE EVERY 5000 MILES

REAR HUBS
GREASE EVERY 5000 MILES

REAR AXLE
DRAIN, RE-FILL WITH "HYPOID" OIL
EVERY 5000 MILES

U.J. SHAFT JOINTS
GREASE EVERY 3000 MILES

U.J. SHAFT SPLINE
GREASE EVERY 3000 MILES

GEARBOX
CHECK EVERY 2500 MILES

PEDAL-BRACKETS
GREASE EVERY 5000 MILES

CLUTCH THRUST
GREASE EVERY 3000 MILES

BRAKE FLUID RESERVOIR
CHECK LEVEL EVERY 5000 MILES

ONTACT BREAKER PIVOT
PPLY SPOT OF OIL EVERY 5000 MILES

DIPSTICK SUMP
CHECK EVERY 300 MILES

DYNAMO
CHECK EVERY 10,000 MILES

WATER PUMP
GREASE 5000 MILES

STEERING BOX
CHECK LEVEL EVERY 5000 MILES

CHANGE OIL EVERY 3000 MILES.
THE FREQUENCY OF THE DRAIN PERIOD
SHOULD BE RELATED TO THE DRIVING
CONDITIONS TO WHICH THE CAR IS
SUBMITTED. A PERIOD OF 3000 MILES
IS RECOMMENDED AS THE INTERVAL FOR
AVERAGE DRIVING CONDITIONS.
IT SHOULD BE REDUCED FOR UNFAVOURABLE
CONDITIONS AND SHOULD BE EXTENDED FOR
DEFINITELY FAVOURABLE CONDITIONS.

FRONT HUBS
RE-PACK HUB CAPS WITH GREASE
EVERY 5000 MILES

FRONT HUBS
RE-PACK HUB CAPS WITH GREASE
EVERY 5000 MILES

SLIDING AXLES
GREASE EVERY 3000 MILES

SLIDING AXLES
GREASE EVERY 3000 MILES
FOR "ONE-SHOT" SYSTEM SEE PAGE 14

TRACK ROD ENDS
GREASE EVERY 5000 MILES

TRACK ROD ENDS
GREASE EVERY 5000 MILES

DRAG LINK ENDS
GREASE EVERY 5000 MILES

LUBRICATION CHART PLUS/4
LUBRICATE AT MILEAGE SHOWN

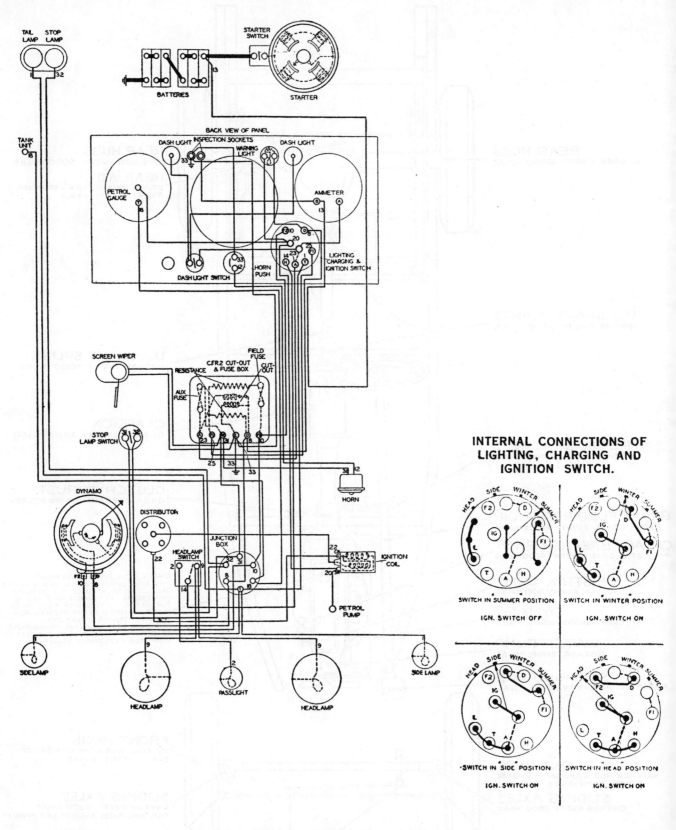

WIRING DIAGRAM MORGAN FOUR/4 SERIES I (1936)

Key to cable colours: 1 Red   2 Red and yellow   3 Red and blue   4 Red and white   5 Red and green   6 Red and brown
7 Red and black   8 Yellow   9 Yellow and blue   10 Yellow and green   11 Yellow and brown   12 Yellow and purple   13 Yellow
and black   14 Blue   15 Blue and white   16 Blue and green   17 Blue and brown   18 Blue and purple   19 Blue and black
20 White   21 White and green   22 White and brown   23 White and purple   24 White and black   25 Green   26 Green and brown
27 Green and purple   28 Green and black   29 Brown   30 Brown and purple   31 Purple   32 Purple and black   33 Black

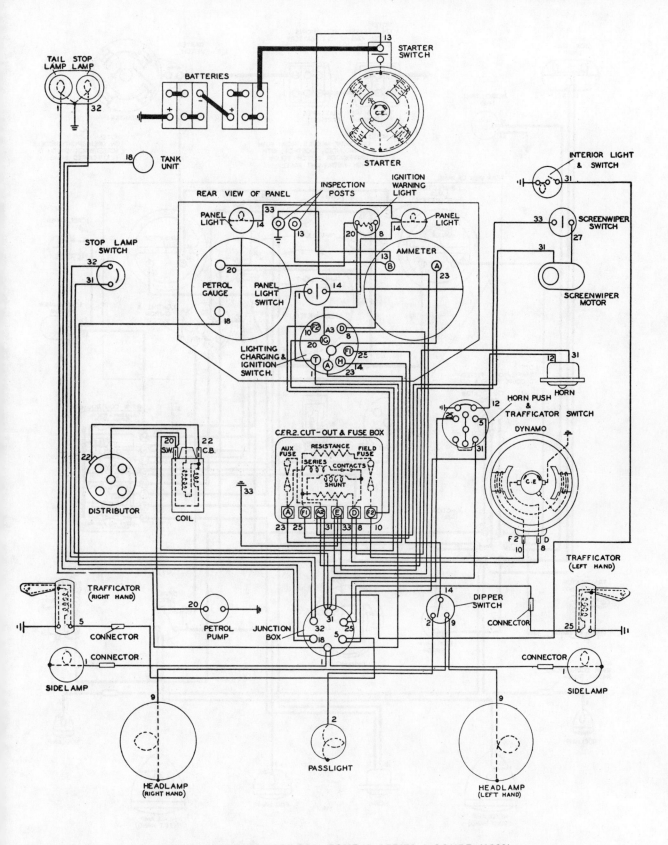

WIRING DIAGRAM MORGAN FOUR/4 SERIES I COUPE (1939)

Key to cable colours : 1 Red   2 Red and yellow   3 Red and blue   4 Red and white   5 Red and green   6 Red and brown
7 Red and black   8 Yellow   9 Yellow and blue   10 Yellow and green   11 Yellow and brown   12 Yellow and purple   13 Yellow
and black   14 Blue   15 Blue and white   16 Blue and green   17 Blue and brown   18 Blue and purple   19 Blue and black
20 White   21 White and green   22 White and brown   23 White and purple   24 White and black   25 Green   26 Green and brown
27 Green and purple   28 Green and black   29 Brown   30 Brown and purple   31 Purple   32 Purple and black   33 Black

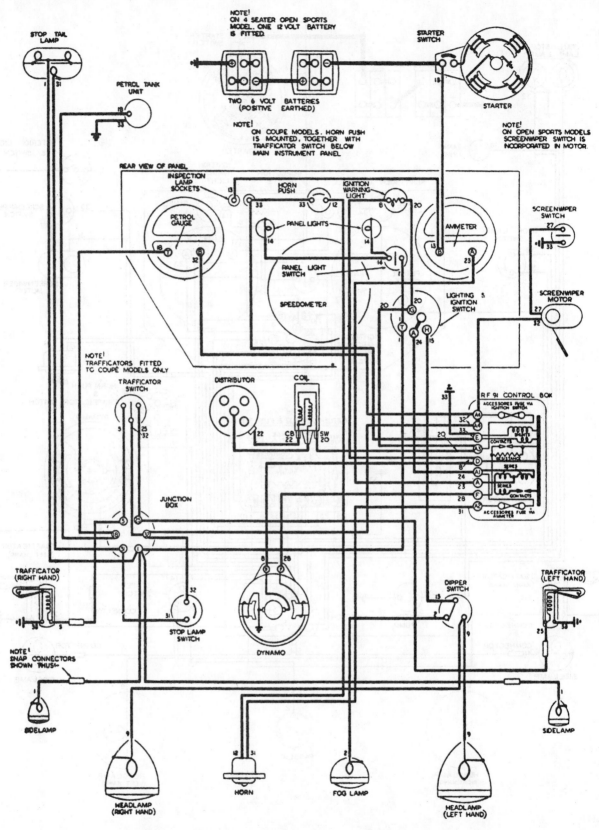

WIRING DIAGRAM MORGAN FOUR/4 SERIES I (1946-47)

Key to cable colours :   1 Red   2 Red and yellow   3 Red and blue   4 Red and white   5 Red and green   6 Red and brown   7 Red and black   8 Yellow   9 Yellow and blue   10 Yellow and green   11 Yellow and brown   12 Yellow and purple   13 Yellow and black   14 Blue   15 Blue and white   16 Blue and green   17 Blue and brown   18 Blue and purple   19 Blue and black   20 White   21 White and green   22 White and brown   23 White and purple   24 White and black   25 Green   26 Green and brown   27 Green and purple   28 Green and black   29 Brown   30 Brown and purple   31 Purple   32 Purple and black   33 Black

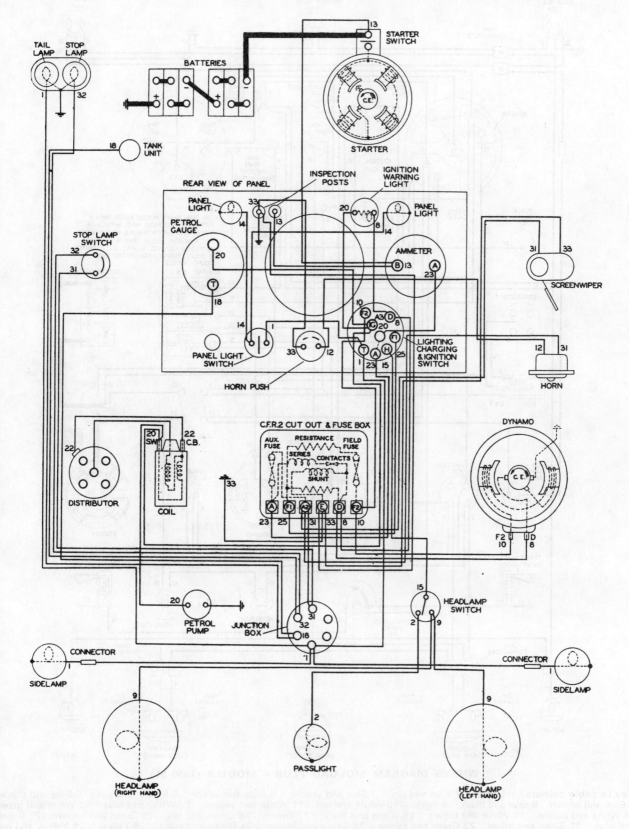

WIRING DIAGRAM MORGAN FOUR/4 SERIES I (1939)

Key to cable colours: 1 Red   2 Red and yellow   3 Red and blue   4 Red and white   5 Red and green   6 Red and brown
7 Red and black   8 Yellow   9 Yellow and blue   10 Yellow and green   11 Yellow and brown   12 Yellow and purple   13 Yellow
and black   14 Blue   15 Blue and white   16 Blue and green   17 Blue and brown   18 Blue and purple   19 Blue and black
20 White   21 White and green   22 White and brown   23 White and purple   24 White and black   25 green   26 Green and brown
27 Green and purple   28 Green and black   29 Brown   30 Brown and purple   31 Purple   32 Purple and black   33 Black

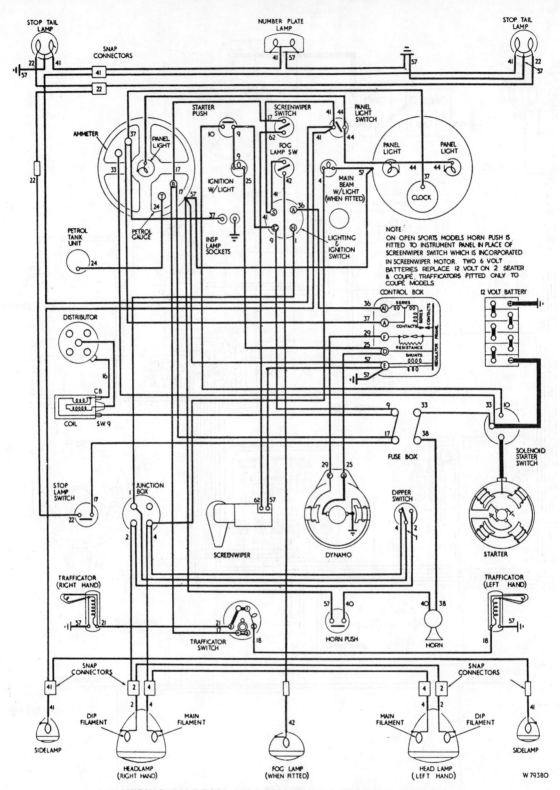

WIRING DIAGRAM MORGAN PLUS 4 MODELS (1950-51)

W 79380

Key to cable colours : 1 Blue 2 Blue and red 3 Blue and yellow 4 Blue and white 5 Blue and green 6 Blue and purple 7 Blue and brown 8 blue and black 9 White 10 White and red 11 White and yellow 12 White and blue 13 White and green 14 White and purple 15 White and brown 16 White and black 17 Green 18 Green and red 19 Green and yellow 20 Green and blue 21 Green and white 22 Green and purple 23 Green and brown 24 Green and black 25 Yellow 26 Yellow and red 27 Yellow and blue 28 Yellow and white 29 Yellow and green 30 Yellow and purple 31 Yellow and brown 32 Yellow and black 33 Brown 34 Brown and red 35 Brown and yellow 36 Brown and blue 37 Brown and white 38 Brown and green 39 Brown and purple 40 Brown and black 41 Red 42 Red and yellow 43 Red and blue 44 Red and white 45 Red and green 46 Red and purple 47 Red and brown 48 Red and black 49 Purple 50 Purple and red 51 Purple and yellow 52 Purple and blue 53 Purple and white 54 Purple and green 55 Purple and brown 56 Purple and black 57 Black 58 Black and red 59 Black and yellow 60 Black and blue 61 Black and white 62 Black and green 63 Black and purple 64 Black and brown.

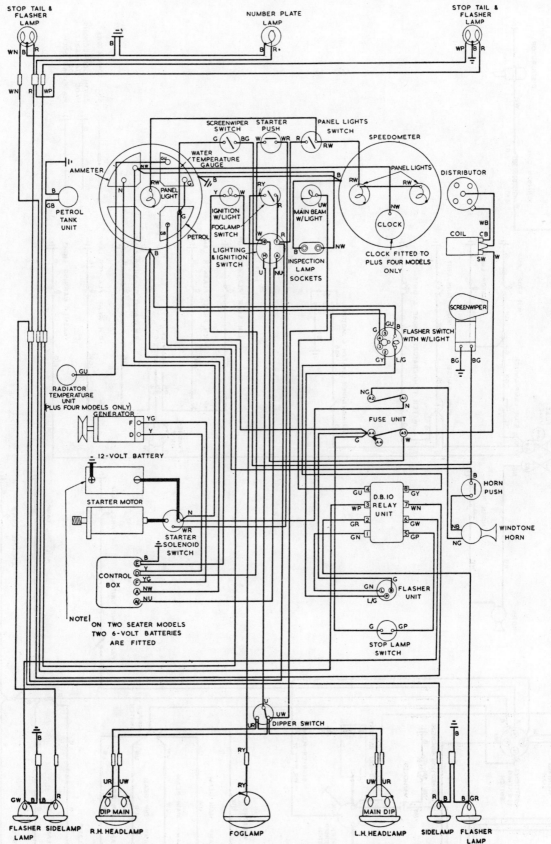

WIRING DIAGRAM MORGAN PLUS 4 AND FOUR/4 MODELS (1956)

Key to cable colours :   B Black   U Blue   N Brown   R Red   P Purple   G Green   S Slate   W White   Y Yellow
D Dark   L Light   M Medium.
When a cable has two colour code letters, the first denotes the main colour and the second denotes the tracer colour.

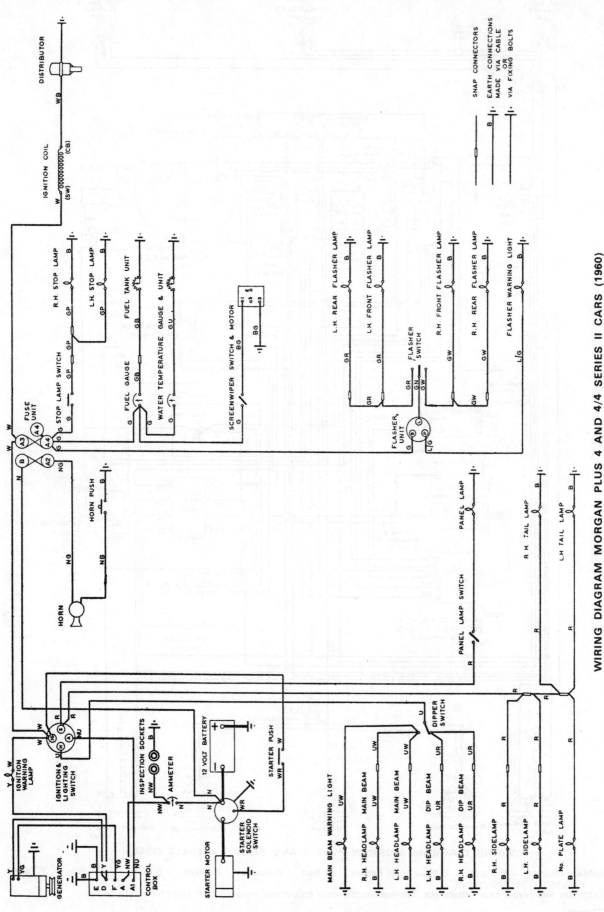

WIRING DIAGRAM MORGAN PLUS 4 AND 4/4 SERIES II CARS (1960)

Key to cable colours: B Black U Blue N Brown R Red P Purple G Green S Slate W White Y Yellow
D Dark L Light M Medium.
When a cable has two colour code letters, the first denotes the main colour and the second denotes the tracer colour.

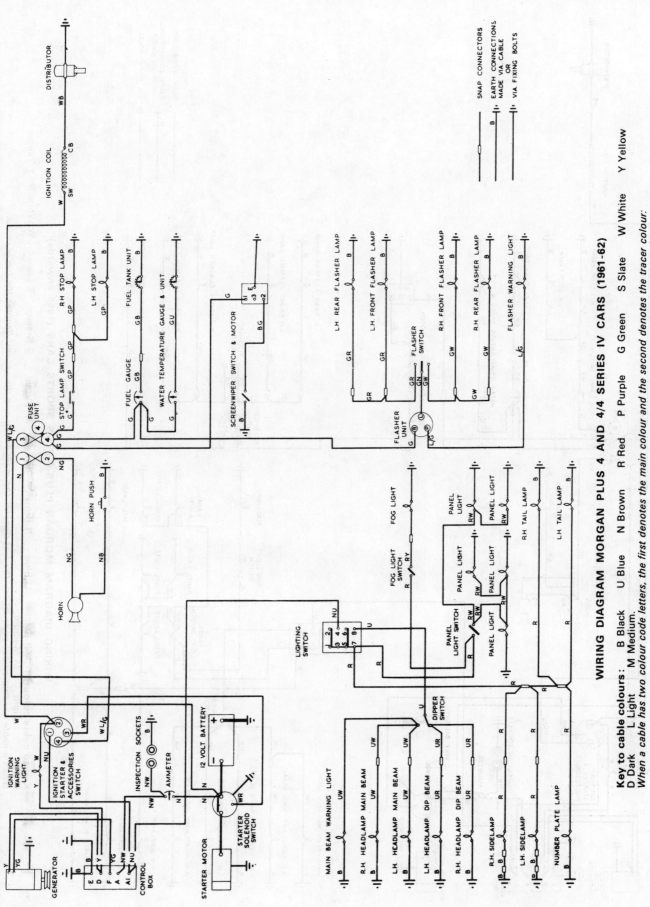

WIRING DIAGRAM MORGAN PLUS 4 AND 4/4 SERIES IV CARS (1961-62)

Key to cable colours: B Black   U Blue   N Brown   R Red   P Purple   G Green   S Slate   W White   Y Yellow
D Dark   L Light   M Medium.
When a cable has two colour code letters, the first denotes the main colour and the second denotes the tracer colour:

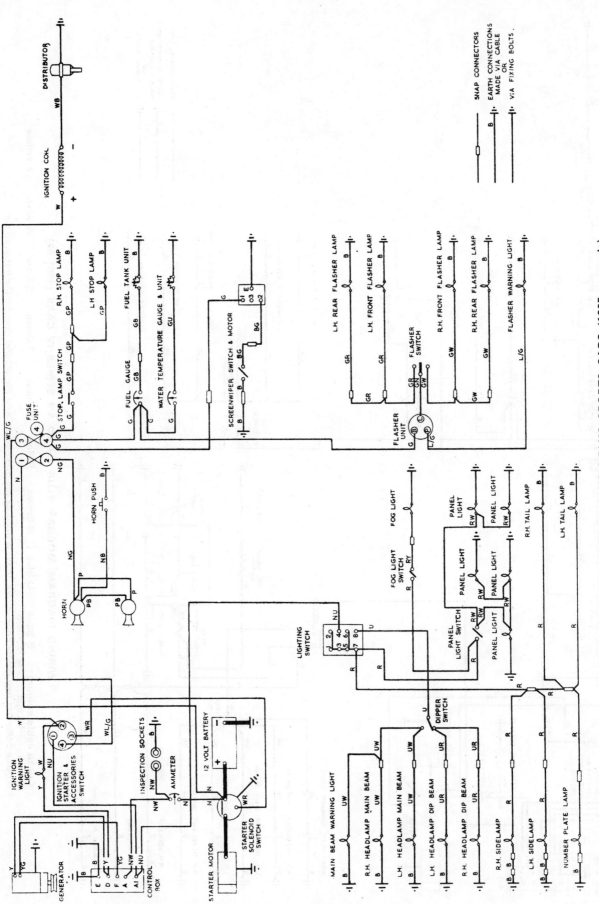

WIRING DIAGRAM MORGAN PLUS-4-PLUS SPORTS CARS (1965-onwards)

Key to cable colours: B Black   U Blue   N Brown   R Red   P Purple   G Green   S Slate   W White   Y Yellow
D Dark   L Light   M Medium.
When a cable has two colour code letters, the first denotes the main colour and the second denotes the tracer colour.

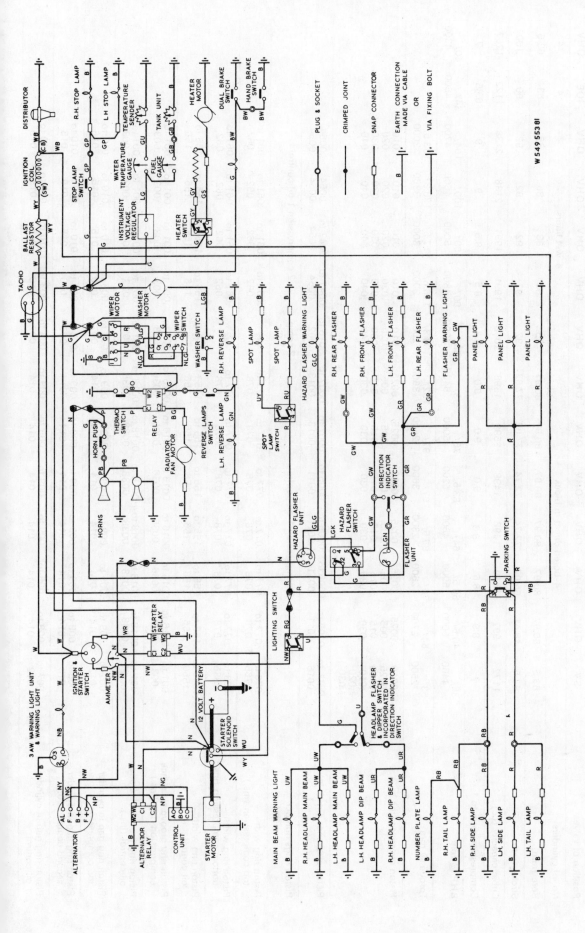

WIRING DIAGRAM FOR FOUR/FOUR FROM 1970

W 549 553 81

PLUG & SOCKET

CRIMPED JOINT

SNAP CONNECTOR

EARTH CONNECTION
MADE VIA CABLE
OR
VIA FIXING BOLT

ENGINE

MODEL	4/4 II	4/4 III	4/4 IV	4/4 V	4/4 V-Comp	1600	1600 Comp	Vanguard	TR2	TR3	TR4	TR4A	4/4 Coventry Climax	4/4 Standard Special
ENGINE TYPE	Ford 100E	105 E	109 E	116 E	116 E GT	2737 E	2737 E GT							
Position of valves	SV	OHV	OHV	OHV	OHV	OHV	OHV	OHV	OHV	OHV	OHV	OHV	IOE	OHV
No. of cylinders	4-bored direct in block								4-wet liners				4	4
Bore (mm)	63.5	80.97	80.97	80.97	80.97	80.97	80.97	85	83	83	86	86	63	63.5
Stroke (mm)	92.5	48.41	65.07	72.74	72.74	77.62	77.62	92	92	92	92	92	90	100
Cubic capacity (cc)	1172	997	1340	1498	1498	1598	1598	2088	1991	1991	2138	2138	1122	1267
Compression ratio to 1	7	8.9	8.5	8.3	9.0	9.0	9.0	6.7	8.5	8.5	9	9	6.85	7
BHP @ rpm	36/4400	40.5/5000	56.5/5000	64/4600	83.5/5200	75/5000	93/5400	68/4200	90/4800	100/5000	100/4600	104/4700	34/4500	40/4300
Torque @ rpm	53/2500	54/2700	76/2500	85.5/2300	97/3600	97/2500	102/3600	108.3/2000	116.6/3000	117.5/3000	128.3/3350	133.5/3000		
Piston oversizes (ins.)	.0010 .0025 .0050 .010 .020 .030	.0025 .005 .015 .030	.0025 .005 .015 .030	.0025 .005 .015 .030	.0025 .005 .015 .030	.0025 .005 .015 .030	.0025 .005 .015 .030	.010 .020 .030 .040	.010 .020 .030 .040	.010 .020 .030 .040	.010 .020 .030 .040	.010 .020 .030 .040		
Piston clearance (ins.)	.0011 to .0016	.0005 to .0011	.0005 to .0011	.0005 to .0011	.0005 to .0011	.0007 to .0013	.0007 to .0013	.0015 to .002	.0047 to .0054	.0047 to .0054	.0054 .0054	.0054 .0054		
Piston rings number	2 compression 1 oil control					2 compression 1 oil control		3 comp. 1 oil	2 compression 1 oil control					
Piston ring width—top compression (ins.)	.076 to .0765	.077 to .078	.077 to .078	.077 to .078	.077 to .078	.077 to .078	.077 to .078	$\frac{5}{64}$	.061 to .062	.061 to .062	.061 to .062	.061 to .062		
Piston ring width—bottom compression (ins.)	.093 to .0935	.077 to .078	.077 to .078	.077 to .078	.077 to .078	.077 to .078	.077 to .078	$\frac{5}{64}$	.061 to .062	.061 to .062	.061 to .062	.061 to .062		
Piston ring width—oil control	.1545 to .1550	.155 to .156	.155 to .156	.155 to .156	.155 to .156	.155 to .156	.155 to .156	$\frac{5}{32}$	.155 to .156	.155 to .156	.155 to .156	.155 to .156		
Piston ring groove clearance compression ring (ins.)	.001 to .003	.0016 to .0036	.0016 to .0036	.0016 to .0036	.0016 to .0036	.0016 to .0036	.0016 to .0036	.001 to .003	.001 to .003	.001 to .003	.001 to .003	.001 to .003		
Piston ring groove clearance oil control (ins.)	.001 to .00 25	.0018 to .0038	.0018 to .0038	.0018 to .0038	.0018 to .0038	.0018 to .0038	.0018 to .0038	.001 to .003	.001 to .003	.001 to .003	.001 to .003	.001 to .003		
Piston ring gap in cylinder—top compression	.007 to .012	.009 to .014	.009 to .014	.009 to .014	.009 to .014	.009 to .014	.009 to .014	.003 to .007	.003 to .010	.010 to .015	.010 to .015	.010 to .015		
Piston ring gap in cylinder—second compression	.008 to .014	.009 to .014	.009 to .014	.009 to .014	.009 to .014	.009 to .014	.009 to .014	.003 to .007	.003 to .010	.010 to .015	.010 to .015	.010 to .015		
Piston ring gap in cylinder—oil control	.007 to .012	.009 to .014	.009 to .014	.009 to .014	.009 to .014	.009 to .014	.009 to .014	.003 to .007	.003 to .010	.010 to .015	.010 to .015	.010 to .015		

The TR2, TR3, TR4 and TR4A columns are grouped under the heading "PLUS/4 and PLUS/4 PLUS".

	4/4 II	4/4 III	4/4 IV	4/4 V	4/4 V-Comp	1600	1600 Comp	PLUS/4 and PLUS/4 PLUS					4/4 Coventry Climax	4/4 Standard Special
ENGINE TYPE	Ford 100E	105 E	109 E	116 E	116 E GT	2737 E	2737 E GT	Vanguard	TR2	TR3	TR4	TR4A		
Oil pressure lb/sq. inch	30	35 to 40	35 to 40	35 to 40	35 to 40	35 to 40	35 to 40	40 to 60	70	70	70	70	40	40 to 60
Gudgeon pin diameter (ins.)	.6876 to .6879	.8120 to .8123	.8120 to .8123	.8120 to .8123	.8120 to .8123	.8120 to .8123	.8120 to .8123	.87510 to .87485	.87510 to .87485	.87510 to .87485	.87510 to .87485	.87510 to .87485		
Gudgeon pin fit in piston (ins.)		up to .0002 clearance						Selective floating fit						
Gudgeon pin fit to con rod (ins.)	up to .0005	.0001 to .0003	.0001 to .0003	.0001 to .0003	.0001 to .0003	.0001 to .0003	.0001 to .0003	.0001	.0001	.0001	.0001	.0001		
Crank pin diameter (ins.)	1.698 to 1.699	1.9370 to 1.9375	1.9370 to 1.9375	1.9370 to 1.9375	1.9370 to 1.9375	1.9370 to 1.9375	1.9370 to 1.9375	2.0861 to 2.0866	2.0861 to 2.0866	2.0861 to 2.0866	2.0861 to 2.0866	2.0861 to 2.0866		
Crank pin undersizes (ins.)	.010, .020, .030, .040 (latter OHV engine only)							.010, .020, .030						
Con rod length—centres (ins.)	6.123 to 6.127	4.611 to 4.612	4.283 to 4.285	4.799 to 4.801	4.799 to 4.801	4.927 to 4.929	4.927 to 4.929	6.248 to 6.252	6.248 to 6.252	6.248 to 6.252	6.248 to 6.252	6.248 to 6.252		
Big end bearing clearance (ins.)	.0005 to .0002	.0005 to .0002	.0005 to .0002	.0005 to .0002	.0005 to .0002	.0005 to .0002	.0005 to .0002	.0006 to .0025	.0016 to .0035	.0016 to .0035	.0028 to .0040	.0028 to .0040		
Big end side clearance (ins.)	.004 to .010	.002 to .008	.002 to .008	.004 to .010	.004 to .010	.004 to .010	.004 to .010	.0075 to .0105	.007 to .014	.007 to .014	.007 to .014	.007 to .014		
Main journal diameter (ins.)	2.0010 to 2.0015	2.1255 to 2.1260	2.1255 to 2.1260	2.1255 to 2.1260	2.1255 to 2.1260	2.1255 to 2.1260	2.1255 to 2.1260	2.4790 to 2.4795	2.4790 to 2.4795	2.4790 to 2.4795	2.4790 to 2.4795	2.4790 to 2.4795		
Main journal undersizes (ins.)	.01, .02, .03							.010, .020, .030, .045						
Main bearing No.	3	3	3	5	5	5	5	3	3	3	3	3	3	3
Main bearing clearance (ins.)	.0000 to .0015	.0005 to .0020	.0005 to .0020	.0005 to .0020	.0005 to .0020	.0005 to .0020	.0005 to .0020	.003 to .005	.0010 to .0025	.0010 to .0025	.0015 to .0025	.0015 to .0025		
Crankshaft end play (ins.)	.002 to .011	.003 to .011	.003 to .011	.003 to .011	.003 to .011	.003 to .011	.003 to .011	.004 to .006	.004 to .006	.004 to .006	.004 to .006	.004 to .006		
Camshaft journal diameter (ins.)	1.56	1.56	1.56	1.56	1.56	1.56	1.56	Front	1.871 to 1.872 others 1.7153 to 1.7158					
No. of camshaft bearings	3	3	3	3	3	3	3	4	4	4	4	4		
Camshaft bearing clearance (ins.)	.001 to .002	.001 to .002	.001 to .002	.001 to .002	.001 to .002	.001 to .002	.001 to .002	.003 to .005	.0026 to .0046	.0026 to .0046	.0026 to .0046	Front .0028 to .0047 Others .0015 to .0029		
Camshaft end float (ins.)	Spring-loaded	.002 to .007	.002 to .007	.002 to .007	.002 to .007	.002 to .007	.002 to .007	.003 to .0075	.003 to .0075	.003 to .0075	.004 to .0075	.004 to .0075		
Valve head diameter—inlet (ins.)	1.15	1.262 to 1.272	1.262 to 1.272	1.432 to 1.442	1.405 to 1.415	1.497 to 1.507	1.497 to 1.507	1.5020 to 1.4980	1.5620 to 1.5580	1.5620 to 1.5580	1.5620 to 1.5580	1.5620 to 1.5580		
Valve head diameter—exhaust (ins.)	1.05	1.183 to 1.193	1.183 to 1.193	1.183 to 1.193	1.124 to 1.125	1.240 to 1.250	1.240 to 1.250	1.283 to 1.279	1.303 to 1.299	1.303 to 1.299	1.303 to 1.299	1.303 to 1.299		
Valve stem diameter—inlet (ins.)	.3095 to .3105	.3095 to .3105	.3095 to .3105	.3095 to .3105	.3095 to .3105	.3095 to .3105	.3095 to .3105	.3110 to .3100	.3110 to .3100	.3110 to .3100	.3110 to .3100	.3110 to .3100		

ENGINE

	4/4 II	4/4 III	4/4 IV	4/4 V	4/4 V-Comp	1600	1600 Comp	PLUS/4 and PLUS/4 PLUS					4/4	
MODEL								Vanguard	TR2	TR3	TR4	TR4A	Coventry Climax	Standard Special
ENGINE TYPE	Ford 100E	105 E	109 E	116 E	116 E GT	2737 E	2737 E GT							
Valve stem diameter—exhaust (ins.)	.3086 to .3096	.3086 to .3096	.3086 to .3096	.3086 to .3096	.3086 to .3096	.3086 to .3096	.3086 to .3096	.3400 to .3399	.3715 to .3705	.3715 to .3705	.3715 to .3705	.3715 to .3705		
Valve seat angle	45°	45°	45°	45°	45°	45°	45°	45°	45°	45°	45°	45°	45°	
Valve stem guide clearance inlet (ins.)	.0008 to .0030	.0008 to .0030	.0008 to .0030	.0008 to .0030	.0008 to .0030	.0008 to .0030	.0008 to .0030	.001 to .003	.001 to .003	.001 to .003	.001 to .003	.001 to .003		
Valve stem guide clearance exhaust (ins.)	.0017 to .0039	.0017 to .0039	.0017 to .0039	.0017 to .0039	.0017 to .0039	.0017 to .0039	.0017 to .0039	.003 to .005	.003 to .005	.003 to .005	.003 to .005	.003 to .005		
Valve spring free length outer (ins.)	1.98	1.48	1.48	1.48	1.48	1.48	1.48	1.97	1.980	1.980	1.95	1.89		
Valve spring free length inner (ins.)								1.63	2.080	2.080	1.89	1.89		
Valve spring free length aux. inner (ins.)								1.54	1.54	1.54	1.56	1.56		
Inlet valve clearance (ins.) (normal operating temperature)	.013	.010	.010	.010	.012	.010	.012	.010 (cold)	.010 (cold)	.010 (cold)	.010 (cold)	.010 (cold)	.006 (cold)	.022 (cold)
Exhaust valve clearance (ins.)	.013	.017	.017	.017	.022	.017	.022	.012 (cold)	.012 (cold)	.012 (cold)	.010 (cold)	.010 (cold)	.008 (cold)	.022 (cold)
Valve timing clearance—inlet (ins.)	.015	.015	.015	.015	.016	.015	.016	.015	.015	.015	.0165	.0165		
Valve timing clearance—exhaust (ins.)	.015	.027	.027	.027	.026	.027	.026	.015	.015	.015	.0165	.0165		
Valve timing inlet opens b t d c	3° 30'	10°	17°	17°	27°	17°	27°	10°	15°	15°	17°	17°	10°	10°
Valve timing inlet closes a b d c	56° 30'	50°	51°	51°	65°	51°	65°	50°	55°	57°	57°	57°	50°	50°
Valve timing exhaust opens b b d c	47° 30'	44°	51°	51°	65°	51°	65°	50°	55°	57°	57°	57°	50°	50°
Valve timing inlet closes a t d c	12° 30'	10°	17°	17°	27°	17°	27°	10°	15°	15°	17°	17°	10°	10°
Oil capacity sump (imperial pints)	5¼	4	4	6¼	6¼	7.2	7.2	11	11	11	11	11	8	11
Torque settings lb/ft. cyl. head nuts	65 to 70	65 to 70	65 to 70	65 to 70	65 to 70	65 to 70	65 to 70	60 to 65	60 to 65	100 to 105	100 to 105	100 to 105		
Torque settings lb/ft. cyl. main bearings	55 to 60	55 to 60	55 to 60	55 to 60	55 to 60	65 to 70	65 to 70	85 to 90	85 to 90	85 to 90	85 to 90	85 to 90		
Torque settings lb/ft. big end bearings	20 to 25	20 to 25	20 to 25	20 to 25	20 to 25	30 to 35	30 to 35	42 to 46	55 to 60	55 to 60	55 to 60	55 to 60		

IGNITION SYSTEM

	4/4 II	4/4 III	4/4 IV	4/4 V	4/4 V-Comp	1600	1600 Comp	Vanguard	TR2	TR3	TR4	TR4A	Coventry Climax	Standard Special
Spark plug make	Champion	Champion	Champion	Champion	Champion	Autolite	Autolite	Champion	Champion	Lodge	Lodge	Lodge	KLG	Champion
Spark plug type 14 mm	L10	N5	N5	N5	N4	AG22	AG22	L10	L10S	CNY	CNY	CNY	F50X	N8
Spark plug gap (in.)	.025	.025	.025	.025	.025	early .023 later .030	early .023 later .030	.032	.025	.025	.025	.025	.025	.025
Ignition timing (static) b t d c	5°	10°	6°	8°	10°	8°	8°	4°	4°	4°	4°	4°	t d c	t d c

CARBURETTER DETAILS / GEARBOX AND REAR AXLE

	4/4 II	4/4 III	4/4 IV	4/4 V	4/4 V-Comp	1600	1600 Comp	PLUS/4 and PLUS/4 PLUS Vanguard	TR2	TR3	TR4	TR4A	4/4 Coventry Climax	4/4 Standard Special
ENGINE TYPE	Ford 100E	105 E	109 E	116 E	116 E GT	2737 E	2737 E GT		TR2	TR3	TR4	TR4A		
Contact breaker gap (in.)	.015	.015	.015	.015	.015	.025	.025	.015	.015	.015	.015	.015	.012 to .015	
Firing order				1—2—4—3				1—3—4—2						
Distributor type	D2A4	DM2	DM2	25D4	25D4	25D4 or Motorcraft	25D4	DVX4A	DM2	DM2	25D4	25D4		
Coil type	LA12	LA12	LA12	LA12	LA12	LA12	LA12	B12	HA12	HA12	HA12	HA12		
CARBURETTER DETAILS														
Make	Solex	Solex	Zenith	Zenith	Weber	Zenith or Ford	Weber	Solex	SU	SU	Stromberg or SU	Stromberg or SU	Solex	Solex
Model	26Z1C2	B30Z1C3	32VN2	33VN	DCD1	C7BH-B	DCD1	32B1	H4	H6	175CD	HS6	30HBFG	30FAI
Choke tube	21	22	26	29	prim 26 sec 27	28	prim 26 sec 27	25					30—23	24
Main jet	110	115	65	92	140 155	150	150 155	135					115	125
Main air correction jet/Compensating jet	160	175	115	112	230 180	150	160 140	190					210	170
Pilot jet/slow running jet	50	40	55	55	50 70	65	50 45	55					55	45
Starter jet/pump jet	130	125	60	50	60	55	65	130					110	100
Standard needle									FV or SM	SM	2A	SM		
GEARBOX AND REAR AXLE														
Gear ratio overall—first	15.07	18.1	18.7 or 14.53	18.7 or 14.53	14.53	14.53	13.5 or 12.3	12.5	12.5	12.5	11.05	11.05	Meadows/Moss 17.1/19.3	16.41
Gear ratio overall—second	8.25	10.54	10.9 or 9.2	10.9 or 9.2	9.2	9.2	8.0 or 7.28	7.3	7.3	7.3	6.5	6.5	12.1/11.95	11.42
Gear ratio overall—third	4.4	6.21	6.44 or 5.8	6.44 or 5.8	5.8	5.8	5.8	5.4 or 4.9	5.1	5.1	5.1	4.5	7/6.7	6.70
Gear ratio overall—fourth	4.4	4.56 or 4.1	4.56 or 4.1	4.56 or 4.1	4.1	4.1	4.1	4.1 or 3.73	3.73	3.73	3.73	3.73	5/5	4.72
Gear ratio overall—reverse	19.71	23.7	22.0 or 16.22	22.0 or 16.22	16.22	16.22	16.22	13.5 or 12.3	12.5	12.5	12.5	11.05	22.6/22.35	21.33
Gearbox capacity (imp. pts.)	1¾	1¾	1¾	1¾	2.13	2.13	2.13	2½	2½	2½	2½	2½	1½/1½	2
Rear axle ratio to 1	4.44	4.56 or 4.1	4.56 or 4.1	4.56 or 4.1	4.56 or 4.1	4.56 or 4.1	4.56 or 4.1	4.1 or 3.73	3.73	3.73	3.73	3.73	5.0	4.72
Rear axle capacity (imp. pts.)	2	2	2	2	2	2	2	2½	2½	2½	2½	2½	1½	2

MODEL	4/4 II	4/4 III	4/4 IV	4/4 V	4/4 V-Comp	1600	1600 Comp	PLUS/4 and PLUS/4 PLUS					4/4 Coventry Climax	4/4 Standard Special
								Vanguard	TR2	TR3	TR4	TR4A		
ENGINE TYPE	Ford 100E	105 E	109 E	116 E	116 E GT	2737 E	2737 E GT							

ELECTRICAL

Battery 12 Volt (2×6V some models)	40AH	36	36	36	36	36	36	54	54	54	54	54	57	57
Battery—earth	+	+	+	+	+	—	—	+	+	+	+	Early + Later —	+	+
Generator type Lucas	C40	C40	C40L	C40L	C40L	C40L	C40L	C39PV2	C39PV2	C39PV2	C40/1	C40/1		
Starter type Lucas	M35G	M35H	M35H	M35G	M35G	M35G	M35G	M418G	M418G	M418G	M418G	M418G		

COOLING SYSTEM

Type - Thermo-syphon Plus	Water pump fan and thermostat												—	Fan
Capacity (imperial pints)	12	12	12	12	12	12	12	16	16	16	16	16	16	16

FRONT SUSPENSION AND STEERING

Springs free length (in.)	$12\frac{1}{4}$	$14\frac{1}{4}$	$14\frac{1}{4}$	$14\frac{1}{4}$	$14\frac{1}{4}$	$14\frac{1}{4}$	$14\frac{1}{4}$	$12\frac{1}{4}$	13	13	13	13		
Camber angle	2°	2°	2°	2°	2°	2°	2°	2°	2°	2°	2°	2°	3°	3°
Castor angle	4°	4°	4°	4°	4°	4°	4°	4°	4°	4°	4°	4°	3°	3°
Kingpin inclination	2°	2°	2°	2°	2°	2°	2°	2°	2°	2°	2°	2°	3°	3°
Toe-in	2°	2°	2°	2°	2°	2°	2°	2°	2°	2°	2°	2°	3°	3°
Tyre pressures lb/sq. in.	16 to 18 add 6 for high speeds												18 to 21	18

DIMENSIONS

Overall length (2-seater)	12' 0"	12' 0"	12' 0"	12' 0"	12' 0"	12' 0"	12' 0"	11' 8"	12' 0"	12' 0"	12' 0"	12' 0"	11' 4"	11' 4"
Overall width (2-seater)	4' 8"	4' 8"	4' 8"	4' 8"	4' 8"	4' 8"	4' 8"	4' 8"	4' 8"	4' 8"	4' 8"	4' 8"	4' 6"	4' 7"
Height—hood up (2-seater)	4' 3"	4' 3"	4' 3"	4' 3"	4' 3"	4' 3"	4' 3"	$4' 4\frac{1}{2}"$	$4' 4\frac{1}{2}"$	$4' 4\frac{1}{2}"$	$4' 4\frac{1}{2}"$	$4' 4\frac{1}{2}"$	4' 2"	4' 4"
Ground clearance	7"	7"	7"	7"	7"	7"	7"	7"	7"	7"	7"	7"	6"	6"
Track—front and rear	3' 11"	3' 11"	3' 11"	3' 11"	3' 11"	3' 11"	3' 11"	3' 11"	3' 11"	3' 11"	3' 11"	3' 11"	3' 9"	3' 9"
Wheelbase	8' 0"	8' 0"	8' 0"	8' 0"	8' 0"	8' 0"	8' 0"	8' 0"	8' 0"	8' 0"	8' 0"	8' 0"	7' 8"	7' 8"
Turning circle	32' 0"	32' 0"	32' 0"	32' 0"	32' 0"	32' 0"	32' 0"	33' 0"	32' 0"	32' 0"	32' 0"	32' 0"	33' 0"	33' 0"
Tyre size	500×16	500×16	560×15	560×15	560×15	560×15	560×15	525×16	525×16	560×15	560×15	560×15	450×17 500×16	450×17 500×16

HINTS ON MAINTENANCE AND OVERHAUL

There are few things more rewarding than the restoration of a vehicle's original peak of efficiency and smooth performance.

The following notes are intended to help the owner to reach that state of perfection. Providing that he possesses the basic manual skills he should have no difficulty in performing most of the operations detailed in this manual. It must be stressed, however, that where recommended in the manual, highly-skilled operations ought to be entrusted to experts, who have the necessary equipment, to carry out the work satisfactorily.

Quality of workmanship :

The hazardous driving conditions on the roads to-day demand that vehicles should be as nearly perfect, mechanically, as possible. It is therefore most important that amateur work be carried out with care, bearing in mind the often inadequate working conditions, and also the inferior tools which may have to be used. It is easy to counsel perfection in all things, and we recognise that it may be setting an impossibly high standard. We do, however, suggest that every care should be taken to ensure that a vehicle is as safe to take on the road as it is humanly possible to make it.

Safe working conditions :

Even though a vehicle may be stationary, it is still potentially dangerous if certain sensible precautions are not taken when working on it while it is supported on jacks or blocks. It is indeed preferable not to use jacks alone, but to supplement them with carefully placed blocks, so that there will be plenty of support if the car rolls off the jacks during a strenuous manoeuvre. Axle stands are an excellent way of providing a rigid base which is not readily disturbed. Piles of bricks are a dangerous substitute. Be careful not to get under heavy loads on lifting tackle, the load could fall. It is preferable not to work alone when lifting an engine, or when working underneath a vehicle which is supported well off the ground. To be trapped, particularly under the vehicle, may have unpleasant results if help is not quickly forthcoming. Make some provision, however humble, to deal with fires. Always disconnect a battery if there is a likelihood of electrical shorts. These may start a fire if there is leaking fuel about. This applies particularly to leads which can carry a heavy current, like those in the starter circuit. While on the subject of electricity, we must also stress the danger of using equipment which is run off the mains and which has no earth or has faulty wiring or connections. So many workshops have damp floors, and electrical shocks are of such a nature that it is sometimes impossible to let go of a live lead or piece of equipment due to the muscular spasms which take place.

Work demanding special care :

This involves the servicing of braking, steering and suspension systems. On the road, failure of the braking system may be disastrous. Make quite sure that there can be no possibility of failure through the bursting of rusty brake pipes or rotten hoses, nor to a sudden loss of pressure due to defective seals or valves.

Problems :

The chief problems which may face an operator are :

1 External dirt.
2 Difficulty in undoing tight fixings.
3 Dismantling unfamiliar mechanisms.
4 Deciding in what respect parts are defective.
5 Confusion about the correct order for reassembly.
6 Adjusting running clearance.
7 Road testing.
8 Final tuning.

Practical suggestions to solve the problems :

1 Preliminary cleaning of large parts – engines, transmissions, steering, suspensions, etc, – should be carried out before removal from the car. Where road dirt and mud alone are present, wash clean with a high-pressure water jet, brushing to remove stubborn adhesions, and allow to drain and dry. Where oil or grease is also present, wash down with a proprietary compound (Gunk, Teepol etc,) applying with a stiff brush – an old paint brush is suitable – into all crevices. Cover the distributor and ignition coils with a polythene bag and then apply a strong water jet to clear the loosened deposits. Allow to drain and dry. The assemblies will then be sufficiently clean to remove and transfer to the bench for the next stage.

On the bench, further cleaning can be carried out, first wiping the parts as free as possible from grease with old newspaper. Avoid using rag or cotton waste which can leave clogging fibres behind. Any remaining grease can be removed with a brush dipped in paraffin. Avoid using paraffin or petrol in large quantities for cleaning in enclosed areas, such as garages, on account of the high fire risk.

When all exteriors have been cleaned, and not before, dismantling can be commenced. This ensures that dirt will not enter into interiors and orifices revealed by dismantling. In the next phases, where components have to be cleaned, use a special solvent or petrol and keep the containers covered except when in use. After the components have been cleaned, plug small holes with tapered hard wood plugs cut to size and blank off larger orifices with greaseproof paper and masking tape. Do not use soft wood plugs or matchsticks as they may break.

2 It is not advisable to hammer on the end of a screw thread, but if it must be done, first screw on a nut to protect the thread, and use a lead hammer. This applies particularly to the removal of tapered cotters. Nuts and bolts seem to 'grow' together, especially in exhaust systems. If penetrating oil does not work, try the judicious application of heat, but be careful of starting a fire. Asbestos sheet or cloth is useful to isolate heat.

Tight bushes or pieces of tail-pipe rusted into a silencer can be removed by splitting them with an open-ended hacksaw. Tight screws can sometimes be started by a tap from a hammer on the end of a suitable screwdriver. Many tight fittings will yield to the judicious use of a hammer, but it must be a soft-faced hammer, if damage is to be avoided, use a heavy block on the opposite side to absorb shock. Any parts of the steering system which have been damaged should be renewed, as attempts to repair them may lead to cracking and subsequent failure, and steering ball joints should be disconnected using a recommended tool to prevent damage.

3 It often happens that an owner is baffled when trying to dismantle an unfamiliar piece of equipment. So many modern devices are pressed together or assembled by spinning-over flanges, that they must be sawn apart. The intention is that the whole assembly must be renewed. However, parts which appear to be in one piece to the naked eye may reveal close-fitting joint lines when inspected with a magnifying glass, and this may provide the necessary clue to dismantling. Lefthanded screw threads are used where rotational forces would tend to unscrew a righthanded screw thread.

Be very careful when dismantling mechanisms which may come apart suddenly. Work in an enclosed space where the parts will be contained, and drape a piece of cloth over the device if springs are likely to fly in all directions. Mark everything which might be reassembled in the wrong position, scratched symbols may be used on unstressed parts, or a sequence of tiny dots from a centre punch can be useful. Stressed parts should never be scratched or centre-popped as this may lead to cracking under working conditions. Store parts which look alike in the correct order for reassembly. Never rely upon memory to assist in the assembly of complicated mechanisms, especially when they will be dismantled for a long time, but make notes, and drawings to supplement the diagrams in the manual, and put labels on detached wires. Rust stains may indicate unlubricated wear. This can sometimes be seen round the outside edge of a bearing cup in a universal joint. Look for bright rubbing marks on parts which normally should not make heavy contact. These might prove that something is bent or running out of truth. For example, there might be bright marks on one side of a piston, at the top near the ring grooves, and others at the bottom of the skirt on the other side. This could well be the clue to a bent connecting rod. Suspected cracks can be proved by heating the component in a light oil to approximately 100°C, removing, drying off, and dusting with french chalk. If a crack is present the oil retained in the crack will stain the french chalk.

4 In determining wear, and the degree, against the permissible limits set in the manual, accurate measurement can only be achieved by the use of a micrometer. In many cases, the wear is given to the fourth place of decimals; that is in ten-thousandths of an inch. This can be read by the vernier scale on the barrel of a good micrometer. Bore diameters are more difficult to determine. If, however, the matching shaft is accurately measured, the degree of play in the bore can be felt as a guide to its suitability. In other cases, the shank of a twist drill of known diameter is a handy check.

Many methods have been devised for determining the clearance between bearing surfaces. To-day the best and simplest is by the use of Plastigage, obtainable from most garages. A thin plastic thread is laid between the two surfaces and the bearing is tightened, flattening the thread. On removal, the width of the thread is compared with the scale supplied with the thread and the clearance is read off directly. Sometimes joint faces leak persistently, even after gasket renewal. The fault will then be traceable to distortion, dirt or burrs. Studs which are screwed into soft metal frequently raise burrs at the point of entry. A quick cure for this is to chamfer the edge of the hole in the part which fits over the stud.

5 **Always check a replacement part with the original one before it is fitted.**

If parts are not marked, and the order for reassembly is not known, a little detective work will help. Look for marks which are due to wear to see if they can be mated. Joint faces may not be identical due to manufacturing errors, and parts which overlap may be stained, giving a clue to the correct position. Most fixings leave identifying marks especially if they were painted over on assembly. It is then easier to decide whether a nut, for instance, has a plain, a spring, or a shakeproof washer under it. All running surfaces become 'bedded' together after long spells of work and tiny imperfections on one part will be found to have left corresponding marks on the other. This is particularly true of shafts and bearings and even a score on a cylinder wall will show on the piston.

6 Checking end float rocker clearances by feeler gauge may not always give accurate results because of wear. For instance, the rocker tip which bears on a valve stem may be deeply pitted, in which case the feeler will simply be bridging a depression. Thrust washers may also wear depressions in opposing faces to make accurate measurement difficult. End float is then easier to check by using a dial gauge. It is common practice to adjust end play in bearing assemblies, like front hubs with taper rollers, by doing up the axle nut until the hub becomes stiff to turn and then backing it off a little. Do not use this method with ballbearing hubs as the assembly is often preloaded by tightening the axle nut to its fullest extent. If the splitpin hole will not line up, file the base of the nut a little.

Steering assemblies often wear in the straight-ahead position. If any part is adjusted, make sure that it remains free when moved from lock to lock. Do not be surprised if an assembly like a steering gearbox, which is known to be carefully adjusted outside the car, becomes stiff when it is bolted into place. This will be due to distortion of the case by the pull of the mounting bolts, particularly if the mounting points are not all touching together. This problem may be met in other equipment and is cured by careful attention to the alignment of mounting points.

When a spanner is stamped with a size and A/F it means that the dimension is the width between the jaws and has no connection with ANF, which is the designation for the American National Fine thread. Coarse threads like Whitworth are rarely used on cars to-day except for studs which screw into soft aluminium or cast iron. For this reason it might be found that the top end of a cylinder head stud has a fine thread and the lower end a coarse thread to screw into the cylinder block. If the car has mainly UNF threads then it is likely that any coarse threads will be UNC, which are not the same as Whitworth. Small sizes have the same number of threads in Whitworth and UNC, but in the $\frac{1}{2}$ in size for example, there are twelve threads to the inch in the former and thirteen in the latter.

7 After a major overhaul, particularly if a great deal of work has been done on the braking, steering and suspension systems, it is advisable to approach the problem of testing with care. If the braking system has been overhauled, apply heavy pressure to the brake pedal and get a second operator to check every possible source of leakage. The brakes may work extremely well, but a leak could cause complete failure after a few miles.

Do not fit the hub caps until every wheel nut has been checked for tightness, and make sure that the tyre pressures are correct. Check the levels of coolant, lubricants and hydraulic fluids. Being satisfied that all is well, take the car on the road and test the brakes at once. Check the steering and the action of the handbrake. Do all this at moderate speeds on quiet roads, and make sure there is no other vehicle behind you when you try a rapid stop.

Finally, remember that many parts settle down after a time, so check for tightness of all fixings after the car has been on the road a hundred miles or so.

8 It is useless to tune an engine which has not reached its normal running temperature. In the same way, the tune of an engine which is stiff after a rebore will be different when the engine is again running free. Remember too, that rocker clearances on pushrod operated valve gear will change when the cylinder head nuts are tightened after an initial period of running with a new head gasket.

Trouble may not always be due to what seems the obvious cause. Ignition, carburation and mechanical condition are interdependent and spitting back through the carburetter, which might be attributed to a weak mixture, can be caused by a sticking inlet valve.

For one final hint on tuning, never adjust more than one thing at a time or it will be impossible to tell which adjustment produced the desired result.

WARNING

If, during any overhaul or service, it is necessary to extract any roll pins and/or circlips they MUST be discarded.

New pins and/or circlips MUST be fitted on reassembly. The refitting of used roll pins and/or circlips could result in failure of a component and possibly create a safety hazard.

Inches / Decimals / Millimetres

Inches	Decimals	Millimetres
1/64	.015625	.3969
1/32	.03125	.7937
3/64	.046875	1.1906
1/16	.0625	1.5875
5/64	.078125	1.9844
3/32	.09375	2.3812
7/64	.109375	2.7781
1/8	.125	3.1750
9/64	.140625	3.5719
5/32	.15625	3.9687
11/64	.171875	4.3656
3/16	.1875	4.7625
13/64	.203125	5.1594
7/32	.21875	5.5562
15/64	.234375	5.9531
1/4	.25	6.3500
17/64	.265625	6.7469
9/32	.28125	7.1437
19/64	.296875	7.5406
5/16	.3125	7.9375
21/64	.328125	8.3344
11/32	.34375	8.7312
23/64	.359375	9.1281
3/8	.375	9.5250
25/64	.390625	9.9219
13/32	.40625	10.3187
27/64	.421875	10.7156
7/16	.4375	11.1125
29/64	.453125	11.5094
15/32	.46875	11.9062
31/64	.484375	12.3031
1/2	.5	12.7000
33/64	.515625	13.0969
17/32	.53125	13.4937
35/64	.546875	13.8906
9/16	.5625	14.2875
37/64	.578125	14.6844
19/32	.59375	15.0812
39/64	.609375	15.4781
5/8	.625	15.8750
41/64	.640625	16.2719
21/32	.65625	16.6687
43/64	.671875	17.0656
11/16	.6875	17.4625
45/64	.703125	17.8594
23/32	.71875	18.2562
47/64	.734375	18.6531
3/4	.75	19.0500
49/64	.765625	19.4469
25/32	.78125	19.8437
51/64	.796875	20.2406
13/16	.8125	20.6375
53/64	.828125	21.0344
27/32	.84375	21.4312
55/64	.859375	21.8281
7/8	.875	22.2250
57/64	.890625	22.6219
29/32	.90625	23.0187
59/64	.921875	23.4156
15/16	.9375	23.8125
61/64	.953125	24.2094
31/32	.96875	24.6062
63/64	.984375	25.0031

Inches to Millimetres

Inches	mm
.001	.0254
.002	.0508
.003	.0762
.004	.1016
.005	.1270
.006	.1524
.007	.1778
.008	.2032
.009	.2286
.01	.254
.02	.508
.03	.762
.04	1.016
.05	1.270
.06	1.524
.07	1.778
.08	2.032
.09	2.286
.1	2.54
.2	5.08
.3	7.62
.4	10.16
.5	12.70
.6	15.24
.7	17.78
.8	20.32
.9	22.86
1	25.4
2	50.8
3	76.2
4	101.6
5	127.0
6	152.4
7	177.8
8	203.2
9	228.6
10	254.0
11	279.4
12	304.8
13	330.2
14	355.6
15	381.0
16	406.4
17	431.8
18	457.2
19	482.6
20	508.0
21	533.4
22	558.8
23	584.2
24	609.6
25	635.0
26	660.4
27	685.8
28	711.2
29	736.6
30	762.0
31	787.4
32	812.8
33	838.2
34	863.6
35	889.0
36	914.4

Millimetres to Inches

mm	Inches
.01	.00039
.02	.00079
.03	.00118
.04	.00157
.05	.00197
.06	.00236
.07	.00276
.08	.00315
.09	.00354
.1	.00394
.2	.00787
.3	.01181
.4	.01575
.5	.01969
.6	.02362
.7	.02756
.8	.03150
.9	.03543
1	.03937
2	.07874
3	.11811
4	.15748
5	.19685
6	.23622
7	.27559
8	.31496
9	.35433
10	.39370
11	.43307
12	.47244
13	.51181
14	.55118
15	.59055
16	.62992
17	.66929
18	.70866
19	.74803
20	.78740
21	.82677
22	.86614
23	.90551
24	.94488
25	.98425
26	1.02362
27	1.06299
28	1.10236
29	1.14173
30	1.18110
31	1.22047
32	1.25984
33	1.29921
34	1.33858
35	1.37795
36	1.41732
37	1.4567
38	1.4961
39	1.5354
40	1.5748
41	1.6142
42	1.6535
43	1.6929
44	1.7323
45	1.7717

Unit Conversions

UNITS	Pints to Litres	Gallons to Litres	Litres to Pints	Litres to Gallons	Miles to Kilometres	Kilometres to Miles	Lbs. per sq. In. to Kg. per sq. Cm.	Kg. per sq. Cm. to Lbs. per sq. In.
1	.57	4.55	1.76	.22	1.61	.62	.07	14.22
2	1.14	9.09	3.52	.44	3.22	1.24	.14	28.50
3	1.70	13.64	5.28	.66	4.83	1.86	.21	42.67
4	2.27	18.18	7.04	.88	6.44	2.49	.28	56.89
5	2.84	22.73	8.80	1.10	8.05	3.11	.35	71.12
6	3.41	27.28	10.56	1.32	9.66	3.73	.42	85.34
7	3.98	31.82	12.32	1.54	11.27	4.35	.49	99.56
8	4.55	36.37	14.08	1.76	12.88	4.97	.56	113.79
9		40.91	15.84	1.98	14.48	5.59	.63	128.00
10		45.46	17.60	2.20	16.09	6.21	.70	142.23
20				4.40	32.19	12.43	1.41	284.47
30				6.60	48.28	18.64	2.11	426.70
40				8.80	64.37	24.85		
50					80.47	31.07		
60					96.56	37.28		
70					112.65	43.50		
80					128.75	49.71		
90					144.84	55.92		
100					160.93	62.14		

Torque Conversions

UNITS	Lb ft to kgm	Kgm to lb ft	UNITS	Lb ft to kgm	Kgm to lb ft
1	.138	7.233	7	.967	50.631
2	.276	14.466	8	1.106	57.864
3	.414	21.699	9	1.244	65.097
4	.553	28.932	10	1.382	72.330
5	.691	36.165	20	2.765	144.660
6	.829	43.398	30	4.147	216.990

GLOSSARY OF TERMS

Allen key   Cranked wrench of hexagonal section for use with socket head screws.

Alternator   Electrical generator producing alternating current. Rectified to direct current for battery charging.

Ambient temperature   Surrounding atmospheric temperature.

Annulus   Used in engineering to indicate the outer ring gear of an epicyclic gear train.

Armature   The shaft carrying the windings, which rotates in the magnetic field of a generator or starter motor. That part of a solenoid or relay which is activated by the magnetic field.

Axial   In line with, or pertaining to, an axis.

Backlash   Play in meshing gears.

Balance lever   A bar where force applied at the centre is equally divided between connections at the ends.

Banjo axle   Axle casing with large diameter housing for the crownwheel and differential.

Bendix pinion   A self-engaging and self-disengaging drive on a starter motor shaft.

Bevel pinion   A conical shaped gearwheel, designed to mesh with a similar gear with an axis usually at 90 deg. to its own.

bhp   Brake horse power, measured on a dynamometer.

bmep   Brake mean effective pressure. Average pressure on a piston during the working stroke.

Brake cylinder   Cylinder with hydraulically operated piston(s) acting on brake shoes or pad(s).

Brake regulator   Control valve fitted in hydraulic braking system which limits brake pressure to rear brakes during heavy braking to prevent rear wheel locking.

Camber   Angle at which a wheel is tilted from the vertical.

Capacitor   Modern term for an electrical condenser. Part of distributor assembly, connected across contact breaker points, acts as an interference suppressor.

Castellated   Top face of a nut, slotted across the flats, to take a locking splitpin.

Castor   Angle at which the kingpin or swivel pin is tilted when viewed from the side.

cc   Cubic centimetres. Engine capacity is arrived at by multiplying the area of the bore in sq cm by the stroke in cm by the number of cylinders.

Clevis   U-shaped forked connector used with a clevis pin, usually at handbrake connections.

Collet   A type of collar, usually split and located in a groove in a shaft, and held in place by a retainer. The arrangement used to retain the spring(s) on a valve stem in most cases.

Commutator   Rotating segmented current distributor between armature windings and brushes in generator or motor.

Compression   The ratio, or quantitative relation, of the total volume (piston at bottom of stroke) to the unswept volume (piston at top of stroke) in an engine cylinder.

Condenser   See capacitor.

Core plug   Plug for blanking off a manufacturing hole in a casting.

Crownwheel   Large bevel gear in rear axle, driven by a bevel pinion attached to the propeller shaft. Sometimes called a 'ring gear'.

'C'-spanner   Like a 'C' with a handle. For use on screwed collars without flats, but with slots or holes.

Damper   Modern term for shock-absorber, used in vehicle suspension systems to damp out spring oscillations.

Depression   The lowering of atmospheric pressure as in the inlet manifold and carburetter.

Dowel   Close tolerance pin, peg, tube, or bolt, which accurately locates mating parts.

Drag link   Rod connecting steering box drop arm (pitman arm) to nearest front wheel steering arm in certain types of steering systems.

Dry liner   Thinwall tube pressed into cylinder bore

Dry sump   Lubrication system where all oil is scavenged from the sump, and returned to a separate tank.

Dynamo   See Generator.

Electrode   Terminal, part of an electrical component, such as the points or 'Electrodes' of a sparking plug.

Electrolyte   In lead-acid car batteries a solution of sulphuric acid and distilled water.

End float   The axial movement between associated parts, end play.

EP   Extreme pressure. In lubricants, special grades for heavily loaded bearing surfaces, such as gear teeth in a gearbox, or crownwheel and pinion in a rear axle.

Fade	Of brakes. Reduced efficiency due to overheating.
Field coils	Windings on the polepieces of motors and generators.
Fillets	Narrow finishing strips usually applied to interior bodywork.
First motion shaft	Input shaft from clutch to gearbox.
Fullflow filter	Filters in which all the oil is pumped to the engine. If the element becomes clogged, a bypass valve operates to pass unfiltered oil to the engine.
FWD	Front wheel drive.
Gear pump	Two meshing gears in a close fitting casing. Oil is carried from the inlet round the outside of both gears in the spaces between the gear teeth and casing to the outlet, the meshing gear teeth prevent oil passing back to the inlet, and the oil is forced through the outlet port.
Generator	Modern term for 'Dynamo'. When rotated produces electrical current.
Grommet	A ring of protective or sealing material. Can be used to protect pipes or leads passing through bulkheads.
Grubscrew	Fully threaded headless screw with screwdriver slot. Used for locking, or alignment purposes.
Gudgeon pin	Shaft which connects a piston to its connecting rod. Sometimes called 'wrist pin', or 'piston pin'.
Halfshaft	One of a pair transmitting drive from the differential.
Helical	In spiral form. The teeth of helical gears are cut at a spiral angle to the side faces of the gearwheel.
Hot spot	Hot area that assists vapourisation of fuel on its way to cylinders. Often provided by close contact between inlet and exhaust manifolds.
HT	High Tension. Applied to electrical current produced by the ignition coil for the sparking plugs.
Hydrometer	A device for checking specific gravity of liquids. Used to check specific gravity of electrolyte.
Hypoid bevel gears	A form of bevel gear used in the rear axle drive gears. The bevel pinion meshes below the centre line of the crownwheel, giving a lower propeller shaft line.
Idler	A device for passing on movement. A free running gear between driving and driven gears. A lever transmitting track rod movement to a side rod in steering gear.
Impeller	A centrifugal pumping element. Used in water pumps to stimulate flow.
Journals	Those parts of a shaft that are in contact with the bearings.
Kingpin	The main vertical pin which carries the front wheel spindle, and permits steering movement. May be called 'steering pin' or 'swivel pin'.
Layshaft	The shaft which carries the laygear in the gearbox. The laygear is driven by the first motion shaft and drives the third motion shaft according to the gear selected. Sometimes called the 'countershaft' or 'second motion shaft.'
lb ft	A measure of twist or torque. A pull of 10 lb at a radius of 1 ft is a torque of 10 lb ft.
lb/sq in	Pounds per square inch.
Little-end	The small, or piston end of a connecting rod. Sometimes called the 'small-end'.
LT	Low Tension. The current output from the battery.
Mandrel	Accurately manufactured bar or rod used for test or centring purposes.
Manifold	A pipe, duct, or chamber, with several branches.
Needle rollers	Bearing rollers with a length many times their diameter.
Oil bath	Reservoir which lubricates parts by immersion. In air filters, a separate oil supply for wetting a wire mesh element to hold the dust.
Oil wetted	In air filters, a wire mesh element lightly oiled to trap and hold airborne dust.
Overlap	Period during which inlet and exhaust valves are open together.
Panhard rod	Bar connected between fixed point on chassis and another on axle to control sideways movement.
Pawl	Pivoted catch which engages in the teeth of a ratchet to permit movement in one direction only.
Peg spanner	Tool with pegs, or pins, to engage in holes or slots in the part to be turned.
Pendant pedals	Pedals with levers that are pivoted at the top end.
Phillips screwdriver	A cross-point screwdriver for use with the cross-slotted heads of Phillips screws.
Pinion	A small gear, usually in relation to another gear.
Piston-type damper	Shock absorber in which damping is controlled by a piston working in a closed oil-filled cylinder.
Preloading	Preset static pressure on ball or roller bearings not due to working loads.
Radial	Radiating from a centre, like the spokes of a wheel.

Radius rod	Pivoted arm confining movement of a part to an arc of fixed radius.
Ratchet	Toothed wheel or rack which can move in one direction only, movement in the other being prevented by a pawl.
Ring gear	A gear tooth ring attached to outer periphery of flywheel. Starter pinion engages with it during starting.
Runout	Amount by which rotating part is out of true.
Semi-floating axle	Outer end of rear axle halfshaft is carried on bearing inside axle casing. Wheel hub is secured to end of shaft.
Servo	A hydraulic or pneumatic system for assisting, or, augmenting a physical effort. See 'Vacuum Servo'.
Setscrew	One which is threaded for the full length of the shank.
Shackle	A coupling link, used in the form of two parallel pins connected by side plates to secure the end of the master suspension spring and absorb the effects of deflection.
Shell bearing	Thinwalled steel shell lined with anti-friction metal. Usually semi-circular and used in pairs for main and big-end bearings.
Shock absorber	See 'Damper'.
Silentbloc	Rubber bush bonded to inner and outer metal sleeves.
Socket-head screw	Screw with hexagonal socket for an Allen key.
Solenoid	A coil of wire creating a magnetic field when electric current passes through it. Used with a soft iron core to operate contacts or a mechanical device.
Spur gear	A gear with teeth cut axially across the periphery.
Stub axle	Short axle fixed at one end only.
Tachometer	An instrument for accurate measurement of rotating speed. Usually indicates in revolutions per minute.

TDC	Top Dead Centre. The highest point reached by a piston in a cylinder, with the crank and connecting rod in line.
Thermostat	Automatic device for regulating temperature. Used in vehicle coolant systems to open a valve which restricts circulation at low temperature.
Third motion shaft	Output shaft of gearbox.
Threequarter floating axle	Outer end of rear axle halfshaft flanged and bolted to wheel hub, which runs on bearing mounted on outside of axle casing. Vehicle weight is not carried by the axle shaft.
Thrust bearing or washer	Used to reduce friction in rotating parts subject to axial loads.
Torque	Turning or twisting effort. See 'lb ft'.
Track rod	The bar(s) across the vehicle which connect the steering arms and maintain the front wheels in their correct alignment.
UJ	Universal joint. A coupling between shafts which permits angular movement.
UNF	Unified National Fine screw thread.
Vacuum servo	Device used in brake system, using difference between atmospheric pressure and inlet manifold depression to operate a piston which acts to augment brake pressure as required. See 'Servo'.
Venturi	A restriction or 'choke' in a tube, as in a carburetter, used to increase velocity to obtain a reduction in pressure.
Vernier	A sliding scale for obtaining fractional readings of the graduations of an adjacent scale.
Welch plug	A domed thin metal disc which is partially flattened to lock in a recess. Used to plug core holes in castings.
Wet liner	Removable cylinder barrel, sealed against coolant leakage, where the coolant is in direct contact with the outer surface.
Wet sump	A reservoir attached to the crankcase to hold the lubricating oil.

INDEX

The following abbreviations are used:

CC   Coventry Climax engine
SS   Standard Special engine
FSV   Ford 100E engine
FOHV   Ford 105E, 109E, 118E, 1600 and GT engines
VTR   Standard Vanguard and Triumph TR engines